OVERSIZE

MARK MILLER'S
INDIAN MARKET
COOKBOOK

MARK MILLER'S INDIAN MARKET COOKBOOK

Mark Miller

Mark Kiffin *and* Suzy Dayton

with
John Harrisson

Ten Speed Press
Berkeley, California

*To those who have gone before
and who show us the path to the future.*

Ten Speed Press
P.O. Box 7123
Berkeley, California 94707

Cover and book design and typography by Fifth Street Design, Berkeley, California.
Photostyling by Fifth Street Design.
Photoediting of back cover photograph by Fifth Street Design.

Food photography by Lois Ellen Frank, Santa Fe, New Mexico.

Props provided for photographic sets by Paulette Tavormina, Santa Fe, New Mexico.

Hand-tinted photographs for chapter openings by Judith Vejvoda, Santa Fe, New Mexico.

Photos on pages 43, 80, 99, 119, 147, 160, 168 courtesy Museum of Santa Fe, New Mexico.
Photos on pages 10, 21, 25, 77, 88, 117, 123, 163, 169 © 1995 Fifth Street Design.

Page 175: Emily Luchetti is the creator of Stars's Chocolate Silk recipe, as published in Stars Desserts, Harper Collins Publishers © 1991.

Library of Congress Cataloging-in-Publication Data

Miller, Mark Charles, 1949-
    [Indian market cookbook]
    Mark Miller's Indian market cookbook / Mark Miller, Mark Kiffin,
and Suzy Dayton with John Harrisson.
        p.   cm.
    Includes Index.
    ISBN 0-89815-620-3
    1. Cookery, American—Southwestern style. 2. Indian cookery.
3. Cookery—New Mexico—Santa Fe.   I. Kiffin, Mark.   II. Dayton,
Suzy.   III.Title.   IV. Title: Indian market cookbook.
TX715.2.S69M55   1995
641.5979—dc20   95–4212
                                                  CIP

Printed in Singapore

1 2 3 4 5 — 99 98 97 96 95

CONTENTS

TAMALES, EMPANADAS, & MORE 64

INTRODUCTION

MAGNIFICENT POLISHED POTS, expressive figurines, troves of heavy silver jewelry and inlaid turquoise brace-lets, graceful sculpture, fetishes and kachina dolls, intricate etchings, and drawings that echo historic petroglyphs. Col-orful artwork and meticulously crafted traditional sand paintings. Dazzling weavings and geometrically perfect embroidery, eye-catching and colorful beadwork, jewelry that's imbued, and graceful and elaborate baskets. Elegant leatherwork, and decorated drums made from rawhide, aspen, and cottonwood. World-class examples of all these art forms are the focus and centerpiece of the single most important exhibition and sale of Native American art anywhere in the world, held in New Mexico every August —Santa Fe's unique Indian Market.

To mark this occasion every year, we create a series of special dinners, our Indian Market Week menus, at Coyote Cafe. This is an ongoing tradition we have continued ever since the restaurant opened in 1987. These menus have been structured to reflect the distinctive and diverse cultural heritage of Santa Fe, and especially the centuries-old Southwest-ern Native American tradition. The menus often feature the most popular dishes we have served in the restaurant during the previous twelve months.

Just as our part of the Southwest has for centuries stood at a trading crossroads for different peoples and cultures, so our menus have developed in this tradition of culinary exchange. In pre-Columbian times, Native American hunter-gath-erer groups evolved over the centuries into flourishing agrarian-based communities in the Rio Grande Valley. These soci-eties traded with Mesoamerican cultures to the south and Plains tribes to the east, among others.

Later, the Spanish established the Camino Real northward into the region from Mexico, using this artery to trade with the Pueblo Indians of New Mexico and other Southwestern Native Americans, as well as to settle the land and conquer. Santa Fe itself was settled by the Spanish in 1610 as the capital of the region. New Mexico was governed by the viceroy of Mexico City for the next two hundred years.

In the early nineteenth century, the historic Santa Fe Trail was established from Missouri to the east, heralding the influx of the "Anglo-American" culture that has mingled with the Native American and Spanish ever since. These indi-vidual strands have been woven into a rich cultural tapestry across the centuries and across the land.

It is this unique tricultural heritage of Native American, European, and Hispanic (with an emphasis on Mexican cul-ture) backgrounds that distinguishes the Southwestern culture as well as its culinary traditions, and it is these cultural influences that are celebrated by the Indian Market Week menus at Coyote Cafe. Each year, during the week, menu changes enable us to develop different culinary themes and avoid the risk of repetition for guests who choose to dine with us more than once (in fact, we have a loyal following of guests who make a point of returning each night during Indian Market Week.)

The dinners during this week are special occasions at Coyote Cafe. We design and print special menus. We strive to create dishes that represent an evolution of living Southwestern culinary traditions. Fortuitously, we are also celebrating a time of harvest in New Mexico, when some of the most important ingredients in Southwestern cuisine from local farms and pueblos are in high season: chiles, squash, and corn. This facilitates our work in the kitchen and contributes to a vibrant week for us at Coyote Cafe. The traditional and cultural activity of Indian Market Week and the high levels of energy that the visitors bring to Santa Fe all culminate in a week that we always look forward to with great anticipation.

Indian Market, a Santa Fe tradition for more than seventy years, is the oldest, largest, and most prestigious exhibition and sale of Native American art in the world. The market, which is sponsored by the Southwestern Association for Indian Arts (SWAIA), one of the nation's leading organizations in promoting and fostering the development of Native American arts, takes place under the turquoise high desert skies of Santa Fe on the Saturday and Sunday after the third Thursday in August. These two days mark the busiest weekend of the year in "The City Different," when more than one hundred thousand visitors from all over the United States and the world flock to town. Several events, benefits, previews, and activities take place during the days before the weekend, so that these bustling few days are known as Indian Market Week.

Indian Market features the juried handcrafted works of about twelve hundred Native American artists (representing over 120 tribes from more than 20 states) who sell their work in booths lining Santa Fe's downtown Plaza and the sur-rounding side-streets. The great majority of the artists are from the Southwest, from the nineteen New Mexican pueblos such as Taos, San Juan, Tesuque, Acoma, Santo Domingo, and Sandia, and tribes such as the Hopi, Apache, Navajo, Pima, and Ute. Modern-day tribes celebrate their histories and identities in specific forms, such as the Cherokees with their beadwork. These artistic traditions hark back to their earlier traditions. In addition to the various types of artwork on sale, Indian Market Week is colorfully celebrated with traditional dances performed in full costume, artists' demonstrations, a benefit auction, and stalls laden with all kinds of Southwestern Native American foods.

Indian Market Week is awash with color, sound, energy, and fragrances. The multicolored booths bedecked with awnings and filled with artwork are a spectacular feast for all the senses. Although the market officially opens at eight in the morning on Saturday, queues form well before dawn, as connoisseurs, dealers, and private collectors, as well as the enthusiastic and curious hope to beat the crowds and corner the most outstanding pieces, or just to browse and view the unique artwork. But Indian Market is more than a unique art show—it's a social event and living reminder of the cultural heritage of Santa Fe. It's a display of a people's belief system. The Indians walk around the plaza and view each other's work, making knowledgeable and critical comments. They are proud of their work and of the differences of each family. A particular potter may be famous for story telling figurines or miniature pots that are very intricate, but only a few inches tall. Painstakingly done, the work represents the person's thoughts and his or her relationship to the outside worlds, both natural and cultural. They demonstarte patience and mastery of form—a sense of aesthetic bravery.

The origins of Indian Market Week go back to the early 1900s, when the Museum of New Mexico in Santa Fe purchased pottery from artisans of the northern New Mexican pueblos. The purpose was not only to augment the museum's collection but also to stimulate the impoverished economies of the pueblos, foster a sense of identity, and encourage the production of pottery and other traditional crafts.

Then, in 1922, anthropologist Edgar Lee Hewett, the museum's founder and first director of the School of American Research, helped organize the inaugural Southwest Indian Fair and Arts and Crafts Exhibition in the courtyard of Santa Fe's Palace of the Governors, on the downtown plaza. The aims of the fair were to revive traditional techniques and authentic regional arts and crafts, which were under threat from the influx of goods from the eastern United States.

The fair committee promoted the event as a means of creating a marketplace for selling artifacts directly to the public, helping to strengthen tribal economies. Its purpose was also to maintain and develop Southwest Native American tribal expression. By setting up a competitive judging system and awarding prizes in different categories, standards of excellence were set and encouraged. Also, artist Maria Martinez went to the World's Fair in New York in the thirties to display her work and show how the pottery was done.

In the same year, 1922, the New Mexico Association on Indian Affairs (NMAIA) was established to fight the infamous Bursum Bill, whose aim was to allocate 60,000 acres (and water rights) belonging to the Rio Grande pueblos to non-Indian squatters. Significantly, the association brought together Native American leaders of the region for the first time since the Pueblo Revolt against the Spanish in 1680, and it was instrumental in publicizing the issues and polarizing public opinion against the bill.

After the defeat of the Bursum Bill in Congress, the NMAIA continued its work, on land issues, nutrition, and health, promoting cultural identity, and "the encouragement and preservation of traditional Southwestern Indian art forms." It absorbed the fair committee and subsequently took over the responsibility for running the Indian Fair. Later, in 1959, the NMAIA changed its name to the Southwestern Association on Indian Affairs to reflect its broader geographical scope.

It was only in the early 1970s that Indian Market expanded into the major arts event that it is today, mainly due to the increasing national attention accorded to the Southwestern Indian arts and culture. In 1972, there were 150 booths and 250 exhibitors; by the 1990s, the numbers had more than quadrupled. Whereas, in the 1960s, Indian Market occupied just the front portal of the Palace of the Governors and the street in front of it (Palace Avenue), today it occupies booths set up around the whole plaza and spills over into every side street.

Indian Market is a special, magical occasion, and at Coyote Cafe we strive to match the spirit of celebration and to reaffirm cultural roots. In seeking to explore diverse avenues of regional culinary history within the framework of modern Southwestern cuisine, many of the recipes we have created over the years may appear complex. If they seem daunting, I encourage you to at least experiment with one or more of the self-contained elements of the recipe, or to make simpler, more familiar substitutions if you wish. Other recipes in this book are not intimidating and are well worth the effort involved. In presenting a full sample of our Indian Market recipes, we hope you will gain insight into the rich panoply of cultures and culinary traditions that make the Southwestern United States a truly remarkable place—the Land of Enchantment.

BREADS

The advent of breads marks the discovery of cuisine, of man's attempt to create a better diet for himself. The almost magical transformation of raw ingredients into bread—from ground wheat to crusty, aromatic, hearty loaves—serves as an allegory of man's progress from the primitive to the cultured, and from the worldly to the spiritual.

Bread is one of our oldest foods, predating even the ancient civilizations of Egypt, Greece, and Rome. Breadmaking exists in almost every culture in the world, and utilizes wheat flour, ground corn, ground nuts, or some form of processed root vegetable, such as yuca or cassava.

Across the United States, quality breads and breadmaking have enjoyed a renaissance during the last few years. This welcome revival of interest is being fuelled by a "breadless generation" that grew up without homemade bread or bread that was made with time-honored techniques and ingredients. This generation had to make do with processed, tasteless spongy white bread. We are relearning the techniques of baking good, flavorful breads, which is reflected in better-quality loaves now available in bakeries, stores, restaurants, and in the home. At Coyote Cafe, we make a special effort to bake tasty breads in the Southwestern tradition.

The history of breadmaking in the Southwest, which has its origins in Central American civilizations, is both long and diverse. For centuries, Native Americans made bread by hand-grinding corn into flour with stone rollers or with some type of stone surface, occasionally incorporating nuts and seeds. This thin, unleavened dough was usually cooked on hot stones, in undergound pits, or even in the hot desert sand.

One of the common types of traditional bread made by the Hopi Indians in the Southwest is the feathery piki. To the Hopi, making piki—tissue paper-thin sheets of blue-grey cornmeal bread—is a ritual and a skill that takes years to master properly. Piki is cooked on specially selected flat stones that heat evenly when placed over a small fire. The bread is made with ground blue cornmeal, water, and ashes from juniper, chamisa (a pungent wild Southwestern plant with yellow blooms), corn cobs, or bean plants. The ashes preserve the color of the blue corn and release the corn's nutrients so they can be more easily metabolized.

Other Native American groups, including those from the pueblos of New Mexico, refer to their own similar versions of bread by different names. When I first visited Santa Fe in the 1970s, I remember being able to buy piki rolled up in an 8- to 10-inch-long scroll from Native American vendors under the portal of the Palace of the Governors in Santa Fe's downtown Plaza. Unfortunately, I haven't seen it sold locally for some time now. Occasionally, round loaf breads from local pueblos are sold here, especially on feast days.

Native American breadmaking traditions changed radically when the Spanish settlers arrived in their region in the seventeenth century, bringing wheat. Food choices are highly symbolic and reflect sociopolitical religious belief systems. Just as corn played a central symbolic role in the belief system and myths of all Mesoamericans (corn was inextricably linked with their creation and fertility myths), so for the Spanish, wheat also played a central role in their belief system. Wheat was not only grown for nutritional value, but was also processed to represent the body of Christ in the Sacrament of the Eucharist. Eventually, white bread made with wheat came to symbolize the Christian, Western culture, as well as status and refinement. Most Native American groups in the Southwest enthusiastically embraced wheat, and for some it soon became more popular than corn, especially in those areas most heavily settled by the Spanish.

These Spanish settlers also introduced adobe ovens, called hornos, for baking bread. These ovens were originally modeled after medieval Spanish ovens, which were derived from those ovens introduced to Spain by the North African Moors. Hornos, shaped liked domed beehives, are about six feet tall and ten feet in circumference at the base. Made out of clay and straw, they are still a familiar sight in New Mexico, especially at the Native American pueblos. A wood fire is built inside the horno to heat it; once the oven is hot, it is sealed with a door. The oven retains the heat for hours, like a modern-day brick pizza oven. Hornos are still used today for baking. The sight and aroma of dark, earthy, adobe-colored breads emerging from these ovens is an enduring image of the Southwest.

Indian fry bread, a contemporary Native American bread made with wheat, is another example of contact with the Spanish culture, and is derived from the Spanish culinary practice of making churros. Fry bread is sold throughout the Southwest, in restaurants, at stands and rodeo booths, at festivals and feast days, and on the Plaza in Santa Fe during Indian Market Week. Fry bread is simply a leavened wheat-flour dough usually shaped into a circle, square, or triangle, and deep-fried in hot lard or oil until puffy and crisp. It's often served with honey or sugar. The more delicate and airy sopaipilla—which looks almost like a balloon—is a close relative. The best fry breads are cooked over campfires in cowboy-style Dutch ovens, and served with a hearty chile stew.

Most of the flour-based recipes that follow call for the dough to be sprinkled with flour or cornmeal before baking to add texture to the bread. If you want to give your breads a shiny, crisp crust, you can brush egg wash on the crust. The basic egg wash consists of an egg, 2 tablespoons of water, and a pinch of salt to help liquefy the egg; however, you can use just the egg white if you'd rather not use the yolk for health reasons. To achieve an especially crusty surface, mist the top with a spray bottle, or while baking place a pan of cold water in the oven.

New Mexican Blue Corn Muffins

Blue, in all its hues, seems to pervade the Southwestern palette, both in nature and design. Consider, for example, the gorgeous, unparalleled, unbounded azure skies; the ever-present aquamarine painting on doors and window frames that stands out from the earth-colored walls; the blue-black to dark indigo dyes of nineteenth-century Native American weavings; bright blue turquoise and beadwork set against silver jewelry; and blue corn. Blue corn has come to symbolize the Southwest like no other food. It is used in tortillas and tortilla chips, enchiladas, blue posole, piki bread, and atole, and it has certainly come into vogue nationwide in recent years. Incidentally, blue food is very rare in nature, and it's not usually considered an appetizing color (only a few restaurants use blue serving plates, for example). It's surprising, then, that so many people take to blue corn like a long-lost friend—or at least as an interesting novelty.

In the Native American belief system, specific significance is attached to different colors of corn, as demonstrated in various forms of artwork. Each color—blue, yellow, white, red, black, and multi-colored corn—symbolizes a particular cardinal directional point (north, west, south, east, zenith, and nadir). Blue corn symbolizes the cardinal point of the West, and is used as such in religious ceremonies and ceremonial dances. Native Americans realized that each color possessed a different genetic make-up. This observation led them to value and attach great meaning to diversity, as they also recognized that diversity promotes strength, versatility, and adaptation.

Blue corn contains more lysine than other corn, which makes it more nutritional (lysine is an amino acid, a protein building-block that helps prevent pellagra, a deficiency disease that affects the skin and nervous system, resulting from a diet overdependent on untreated corn).

Years ago, I was curious about the flavor of fresh blue corn, and one summer, my friend Elizabeth Berry grew some for me so I could taste it. Fresh blue corn does not have a particularly pleasant or sweet taste, but when dried and ground its delicate and subtle flavors emerge. Many of the varieties of Indian dried corns are much tastier and have a higher nutritional value than the modern-day fresh sweet corns that we eat.

These muffins are perfect for brunch. They look great, and are a change from the usual yellow-corn muffins. For a variation, fill muffin molds one-third full, add 1 teaspoon of a poblano pesto to the center, and top with more dough before baking to add color and flavor, or mix ¼ cup lightly toasted pine nuts into the dough. Note:to make corn bread, simply pour the batter into a 9 x 9 -inch pan and bake.

Yield: 12 large muffins

⅔ cup blue cornmeal
⅓ cup yellow cornmeal
3¼ cups unbleached all-purpose
  flour
¼ cup sugar

1 teaspoon salt
1 tablespoon baking powder
2 eggs, separated
1 cup milk, warmed to about
  100 degrees

3 tablespoons honey
8 tablespoons unsalted butter,
  melted and cooled to about
  100 degrees

Preheat the oven to 350 degrees. In a large mixing bowl, mix together the blue and yellow cornmeal, flour, sugar, salt, and baking powder, and set aside.

In a separate bowl, whisk together the egg yolks, milk, honey, and butter, and set aside. In a third bowl, whip the egg whites with an electric mixer, just until stiff.

Gently fold the honey-milk mixture into the dry ingredients with a spatula, with a few quick strokes. When the mixture is almost incorporated, fold in the egg whites, being careful not to overmix.

Grease a muffin pan and spoon the batter into 12 molds. Bake in the preheated oven for about 20 to 25 minutes, or until golden brown and a toothpick comes out clean when inserted in the middle of a muffin.

Remove the muffin pan from the oven and allow the muffins to cool for 5 minutes in the pan. Turn out onto a rack to finish cooling.

Jalapeño Corn Bread

Corn bread is the oldest bread of the Americas; corn was domesticated six thousand years or so before wheat was introduced to the New World by the Spanish in the sixteenth century. Corn (like wheat, rice, and other grains) was developed from a wild grass; it is descended from teosinte, a Central American grass whose "cobs" measured less than an inch long and only half an inch wide. Over the next three to four thousand years, Mesoamericans genetically selected larger ears which developed into modern-day corn. Corn became one of the staples of successive Mesoamerican civilizations, and its planting became widespread in pre-Columbian North America. By the time the pilgrims landed in New England and the Spanish moved northward from Mexico to colonize the Southwest, bread made with corn was a staple of the Native American cultures from what is now Arizona to Maine. Corn bread was quickly adopted by the settlers both in the East and the West, and is as much an integral part of New England cooking today as it is in the South, in Texas, and in the Southwest, where it's the classic accompaniment to bowls of chili.

Modern corn bread contains wheat flour as well as cornmeal, because the higher gluten content of the flour gives the bread more structure. Consequently, corn bread holds its shape better during the baking process. In parts of Texas and the Southwest, it's common to find cheese, chiles, and herbs added to the batter to give the corn bread further texture and flavor. In this recipe, for example, you can add ½ cup of most kinds of grated or smoked cheese. You can also substitute one or two fresh or roasted poblano chiles for the jalapeños. If possible, buy organic stone-ground cornmeal because stone grinding retains more of the nutritional value and flavor of the corn than regular commercial grinding, which is done with metal rollers that overheat the cornmeal and cause nutritional and flavor loss. Stone-ground cornmeal should be used as soon after purchasing as possible because, like other minimally processed flours and meals, it loses its freshness more quickly than those that are commercially ground.

Yield: one 9-inch pan

1½ cups all-purpose flour
1¼ cups cornmeal, preferably stone ground
1 tablespoon baking powder
2 teaspoons salt

½ cup unsalted butter, melted and cooled to 100 degrees
1½ cups milk
3 eggs, separated
¼ cup honey

3 eggs, separated
3 or 4 jalapeño chiles, stemmed, seeded, and minced
3 tablespoons sugar

Preheat the oven to 375 degrees. In a large mixing bowl, combine the flour, cornmeal, baking powder, and salt. In a separate mixing bowl, stir together the butter, milk, honey, yolks, and jalapeños. In a third bowl, beat the whites with an electric mixer until soft peaks form, then add the sugar and continue beating until stiff. Make a well in the middle of the dry ingredients. Pour in the liquid ingredients and gently combine just until mixed. Fold in the egg whites.

Pour the batter into a greased round or square 9-inch pan. Bake in the preheated oven for 20 to 25 minutes, or until golden brown and a tester comes out clean when inserted. ◗

Green and Red Chile Brioche

In the French hierarchy of breads, one of the most elegant, feathery light, and sinfully rich is the classic brioche. Brioche is made with eggs, butter, and flour and is traditionally baked in fluted, round tin molds, flared outward at an angle and accented with a small glazed topknot. Rolled-out brioche dough can also be used to "wrap" other foods before cooking, especially sausages (as with saucissons en brioche, *a specialty of Lyon) and the classic Russian masterpiece (via France) coulibiac of salmon. The richness of brioche provides a great medium for the subtle fire and flavor of chiles, and in this recipe, the mosaic of red and green chiles creates a colorful visual effect.*

This bread is ideal for brunch, especially when toasted and topped with smoked salmon or caviar. Note: *this recipe requires advance preparation and planning; it should be started a day ahead. This bread is not as difficult to make as it may appear at first glance, and it freezes well. For a variation, add 1 tablespoon mixed herbs, ⅓ cup minced sun-dried tomatoes, or ½ cup chopped olives.*

Yield: 1 standard loaf

¾ **cup milk, warmed to about 100 degrees**
1¼ **cups plus 2⅓ cups unbleached all-purpose flour**
2 **tablespoons fresh yeast, or 1 tablespoon active dry yeast**

½ **cup unsalted butter**
¼ **cup sugar**
1 **teaspoon salt**
3 **eggs**

2 **green New Mexico or Anaheim chiles, roasted and peeled (page 192), seeded, and chopped**
2 **tablespoons ground chile molido or other pure red chile powder**

Egg Wash *(optional)*

1 egg

2 tablespoons water

Pinch of salt

To prepare the dough, pour the milk into a mixing bowl, add the 1¼ cups flour and yeast, and mix together to form a dough. Cover with plastic wrap and allow this fermenting "sponge" to rise in a warm place for 20 to 30 minutes, or until it has doubled in size.

Meanwhile, with an electric mixer, cream together the butter, sugar, and salt at medium speed. Beat in the eggs alternately with the remaining 2⅓ cups of flour, and mix until the dough becomes smooth. With the mixer running, add the sponge, chiles, and chile molido and beat until smooth. Continue to beat the mixture at medium speed for 3 minutes to develop the gluten.

Transfer the dough to a lightly buttered bowl large enough to allow it to double in size. Cover the bowl securely with plastic wrap and refrigerate overnight.

The next day, remove the dough from the refrigerator and place on a lightly floured work surface. Divide the dough into 8 equal pieces and roll into balls, working quickly so that the butter in the dough does not melt and make them difficult to shape.

Place the balls of dough into a greased 9 by 5-inch baking pan so that they are staggered alternately and just barely touch each other. Cover the baking pan with a damp towel and let the dough rise in a warm place for 1 hour, or until it has doubled in size.

Preheat the oven to 350 degrees. If a shiny crust is desired, mix together the egg wash and brush it over the dough. Bake in the preheated oven until the crust is a deep rich brown color, approximately 40 minutes. Remove from the oven and allow to cool in the pan for 10 minutes. Turn out onto a rack to finish cooling.

Roasted Garlic-Chipotle Bread

This bread is full of smoked, fiery chipotle chiles that linger on the palate, and round, deep garlic tones that are sweet and pungent. It is the perfect bread to accompany hearty grilled beef or lamb dishes, or picante bowls of chili. The flavors of the bread are very much a Norteño (northern Mexican) and Tex-Mex combination, redolent of the campfire and open range. Chipotle chiles (smoked dried jalapeños) are one of my closest culinary allies and favorite kitchen seasonings, and are available dried or canned. The canned chiles come packed in adobo sauce, a pickling brine of tomatoes, vinegar, and spices. In this recipe, we use dried chipotles that are rehydrated and puréed, but canned chipotles will do just as well.

Wheats are classified as "hard" or "soft," depending on their gluten content. Pastry flour is processed mostly from soft (low-gluten and high-starch) wheat. Bread flour is derived from hard wheat (which accounts for three-quarters of the North American crop), and has a high-gluten content. Gluten gives the bread structure and results in a light and airy texture (all-purpose flour is a blend of high-gluten hard wheat and low-gluten soft wheat). If you prefer, you can divide the dough into rolls; for a fast-and-easy buffet item or appetizer, serve them with a herbed fresh goat cheese spread.

Yield: 2 loaves

3 cups unbleached bread flour
2 tablespoons fresh yeast,
   or 1 tablespoon dry yeast
¼ cup sugar
1 teaspoon ground cinnamon

2 teaspoons salt
2 cups warm water,
   about 100 degrees
2¾ cups unbleached all-purpose
   flour

1 large head garlic, roasted
   (page 192), peeled, and chopped
4 dried chipotle chiles, rehydrated
   and puréed (page 192)
3 tablespoons cornmeal

In a large mixing bowl, mix together the bread flour, yeast, sugar, cinnamon, salt, and water. Cover with a damp towel or plastic wrap and allow this fermenting "sponge" to rise in a warm place for 20 to 30 minutes, or until it has doubled in size.

Combine the all-purpose flour (adjusting the amount if necessary), garlic, and chile purée, mixing together to form a soft dough.

Transfer the dough to a lightly floured work surface. Knead the dough for 5 to 10 minutes, or until smooth and elastic. Place the dough in a lightly oiled bowl and turn it to coat thoroughly. Cover with a damp towel and let the dough rise for 45 minutes to 1 hour or until it has doubled in size.

Punch the dough down and divide it into 2 pieces, shaping it into round loaves. Place the loaves on a baking sheet that has been sprinkled with the cornmeal, and allow the dough to rise again in a warm place for 1 hour, or until it has doubled in size.

Preheat the oven to 400 degrees. Sprinkle the loaves with a little flour and slash the tops with a sharp knife or razor blade, making cuts about 3 inches long and ½ inch deep. Bake in the preheated oven for 25 minutes, or until the loaves sound hollow when tapped on the bottom. Remove from the oven and turn out onto a rack to cool.

Wild Rosemary-Pecan Bread

Pecans have a wonderful, rich buttery flavor. They are related to hickory nuts and are native to North America. Pecans are commonly used to make candied brittle, ice cream, and pies, and because they are most famous as the main ingredient in the Southern classic, pecan and praline pie, most people think pecans are exclusively from the South. In fact, the Mesilla Valley along the Rio Grande near Las Cruces in southern New Mexico is a major growing area. If possible, make sure you're buying pecans from the current year's crop, because it's not uncommon to find nuts of uncertain vintage and dubious quality. The richness of the pecans contrasts very well with the sharpness of the rosemary.

Hiking across the open range or driving along the backroads of the Southwest in the summer, you will frequently be struck by the evocative aroma of wild herbs basking in the hot sunshine, especially after an afternoon thunderstorm. Wild sage and rosemary are two of the most wonderfully pungent herbs.

Yield: 2 loaves

5 cups unbleached bread flour
2 tablespoons fresh yeast, or
   1 tablespoon active dry yeast
2 tablespoons sugar
2 cups warm water, about
   100 degrees
1 cup pecans, chopped
¾ cup whole-wheat flour
2 tablespoons peanut oil
2 teaspoons salt
2 tablespoons finely chopped fresh
   wild rosemary
3 tablespoons cornmeal

Preheat the oven to 350 degrees. In a large mixing bowl, mix together the bread flour, yeast, sugar, and water. Cover with a damp towel or plastic wrap and allow this fermenting "sponge" to rise in a warm place for 20 to 30 minutes, or until it has doubled in size.

Meanwhile, place the pecans on a baking sheet and toast in the preheated oven for 15 minutes, until browned. Turn off the oven.

Stir down the sponge and add the pecans, whole-wheat flour, oil, salt, and rosemary, stirring until smooth.

Transfer the dough to a lightly floured work surface. Knead the dough for 5 to 10 minutes, until smooth and elastic. Place the dough in a lightly oiled bowl and turn it to coat thoroughly. Cover with a damp towel and let the dough rise in a warm place for 45 minutes to 1 hour, or until it has doubled in size.

Punch down the dough and divide it into 2 pieces, shaping them into round loaves. Place the loaves on a baking sheet that has been sprinkled with the cornmeal, and allow the dough to rise again for 1 hour, or until it has doubled in size.

Preheat the oven to 400 degrees. Sprinkle the loaves with a little flour and slash the tops with a sharp knife or razor blade, making cuts about 3 inches long and ½ inch deep. Bake in the preheated oven for 20 to 25 minutes, or until golden and the loaves sound hollow when tapped on the bottom. Remove from the oven and turn out onto a rack to cool.

Ancho-Black Bean Bread

One of my favorite credos in life is "More is better." In breadmaking, more flavor and more texture is definitely better. I like to flavor breads with many diverse elements, and this dark, dense bread, which is very popular at Coyote Cafe, is a good example. If you're serving full-flavored foods or "full-contact" cuisine, you can't have fussy bread; it must be able to support the other flavors of the meal. Remember: real cowboys don't eat croissants!

This bread has a robust flavor and is very nutritious, and it contains two Southwestern staples—chiles and black beans. It offers unexpected tastes, but not only because of the beans, which are an unusual ingredient in bread. In addition, the ancho and chipotle chiles round out the flavors with a sweet, smoky, and woodsy quality. Ancho chiles are one of the most versatile and flavorful of dried chiles, and they take on various characteristics depending on how they're used. Mixed with black beans in this recipe, they give the bread life and character. This bread was created by one of our bakers, Ron Beattie.

Yield: 2 loaves

2 large or 3 medium-sized dried ancho chiles (about 1½ ounces)
1 dried chipotle chile
1½ cups cooked black beans, puréed with ½ cup of their cooking liquid
1 teaspoon cumin seed, toasted (page 192), and ground
2 teaspoons salt
2½ tablespoons peanut oil
1½ tablespoons molasses
½ tablespoon active dry yeast
2½ cups whole-wheat flour
2½ cups unbleached bread flour
1 egg, beaten
2 tablespoons cornmeal

Rehydrate the ancho chiles and the chipotle together in warm water (see page 192). Once rehydrated, reserve 1 cup of the soaking liquid. Purée the rehydrated chiles and transfer to a mixing bowl. Add the black bean purée, cumin, salt, and oil, and mix together. Set aside.

In a separate large mixing bowl, whisk together the chile soaking liquid and the molasses. Making sure the temperature of the soaking liquid is lower than 115 degrees, gradually whisk in the yeast. Then gradually mix in the whole-wheat flour and bread flour in equal increments, just until the mixture reaches a thick, mudlike consistency (you will be using more of the flour later). Cover with a damp towel and allow this fermenting "sponge" to rise at room temperature for 20 minutes.

Stir the chile and bean purée mixture into the sponge. Gradually add equal increments of both flours to the mixture, mixing well until a firm (but not stiff) dough forms.

Transfer to a lightly floured work surface and knead the dough for 5 to 10 minutes, until soft and supple. Place the dough in a lightly oiled bowl and turn it to coat thoroughly. Cover with a damp towel and let the dough rise in a warm place for 1 hour, or until it has doubled in size.

Punch the dough down again and divide it into 2 pieces, shaping it into round loaves. Place the loaves on a floured baking sheet, cover with a damp towel and allow them to rise once more in a warm place for 30 minutes, or until they have increased in size by one-third. Meanwhile, preheat the oven to 400 degrees and place a baking sheet in the oven to heat.

When the loaves have risen, brush with the beaten egg. Sprinkle the cornmeal on the heated baking sheet and place the loaves on the sheet. Bake in the oven for 20 to 25 minutes, until the loaves sound hollow when tapped on the bottom.

For crusty loaves, spray water with a mister into the oven two or three times within the first 10 minutes of baking. Remove the loaves from the oven and turn out onto a rack to cool.

Green Chile-Apple Bread

One vivid memory I have from growing up in New England is of the apple orchards and the bushels of ripe red fruit displayed in old-fashioned wooden baskets by the roadside in the fall. Sometimes, you could smell the heady sweet aromas of fresh cider being pressed, and we'd take home enough baskets of fruit to keep us in apple pies, applesauce, baked apples, and apple spice cakes for a while. When I moved to New Mexico I was surprised to discover there were plenty of fine apple orchards along the Rio Grande Valley, where the first ones had been planted by Spanish settlers centuries ago. There's something about the brisk autumnal air of New Mexico and New England (especially after the first frost) that brings out the remarkable flavor and dry crispness of apples.

And what better ingredient to pair apples with than chiles! Fall also marks the end of the chile harvest in New Mexico, and for a while, rural roadside stands sell both apples and chiles. Their common seasonality and complementary flavor tones make them a natural pairing in the local cuisine. In fact, Coyote Cocina (the food line produced by Coyote Cafe) markets a wonderful green chile applesauce that perks up pork, sausages, and just about anything else you serve it with. Ron Beattie also created this bread.

Yield: 2 loaves

2 cups unbleached bread flour
2 tablespoons fresh yeast, or
  1 tablespoon active dry yeast
3 tablespoons honey
¾ cup warm water, about
  100 degrees

1½ cups unbleached all-purpose
  flour
1½ teaspoons salt
3 green New Mexico or Anaheim
  chiles, roasted and peeled
  (page 192), seeded, and chopped

3 Granny Smith apples, unpeeled,
  cored and puréed
3 tablespoons cornmeal

In a large mixing bowl, mix 1 cup of the bread flour together with the yeast, honey, and water. Cover with a damp towel or plastic wrap and allow this fermenting "sponge" to rise in a warm place for 20 to 30 minutes, until doubled in size.

Stir down the sponge and add the remaining bread flour, the all-purpose flour (adjusting the amount if necessary), salt, chopped chiles, and puréed apples, stirring until the dough is soft and smooth.

Transfer the dough to a lightly floured work surface. Knead the dough for 5 to 10 minutes, until smooth and elastic. Place the dough in a lightly oiled bowl, and turn it to coat thoroughly. Cover with a damp towel and let the dough rise in a warm place for 45 minutes to 1 hour, or until it has doubled in size.

Punch the dough down and divide it into 2 pieces, shaping them into round loaves. Place the loaves on a baking sheet that has been sprinkled with the cornmeal, and allow the dough to rise again in a warm place for 45 minutes, or until doubled in size.

Preheat the oven to 400 degrees. Sprinkle the loaves with a little flour and slash the tops with a sharp knife or razor blade, making cuts about 3 inches long and ½ inch deep. Bake in the preheated oven for 25 minutes, or until the loaves sound hollow when tapped on the bottom. Remove from the oven and turn out onto a rack to cool.

Lemon-Sage Bread

Sage and lemon are two aromatic, contrasting flavors. The sage, with its grassy, pungent quality, evokes the Southwestern range and is distinctly different than the crisp, sharp, high tones of the lemon. If the sage provides the bass, earth tones the lemon hits the clear high notes. One is the smell of nature, the other of "civilization."

The perfume of lemon, orange, oleander, and rose infuses the air of the majestic, medieval Moorish gardens in Spain, such as the magnificent Alhambra in Grenada. The Moors had imported citrus fruit from the Middle East, and in turn, the Spanish brought them to the New World. Citrus fruit and stone fruit (such as peaches and apricots) were grown in the gardens of the early Spanish missions throughout the Southwest and California, not only for sustenance but also because a domesticated garden symbolized the civilized Christian world, in contrast to the American wilderness with all that sage and emptiness.

Since I opened my Red Sage restaurant in Washington, DC, in early 1992, I have often been asked whether such a herb actually exists. Yes, there is a type of sage that has red blooms, rather like Indian paintbrush's.

As a variation, you can add walnuts or hazelnuts to this bread. Use any leftovers for stuffing quail or game birds.

Yield: 2 loaves

3 cups unbleached bread flour
1 tablespoon active dry yeast
¼ cup sugar
2 cups warm water,
  about 100 degrees

¼ cup cornmeal
2 tablespoons peanut oil
½ cup finely chopped fresh sage
Zest of 2 lemons, minced
1 tablespoon salt

2½ to 3 cups unbleached
  all-purpose flour
3 tablespoons cornmeal

In a large mixing bowl, mix together the bread flour, yeast, sugar, and water. Cover with a damp towel or plastic wrap and allow this fermenting "sponge" to rise in a warm place for 20 to 30 minutes, or until it has doubled in size.

Stir down the mixture and add the cornmeal, oil, sage, lemon zest, salt, and the all-purpose flour (adjusting the amount as necessary), stirring until the dough is soft and smooth.

Transfer the dough to a lightly floured work surface. Knead the dough for 5 to 10 minutes, until smooth and elastic. Place in a lightly oiled bowl and turn the dough to coat thoroughly. Cover with a damp towel and let the dough rise for 45 minutes to 1 hour, or until it has doubled in size.

Punch down the dough and divide it into 2 pieces, shaping them into round loaves. Place the loaves on a baking sheet that has been sprinkled with the cornmeal, and allow the dough to rise again in a warm place for about 45 minutes, or until it has doubled in size.

Preheat the oven to 400 degrees. Sprinkle the loaves with a little flour (or an egg beaten with 2 tablespoons water if you prefer) and slash the tops with a sharp knife or razor blade, making cuts about 3 inches long and ½ inch deep. Bake in the preheated oven for 20 minutes, or until the loaves sound hollow when tapped on the bottom. Remove from the oven and turn out onto a rack to cool.

Pumpkin Seed Pipián Bread

Seeds and nuts have always been an important part of the gathering tradition of the Native Americans of the Southwest. They were often used for seasonings, and the oils of nuts and seeds, which were made into butters and pastes, provided valuable calories and extra nutrition. Seeds and nuts were also ground for flour and used as a thickening agent for soups and stews. The seeds of the indigenous pumpkin were particularly revered; high in oil content, calories, and rich flavor, they were stored for the winter months when there was a scarcity of fresh foods.

Squash and pumpkin seeds are the most commonly used seeds in the cuisines of Mexico and the Southwest. In Mexico (where they are called pepitas), pumpkin seeds form the base of pipián sauces, which are similar to the Italian pestos but without the cheese. Pipiáns are made from ground seeds and nuts, spices, and chiles, and date from pre-Columbian times.

Seeds and nuts also feature in European culinary traditions of breadmaking—and especially in hearty German multigrain breads, for example.

Yield: 2 loaves

3½ cups unbleached bread flour
2 tablespoons fresh yeast, or
   1 tablespoon active dry yeast
⅓ cup honey
¾ cup warm water,
   about 100 degrees

1½ cups pumpkin purée
½ cup finely ground pumpkin seeds
½ teaspoon ground allspice
1 teaspoon ground ginger
2 teaspoons ground cinnamon

1 tablespoon salt
2½ cups unbleached all-purpose
   flour
3 tablespoons cornmeal

Egg Wash

1 egg, beaten

2 tablespoons water

Pinch of salt

In a large mixing bowl, mix 1½ cups of the bread flour together with the yeast, honey, and water. Cover with a damp towel or plastic wrap and allow this fermenting "sponge" to rise in a warm place for 20 to 30 minutes, or until it has doubled in size.

Add the pumpkin purée, 6 tablespoons of the ground pumpkin seeds (reserving 2 tablespoons for later), the allspice, ginger, cinnamon, salt, remaining bread flour, and all-purpose flour (adjusting the amount as necessary), and mix together to form a soft, smooth dough.

Transfer the dough to a lightly floured work surface. Knead the dough for 5 to 10 minutes, until smooth and elastic. Place the dough in a lightly oiled bowl and turn it to coat thoroughly. Cover with a damp towel and let the dough rise for 45 minutes to 1 hour, or until it has doubled in size.

Punch down the dough and divide it into 2 pieces, shaping them into round loaves. Place the loaves on a baking sheet that has been sprinkled with the cornmeal, and allow the dough to rise again in a warm place for about 45 minutes, or until it has doubled in size.

Preheat the oven to 400 degrees. Prepare the egg wash by beating the egg, water, and salt together, and brush the loaves with it. Sprinkle the remaining 2 tablespoons ground pumpkin seeds over the loaves. Bake in the preheated oven for 25 minutes, or until the loaves sound hollow when tapped on the bottom. Remove from the oven and turn out onto a rack to cool.

Wild Oregano Breadsticks

Oregano (from the Greek, "joy of the mountain") is also known as wild marjoram. Oregano is stronger and more pungent than marjoram (to which it is related), and less sweet. In turn, Mexican oregano is stronger than the Italian or Greek variety, and is usually available in dried form at Mexican, Latin, or good Southwestern markets. Wild oregano grows along the arroyos and washes of the semiarid high desert of the Southwest and is similar to Mexican oregano. It's another herb that exudes a particular aroma that reminds one of the high chaparral and the open range.

Wild oregano is also used for teas and medicinal purposes in Mexico and the Southwest, like many other wild herbs. The early Hispanic culture learned these curative remedies and practices from the Native Americans of the region. Even today, there are shops in Santa Fe that carry traditional teas and herbal remedies that are still used.

When baking these breadsticks, make sure they thoroughly dry out and become crisp. If necessary, lower the heat of the oven and cook them a little longer. These breadsticks are ideal with barbecued foods.

Yield: about 30 breadsticks

5 to 6 cups all-purpose flour
1 tablespoon active dry yeast
1 tablespoon sugar

2 cups warm water, about 100 degrees
6 tablespoons unsalted butter, softened

½ cup finely chopped fresh wild oregano or Mexican oregano
1 tablespoon salt
3 tablespoons cornmeal

In a large mixing bowl, mix together 3 cups of the flour, the yeast, sugar, and water. Cover with a damp towel or plastic wrap and allow this fermenting "sponge" to rise in a warm place for 20 to 30 minutes, or until it has doubled in size.

Add the butter, oregano, salt, and remaining 2 to 3 cups of flour (adjusting the amount as necessary), and mix together to form a soft, smooth dough.

Transfer the dough to a lightly floured work surface. Knead the dough for 5 to 10 minutes, until smooth and elastic. Shape the dough into a rectangle about 12 by 15 inches, cover with a damp towel, and let it rise in a warm place for 45 minutes to 1 hour, or until it has doubled in size.

Preheat the oven to 450 degrees. Cut the dough into 30 long, thin pieces. Stretch and roll into breadsticks the length of the baking sheet you will be using. Sprinkle two baking sheets with the cornmeal and place the breadsticks on them, about 1½ to 2 inches apart. Bake in the preheated oven for 15 to 20 minutes, or until the breadsticks are golden brown and crisp.

SOUPS

Sopa de Pato
Roasted Duck Soup with Wild Mushrooms and Vegetables

Sopa de Calabacitas
Yellow Summer Squash Soup with Red Chile Crema

Sopa de Palomino
Roasted Cherry Tomatoes and Garden Greens Soup

Sopa de Tarascan
Roasted Tomato, Bean, and Chile Soup from Pátzcuaro

Sopa de Limón
Yucatán-Style Chicken and Chile Soup with Lime

Summer Sweet Corn and Yellow Squash Soup
Garnished with Fresh Squash Blossoms and Herbs

Fresh Corn Soup
with Chile Pasado, Gulf Shrimp, and Queso Fresco

Plains Venison Jerky Soup
Rich Venison Broth Flavored with Mustard Greens, Corn, and Squash

Albóndigas Oaxacan-Style
in a Rich Tomato-Smoked Chile Sauce

Mission White Bean Soup
*Clear Vegetable Broth with Dried Green Chile, Sun-Dried
Tomatoes, and Aged Anejo Cheese*

Yellow Tomato Gazpacho
with Crab and Sweet Pepper Sauce

Sopa de Calabacitas
Yellow Summer Squash Soup with Red Chile Crema

There are literally hundreds of types of squash, from the familiar zucchini to exotic varieties such as the bitter-tasting, round buffalo squash that can still be found growing wild in the arroyos around Santa Fe. Squash is one of the oldest and most important domesticated plants of the New World. Its use as a cultivated food dates back to at least 7000 BC in Central America, from where it spread to the Southwest via traders who brought seeds with them.

Squash was not only used as a food. Certain varieties—gourds, that is—were grown specifically so they could be dried and used as containers for storing seeds or holding water, and as rattles. Squash was an important plant in the Southwestern culture. It was cultivated by the Hohokam Indians of southern Arizona around two thousand years ago, and by the Anasazi ("Ancient Ones") of the Four Corners region of the Southwest about one thousand years ago. The Hopis and the Pueblo Indians of the Rio Grande Valley commonly preserved summer squashes for the winter months by cutting them into sections and drying them in the sun. The Navajos also grew squash extensively, and depicted them in jewelry and in the sand paintings for religious ceremonies. Southwestern ribbed squash pottery bowls can still be purchased at Santa Fe's Indian Market.

I prefer to use water in most vegetable soups rather than meat stocks, which can overpower the subtle and distinctive flavors of vegetables such as squash. The technique of slowly cooking the squash with herbs in a covered pan with a small amount of moisture gives it a heady but delicate perfume. If you like, you can garnish the soup with fresh basil.

Yield: 4 servings

1½ pounds yellow crookneck squash (or summer squash), cut into large dice
¾ cup chopped white onion
2 tablespoons unsalted butter

3 sprigs fresh marjoram
1 cup water
½ cup heavy cream
½ teaspoon salt, or to taste

1 cup Red Chile Crema (recipe follows)

Place the squash, onion, butter, marjoram, and water in a saucepan and bring to a simmer. Cover and continue to simmer slowly for 25 minutes.

Let cool, remove the marjoram sprigs and any detached leaves, and transfer the mixture to a blender. Purée and return to the saucepan. Add the cream, season with salt, and thin with a little water if necessary. When ready to serve, top with a spoonful of Red Chile Crema.

Red Chile Crema

Crema is the Mexican (and Southwestern) equivalent of crème fraîche, and has more tang than commercial sour cream. An alternative to making this recipe is to buy ready-made crema or crème fraîche at a natural food store or from the dairy section of a gourmet or Latin specialty store.

Yield: about 1⅛ cups

1 cup heavy cream (preferably unpasteurized)

1 tablespoon buttermilk (preferably unpasteurized)
1 clove garlic, roasted (page 192)

1 tablespoon canned chipotle chile in adobo sauce

Heat the cream in a saucepan to about 70 degrees; do not overheat or it will kill the "starter" in the buttermilk. Remove from the heat and transfer to a clean bowl. Add the buttermilk, cover with cheesecloth, and keep overnight in a warm place (at least 75 degrees) to set.

The consistency of the crema should be like loose sour cream. If any mold has developed, do not use and start again.

Purée the crema with the garlic and chipotle chile. Store in an airtight container for up to 2 days.

Sopa de Palomino
Roasted Cherry Tomatoes and Garden Greens Soup

This is a painted, or two-color soup, named after the two-toned palomino breed of horse. I always enjoy creating painted soups, because I like to contrast the strong, pure flavors of different vegetables and their striking, vibrant colors. It's also fun to pair sweet and hot or mild and pungent flavors. With this recipe, for example, you can use spinach and romaine or asparagus and peas for the greens half of the soup.

Always use vegetables that are in peak season, and don't overcook them or you risk losing their intense colors and flavors. The other important thing to remember to ensure success is that the two soups must be of the same consistency and viscosity, so they remain distinct and don't run into each other. Try to avoid swirling the two types of soup together, so they don't get mixed up in the bowl, and eat each one separately. Take a spoonful of one, then the other, so you taste the contrast of flavors.

Store-bought cherry tomatoes usually have the virtue of being fully ripe and sweet, even during the winter. They may be more expensive than plum or regular tomatoes, but they offer the flavor and ripeness that is essential for this recipe. Of course, home-grown sweet garden tomatoes would be perfect, too. The roasting process evaporates the tomatoes' moisture, concentrating the flavors and leaving increased sweetness. If desired, garnish with a little Red Chile Crema (page 34) or fresh cilantro or parsley sprigs.

Yield: 4 servings

Tomato Soup

6 cups cherry tomatoes
¼ cup olive oil
½ cup diced shallots

½ teaspoon roasted garlic (page 192)
1 tablespoon sugar, or to taste
1½ cups water

2 teaspoons fresh lime juice
Salt and freshly ground black pepper to taste

Greens Soup

5 cups water
¾ teaspoon salt
4 cups spinach leaves
4 cups chard leaves
2 cups watercress leaves
1 cup romaine lettuce leaves

½ cup parsley leaves
¾ cup diced poblano chiles
3 serrano chiles, seeded
½ cup basil leaves
½ teaspoon toasted and ground cumin (page 192)

¼ teaspoon toasted and ground coriander (page 192)
Freshly ground black pepper to taste

Preheat the oven to 375 degrees. To prepare the Tomato Soup, toss the cherry tomatoes in half of the oil and place them in a shallow baking pan. Roast in the oven for 6 to 8 minutes, stirring occasionally, or until their skins split.

Meanwhile, heat the remaining oil in a sauté pan or skillet and sauté the shallots over medium-high heat until lightly caramelized, about 6 to 8 minutes. Add the garlic and sugar and sauté for 2 minutes longer. Add the roasted tomatoes, the liquid from the roasting pan, and the water, and simmer for 6 to 8 minutes.

Transfer the soup to a blender and purée. Stop puréeing once the texture is smooth; do not over-blend. Strain the soup through a coarse sieve into a clean saucepan, discarding the skins and seeds. Add the lime juice, season with salt and pepper, and keep the Tomato Soup warm while preparing the Greens Soup.

In a saucepan, bring the water to a boil over high heat, add the salt and the spinach, chard, watercress, romaine, and parsley. Stir continuously for 1 to 2 minutes or until the greens are completely wilted but still vibrant in color. Drain well, reserving the water.

Transfer the greens in batches to a blender, together with just enough of the reserved water to make puréeing possible. Purée with the poblano and serrano chiles and basil leaves. Strain into a clean saucepan, and with the reserved water adjust the consistency of the soup to match that of the Tomato Soup.

Stir in the cumin, coriander, and pepper and heat through. Serve as soon as possible to preserve the fresh colors and flavors. Carefully ladle both soups simultaneously into serving bowls; each soup should occupy half of the bowl.

Sopa de Tarascan

Roasted Tomato, Bean, and Chile Soup from Pátzcuaro

This rich soup takes its name from the Tarascan culture that occupied the present-day Morelia region west of Mexico City. It reached its zenith in the fourteenth and fifteenth centuries, and was one of the few societies in Mexico that the Aztecs never conquered. The legendary belligerence of the Tarascan warriors was also the reason their civilization was one of the last to be overrun by the Spanish conquistadores. Perhaps it was a diet of chiles that fired the fierce Tarascan temperament! They certainly enjoyed a spicy cuisine and this hearty soup remains popular around Pátzcuaro, the city that lies in the heart of the Tarascan territory and where they still speak the Tarascan dialect.

Pátzcuaro is a beautiful city with wonderful colonial architecture. It's famous for its Day of the Dead festivities every November, its spectacular copperwork, and beautiful pottery that fills a local museum. The first time I tasted this soup, I was sitting at a busy café where local families were enjoying their Sunday afternoon meal after church. In fact, all the restaurants surrounding the central square, or zócalo, serve a version of this dish.

This is one of my all-time favorite vegetarian soups. It makes a great one-course meal with some freshly baked crusty bread, such as Wild Rosemary-Pecan Bread (page 23), and it's an ideal cold-weather dish—just the thing after a hard day's skiing! Adding some softened sun-dried tomatoes to the blender will further intensify the soup's flavor.

Yield: 4 servings

8 ounces dried red kidney beans
2 sprigs epazote, finely chopped (optional)
1 teaspoon salt plus additional, to taste
2 teaspoons toasted dried oregano (page 192)
Water to cover beans plus 1 to 2 cups

1 pound Roma tomatoes, halved and seeded
1½ tablespoons olive oil
½ large white onion, sliced
2 cloves garlic, roasted (page 192)
2½ tablespoons canned chipotle chiles in adobo sauce

½ cup peanut oil
2 dried pasilla de Oaxaca chiles or ancho or mulato chiles
8 ounces soft Mexican ranchero cheese or mozzarella or Muenster cheese, cut into thin slices

Place the beans in a saucepan with the epazote, 1 teaspoon of the salt, and oregano, and add enough water to cover by 2 or 3 inches. Cover the pan and bring to a boil. Reduce the heat to a simmer and cook until the beans are tender, about 1 to 1½ hours, adding more water as necessary.

Preheat the oven to 350 degrees. Place the tomato halves on a baking sheet and roast in the oven for 45 minutes. In a sauté pan or skillet, heat the oil and sauté the onion until translucent. Transfer to a blender or food processor with the roasted tomatoes, cooked beans, roasted garlic, and chipotle chiles, and blend. Add the 1 to 2 cups of water and blend to a souplike consistency. Strain through a medium to coarse sieve into a saucepan, and season with salt. Heat the soup in a heavy-bottomed saucepan over low heat, and be careful not to let it burn.

Meanwhile, heat the peanut oil in a skillet or sauté pan and lightly fry the chiles for several seconds until their aroma develops; do not overcook or let them become crisp, or they will taste bitter. Remove, drain on paper towels, and cut the chiles into strips.

Ladle the soup into warm serving bowls, sprinkle the chile strips over, and then cover with the cheese. Place the bowls on the bottom rack under a low broiler or in a hot oven to melt and lightly brown the cheese.

OPPOSITE PAGE *Plains Venison Jerky Soup*

Sopa de Limón

Yucatán-Style Chicken and Chile Soup with Lime

A land that has etched itself on my memory—its people, jungles, sounds, heat, and smells—is the Yucatán region of Mexico. The presence of the Mayans still seems to breathe in the shadows of the ruins and beneath the desolate trees that stand under the hot sun. The Yucatán is filled with pre-Columbian architecture and monuments—I can still see the magnificent pyramids of Chichén Itzá, the ruins of an ancient astronomical observatory overlooking the azure ocean at Tulúm, and the Temple of the Sorcerer at Uxmal. It is a shame that most visitors to the Yucatán miss these sites and congregate instead on the beaches of Cancún and Cozumel.

The cuisine and culture of the Yucatán today is related to that of the Mayan civilization. This region has probably preserved its historic traditions more successfully than other regions because it was largely untouched by the Spanish, who found the land unsuitable either for cattle ranching or mining.

This soup, together with pollo pibil (the region's famous chicken dish), are the two best-known dishes of the Yucatán. Just about every restaurant and roadside stand there has its own version of this dish, and some are even served in coconut shells. I recall first tasting this refreshing soup almost twenty years ago, in the ferocious midday heat and humidity of Mérida. It certainly raised a sweat, which was welcome natural air-conditioning!

If at all possible, use the smaller Mexican or key limes that often have a thin, mottled green and yellow skin. These tend to be juicier, sweeter and more aromatic than the larger Persian limes, which are more oval in shape and resemble green lemons. To create a more convivial meal-time environment, this soup can be served in a tureen at the table and then ladled out, with the garnishes passed around in separate bowls so that everyone can add them to their soup according to their taste.

For a vegetarian or meatless soup, substitute Vegetable Stock (page 193) for the Chicken Stock, and vegetables, scallops, or oysters for the chicken. To cut down on the oil content, you can bake the tortilla strips in the oven until crisp. Just sprinkle the unbaked strips with a little fresh lime juice before baking.

Yield: 4 servings

8 ounces boneless and skinless chicken breast
1 pound Roma tomatoes
6 cups Chicken Stock (page 193)
10 cloves garlic, roasted (page 192) and minced

4 serrano chiles, sliced in rings, with seeds
1 bunch cilantro, tied except for 12 sprigs reserved for garnish
¼ cup canola oil
3 corn tortillas, julienned
⅔ cup diced white onion

1 poblano chile, roasted (page 192), seeded, and julienned
2½ tablespoons fresh lime juice
1 teaspoon toasted and ground Mexican oregano (page 192)
4 lime wedges

Grill or broil the chicken until cooked and browned, but still moist. Shred by hand into ¼ by 2-inch strips and set aside.

In a heavy cast-iron skillet or on a griddle or *comal* (a flat or slightly curved cooking surface made of earthenware or very thin metal, and usually placed over a charcoal fire), dry-roast the tomatoes over medium-high heat until blackened all over. Roughly chop the tomatoes and transfer to a saucepan. Add the stock, garlic, serranos, and cilantro and simmer over low heat for 20 to 30 minutes. Remove the cilantro.

Meanwhile, heat the canola oil in a medium-sized skillet and fry the tortilla strips over medium-high heat until crisp, about 20 to 30 seconds. Remove and drain on paper towels. Remove all but 1 tablespoon of the oil from the pan. Add the onion to the skillet and sauté over medium-high heat until translucent, about 5 minutes.

Transfer the onion to 4 serving bowls and add the poblano chile and the reserved chicken. Ladle in the warm soup and stir in the lime juice. Garnish each serving with the tortilla strips, a pinch of toasted oregano, and 3 cilantro sprigs. Serve with a lime wedge.

Summer Sweet Corn and Yellow Squash Soup
Garnished with Fresh Squash Blossoms and Herbs

I always carry with me the Southwestern image of summer fields of tall, green corn stalks, with their golden tassles blowing in the breeze, set between the brick red-colored earth and the deep turquoise sky that stretches forever. We look forward to the all-too-brief three-month corn season, whose arrival is signaled by the farmers' pick-ups parked by the roadside, full of young tender sweet corn that was harvested in the early morning hours. I can never resist stopping on my way to the restaurant and buying some to eat for lunch.

There are literally more than one hundred varieties of corn, and many were developed by Southwestern Native Americans over the centuries. These varieties of corn were adapted to the different microclimates, diverse ecological conditions (from dry desert climates to high altitudes), and the restrictive, short growing season. Corn played a central symbolic role for most Native Americans, and festivals that celebrate the planting and harvesting of corn are still held at pueblos such as San Felipe and San Ildefenso in northern New Mexico. During the festivals, beautiful and intricate corn dances honor this principal gift of the gods. The dances symbolize growth, fertility, regeneration of the corn and the tribe, and the interdependence of man and nature.

Corn and squash are often grown together—companions in the field as well as in the pot! Squash blossoms, like corn, hold religious and cultural significance to Native Americans of the region, and are symbols of fertility and fruition. Hopi squash blossom kachinas are believed to bring much-needed rain as well as health and prosperity. Navajo silversmiths have always used squash blossom designs in their work, and handsome necklaces bearing these images are worn around the Plaza during Santa Fe's Indian Market Week.

This recipe weaves together the delicate, naturally sweet flavors of corn, squash, and squash blossoms that complement each other so well. Avoid buying overly large squash, because they may contain bitter seeds.

Yield: 4 servings

1 tablespoon olive oil
1⅓ cups diced white onion
1½ cups fresh corn kernels
  (from 2 ears)

1 pound yellow summer squash,
  preferably crookneck, cut into
  large dice
½ cup water
2 sprigs fresh marjoram
4 fresh sweet basil leaves

Salt to taste
1 tablespoon unsalted butter
8 large squash blossoms
4 teaspoons chiffonade of fresh
  basil or chives

Heat the oil in a saucepan and sauté the onion over medium-low heat until translucent, about 6 to 8 minutes. Add the corn, squash, water, marjoram, and basil, and bring to a simmer, covered. Continue to steam until the squash is tender, about 10 minutes. Remove from the heat and discard the marjoram sprigs and basil leaves.

Transfer to a blender and purée; add a little water (1 to 2 tablespoons) if necessary to thin. Strain through a sieve, pressing down to extract all of the liquid; discard the solids. Return to a clean saucepan, season with salt, and keep warm over very low heat.

Heat the butter in a sauté pan and sauté the squash blossoms very gently over low heat until just cooked through, about 30 seconds.

Ladle the soup into serving bowls and garnish with the squash blossoms and herbs.

Fresh Corn Soup

with Chile Pasado, Gulf Shrimp, and Queso Fresco

Chile pasado is the name given to ripened red New Mexico or Anaheim chiles that are fire-roasted while fresh, then peeled and dried. This process concentrates the natural flavors and heat of the chiles, making them sweeter and hotter than regular dried red New Mexico chiles that you see strung in ristras. Because they are peeled, they are also less bitter. The flavor of chile pasado is distinctive—with the tones of apple, cherry, and licorice combined. Chiles pasado are relatively rare and expensive, but a little goes a very long way. (See "Sources," on page 199, for ordering information.) As an alternative, you can use dried red or even dried green New Mexico chiles.

The combination of corn and shrimp is a traditional Southern classic, dating back to the time when Native Americans from the Carolinas and the Gulf Coast used them in their extensive repertoire of ingredients. Queso fresco is a fresh, unripened moist cheese made from partially skimmed milk. Slightly salty and with a sharp flavor, mild feta or a mild dry goat cheese can be substituted for it. The best and most authentic fresh queso fresco I know of is made by Paula Lambert's Mozzarella Co. in Dallas, which ships to individuals as well as restaurants (see "Sources," page 199). Use yellow corn tortillas if blue ones are unavailable.

Yield: 4 servings

4 cups fresh corn kernels
  (from 6 ears)
1 cup water
¼ cup unsalted butter
3½ cups milk
½ teaspoon salt, or to taste

¼ cup canola oil
4 blue corn tortillas, julienned
8 extra-large shrimp (about
  8 ounces), peeled and deveined
6 tablespoons crumbled queso
  fresco or mild feta cheese

2 chiles pasado, lightly toasted
  (page 192) and finely diced
2 tablespoons finely chopped fresh
  cilantro

Place the corn and water in a blender and purée until smooth. Strain through a sieve, pressing down to extract all of the liquid; discard the solids.

Melt the butter in a saucepan over low heat; do not let it get hot. Add the purée and cook over medium heat for 5 minutes, stirring frequently. Add the milk and salt, and bring to a boil. Reduce the heat and simmer gently for 15 minutes, or until the soup has thickened slightly, stirring occasionally.

Meanwhile, heat the canola oil in a medium-sized skillet and fry the tortilla strips over medium-high heat until crisp, about 20 to 30 seconds. Remove and drain on paper towels.

Remove all but 1 tablespoon of the canola oil from the pan, season the shrimp with a little salt, and sauté over medium-high heat until cooked through, about 4 to 5 minutes per side. Remove and reserve.

In the center of each serving bowl, place a small mound of the queso fresco, covered with tortilla strips. Carefully ladle the soup into the bowls around the queso fresco and tortilla strips. Place 2 cooked shrimp, entwined together, on top of the tortilla strips. Sprinkle each serving with the chile pasado and cilantro.

OPPOSITE PAGE *Mission White Bean Soup*

Plains Venison Jerky Soup

Rich Venison Broth Flavored with Mustard Greens, Corn, and Squash

The Sioux, Blackfoot, and other Plains Indians made jerky as a winter provision by curing strips of buffalo or venison with wild herbs and berries and hanging them in the sun to dry, or by slow-drying them over fires. The tradition of drying food was also used by the Native Americans of the Northwest, who preserved salmon in much the same way. You still find salmon jerky sold in the Northwest and along the Canadian coast up to Alaska. The Pueblo Indians of the Southwest, who relied mainly on agriculture for their food supply, traded dried corn, squash, and beans to the Plains Indians for jerky, thus supplementing their largely vegetarian diets and getting a winter source for meat while providing Plains Indians with nutritional vegetables to supplement their diet.

Jerky is best bought in health food stores or in old-fashioned general stores, especially in hunting territory, because the product tends not to be over-salted or flavor-enhanced with MSG. In the Western United States, you can find fresh jerky that's made locally, and you really can tell the difference. You can substitute a good-quality beef or venison jerky for the homemade jerky in this recipe. However, if you are making the jerky at home, note that it should be prepared at least a day ahead of time. You can also make it from lean beef, such as bottom round, if venison is unavailable. The venison stock can be made from bones and scraps or an inexpensive cut of venison obtained from the butcher, or you can use a rich beef stock.

Yield: 4 servings • *Photo page 36*

Venison Jerky

3 pounds boneless venison shoulder or leg, or beef bottom round

2 tablespoons juniper berries, coarsely ground (optional)

½ cup chile caribe (red chile flakes), coarsely ground

½ cup brown sugar

¼ cup freshly ground black pepper

2 tablespoons salt

Soup

½ cup diced turnips

½ cup diced butternut or acorn squash

6 cups (1½ quarts) Venison Broth (recipe follows)

½ cup corn kernels, roasted (page 192)

4 Roma tomatoes (about 8 ounces), roasted (page 192) and chopped

2 cups mustard greens

1 cup arugula

¼ teaspoon salt

1 tablespoon minced fresh marjoram

To prepare the venison jerky, briefly freeze the venison first so that it becomes firm and easier to slice; then slice thinly. Mix the next five ingredients together in a mixing bowl and rub them on the venison. Place the slices of meat on oven racks and slowly dehydrate in an oven set at its lowest temperature (100 to 150 degrees). This process should take at least 8 hours, and may take up to 12 hours.

Bring a saucepan of lightly salted water to a boil. Blanch the turnips and squash in the boiling water for 5 minutes, remove, and drain.

In a large stockpot, bring the Venison Broth to a simmer over high heat. Reduce the heat, add the blanched turnips and squash, and the corn, tomatoes, mustard greens, arugula, jerky, and salt. Simmer for 20 minutes over medium heat to blend the flavors and soften the jerky. Remove the jerky, shred into strips, and return to the soup. Stir in the marjoram and serve immediately.

Venison Broth

2 tablespoons unsalted butter
2 tablespoons peanut oil
1 onion, diced
1 small carrot, diced
4 or 5 large cloves garlic, chopped

1 leek, diced
1 celeriac (celery root), diced
4 cups (1 quart) red wine
¼ cup tomato purée
7 juniper berries, crushed

1 bunch fresh thyme, tied
16 cups (1 gallon) Venison Stock or Beef Stock (pages 193–194)

To prepare the Venison Broth, heat the butter and oil in a heavy-bottomed saucepan and sauté the onion, carrot, garlic, leek, and celeriac over medium-high heat until caramelized, about 20 minutes. Deglaze with the red wine and add the tomato purée. Add the juniper berries and thyme and reduce the liquid over high heat to 1 cup. Add the Venison Stock and bring to a boil. Skim the liquid and simmer for about 2 hours, until the liquid is reduced to 1½ quarts (6 cups). Strain.

Albóndigas Oaxacan-Style

in a Rich Tomato-Smoked Chile Sauce

Albóndigas are Mexican dumplings or meatballs that are eaten as appetizers or added to soups. They are usually made with veal, pork, beef, or a combination of meats, and in coastal areas they're made with seafood, usually shrimp. Most visitors to the southern city of Oaxaca (pronounced wah-HA-cah) are unaware of the state's wonderful coastline that lies a tortuous day's drive away through winding mountain roads. In addition to its folk art and weaving, the state of Oaxaca is famous for its mole sauces and rich culinary heritage, which is based on strong, complex flavors. This recipe is my version of the type of seafood albóndigas you'll find in restaurants in towns like Puerto Angel or Puerto Escondido.

It's interesting that many cuisines in all parts of the world have their meatballs or dumplings—from Italy to China and Mexico. These albóndigas are easy to make and can be prepared and half-cooked ahead of time. Take care not to overcook them, or they will become tough and dry.

Yield: 4 servings

12 ounces large shrimp, peeled and deveined
¼ cup fresh corn kernels, roasted (page 192)
1½ tablespoons minced white onion
1½ tablespoons minced tomato, peeled and seeded
4 teaspoons all-purpose flour
1 egg yolk

1½ tablespoons ancho chile purée (page 192)
½ tablespoon ground coriander
½ tablespoon ground cinnamon
⅔ teaspoon toasted and ground dried Mexican oregano (page192)
⅔ teaspoon salt
2 tablespoons olive oil
½ cup thinly sliced white onion
4 cloves garlic, minced

1 carrot, diced
12 Roma tomatoes (about 1½ pounds), blackened (page 192) and chopped
3 canned chipotle chiles, julienned
6 cups Fish Stock (page 193) or clam juice
¼ cup fresh corn kernels
12 cilantro sprigs, for garnish

In a blender or food processor, pulse the shrimp until a rough paste forms. Transfer to a stainless steel mixing bowl and add the corn, minced onion, minced tomato, flour, egg yolk, ancho purée, coriander, cinnamon, oregano, and salt. Mix well and set over ice water.

Heat the olive oil in a large saucepan and sauté the sliced onion, the garlic, and the carrot over medium heat for 10 to 15 minutes. Add the blackened tomatoes and chipotles, cover, and cook for 15 to 20 minutes longer. Add the stock and corn, and bring to a boil. Reduce the heat to a simmer.

Divide the shrimp into 12 rounded spoonfuls and poach in the liquid for about 5 minutes; do not let the liquid boil. Ladle into soup bowls and garnish with the cilantro.

OPPOSITE PAGE *Yellow Tomato Gazpacho*

Today's enthusiasm for salads stems from a heightened awareness that greens are necessary for a healthy, balanced diet. Greens provide roughage and nutrition, and they should also add flavor. Growing up in New England, the only salad I knew was based on iceberg lettuce, and it was little wonder that everyone slathered on heavy, thick dressings to give their salad some flavor. These days, there's a tremendous variety of interesting, tasty greens available year-round, although if today's salad bars are anything to go by, dressings still haven't caught up. They are still the same creamy and highly caloric ranch, blue cheese, Thousand Island, Russian, and French dressings that parents bought years ago to get their kids to eat salads. As a matter of fact, modern nutritional studies show that dressings account for more "hidden" calories in a meal than any other food. So be careful!

For the most part, Native American diets were balanced and nutritional, and gathering and eating wild greens was an important aspect of their healthful fare. Numerous varieties of edible wild greens grow along the arroyos and canyons and on the craggy mesas and wooded mountainsides. Delicacies such as dandelion greens, salt greens, young thistles,

nettles, tumbleweed shoots, and tansy mustard greens were eaten raw, added to stews, or steamed to accompany other foods. In addition to playing a nutritious dietary role, many of these wild greens (as well as herbs) were used by Native Americans medicinally or in teas.

Before domesticated greens were cultivated in the Southwest, the Native Americans of the region collected these wild greens from early spring through the late fall. The early Spanish settlers in the region learned these practices and continued the tradition of gathering greens. They referred to the wild greens they gathered as verdelitas, a word still used today in New Mexico's Hispanic communities and in Mexican markets.

Greens and vegetables also play a major role in Mexican cuisine. A great many vegetables, including greens, were grown by the Aztecs in the "floating gardens" that surrounded their capital, Tenochtitlán, which is now Mexico City. When you visit Mexico City, the great food markets such as the Mercado Merced have an almost overwhelming display of greens, as well as cacti and edible flowers and leaves from scores of plants. At every big city produce market, you find all kinds of unusual greens, sold mostly by

women who travel in at the crack of dawn from the countryside and the small outlying towns. These women also sell less common types of plants, grown in small home gardens or gathered in the wild, that are used in the local cuisine.

Different greens and vegetables are grown in each region of Mexico, due to different microclimates, eating habits, traditions, and even the demands of local festivals. Many distinctively flavored greens and leaves, such as avocado, orange, and fig leaves, hoja santa, epazote, and romalitos, are not yet commercially available in North America. One of the best reference books on the subject is Lucinda Hutson's Herb Garden Cookbook (Gulf Publishing, 1992).

Salads have not played an important role in the relatively recent rise in popularity of Southwestern cuisine, in part because of the extremes in climate and the short growing season. In fact, all too often, what you find served as salad in the region consists of watery iceberg lettuce and bland tomato slices. The good news is that things are changing, and increasingly we are seeing mixes of interesting greens in our salad bowls, which echoes the way wild greens were gathered and eaten all those centuries ago. High-quality greens are now being grown by organic farmers, often in solar greenhouses that provide a year-round supply. These trends are important, because salads can play a significant role in providing a refreshing counterbalance to the earthier foods in the Southwestern repertoire.

At Coyote Cafe, we favor a version of the Mediterranean mesclun mix. (Mesclun *is actually the word in the French languedoc dialect for "mix."*) A mixture of greens that includes a selection of baby romaine, oak leaf lettuce. arugula, baby spinach, frisée, mizuna, Bibb, radicchio, dandelion greens, or all of these provides an intriguing range of textures, complex flavors, and attractive colors.

You should feel free to use fresh herbs such as cilantro, basil, mint, chives, and epazote in these salad recipes; they can be grown year-round in a window box if you don't have the luxury of a garden.

Ensalada of Wild Chanterelles
with Warm Baby Greens and Wild Boar Bacon

Warm salads are a great way of combining two courses—salads and appetizers—in one. The trick for a successful warm salad is to have the dressing in the saucepan, hot and ready. It also helps to have a big stainless steel salad bowl that can be preheated, and warm plates. Warm salads need greens that hold up well to a heated bowl and warm dressing; nothing's worse than an overdressed blob of fragile greens that have wilted at the faintest suggestion of a heated dressing.

Javelinas, or wild boars, roam the Southwest range in states such as Texas and Arizona. They're range-raised for bacon by the Broken Arrow Ranch in Ingram, Texas. Don't overlook wild boar. It has less fat and a more subtle flavor than regular bacon.

Chanterelle mushrooms have a nutty, delicate flavor and are most commonly available in the late spring and summer. When shopping, buy chanterelles that are dry and spongy, rather than moist or watery. A mixture of the orange and black varieties, sliced lengthwise, makes a striking presentation.

Yield: 4 servings

Dressing

1 tablespoon Spanish sherry wine vinegar
1 shallot, minced

1 teaspoon salt
1 teaspoon freshly ground black pepper

½ cup extra virgin olive oil
½ cup hazelnut or walnut oil

Salad

1 tablespoon olive oil
4 ounces wild boar bacon, applewood-smoked bacon, prosciutto, or smoked prosciutto, sliced and cut into large dice
8 ounces chanterelle mushrooms, sliced lengthwise

Salt and freshly ground black pepper to taste
3 heads baby red oak leaf lettuce (about 5 cups)
3 heads baby green oak leaf lettuce (about 5 cups)
1 head baby frisée (about 1 cup)

¼ cup chopped roasted hazelnuts (page 192), for garnish
1 teaspoon chopped fresh thyme
1 tablespoon sliced fresh chives

To prepare the dressing, place the vinegar, shallot, salt, and pepper in a mixing bowl. Using a whisk, slowly add both oils in a steady stream, whisking continuously until emulsified. Whisk again before dressing the greens.

Heat the olive oil and sauté the bacon over medium heat for 2 minutes. Add the chanterelles and sauté until tender; season with salt and pepper. Add 2 tablespoons of the dressing to the pan and remove from the heat.

Warm a stainless steel bowl and 4 serving plates. Place the greens in the warm bowl, add enough dressing to coat the leaves, and mix well. Divide between the serving plates, and place the mushroom and bacon mixture on top and in the center of the greens. Garnish with the hazelnuts, thyme, and chives, and a sprinkling of freshly ground black pepper.

Mark's Caesar Salad

with Hearts of Romaine, Garlic Croutons, and Parmesan

Remember how McDonald's used to update the gazillions of burgers they'd sold on the sign outside? We're thinking of installing a sign outside Coyote Cafe: 500,000 CAESAR SALADS SERVED! I'm not exactly sure how many we've made to order at my restaurants since I first put on chef whites back in the 1970s, but it must be about that number. I do know it equals to a whole lot of romaine lettuce—maybe a quarter of a million heads.

Recently, I've seen some Southwestern versions of this salad that contain sliced chicken breast or shrimp. It's an innovative twist that can turn a Caesar into a whole meal. Make sure you use high-quality anchovies packed in olive oil and croutons made from fresh (not old or stale) bread. The bread for the croutons should be firm and not too airy or squishy.

This recipe works best with small heads of romaine lettuce. Discard the tough outer leaves and white stalks, and use only the small inner leaves (about 8 to 10 per plate). I prefer to keep the leaves whole, in the traditional manner, rather than cut or tear them. That way, you can pick up the leaves and eat them with your fingers—something that seems to make it tastier and sexier.

Yield: 4 servings

Garlic Croutons

¼ cup extra virgin olive oil
2 cloves garlic, minced

½ loaf white bread, crust removed, cut into ½-inch dice

Dressing

1½ cups extra virgin olive oil
6 cloves garlic
8 egg yolks
8 to 10 anchovies (packed in oil), drained

1 tablespoon Dijon-style mustard
2 tablespoons fresh lemon juice
2 tablespoons sherry vinegar
1 tablespoon freshly grated Parmesan cheese

Freshly ground black pepper to taste

3 heads romaine lettuce, outer leaves removed

¾ cup shaved (or grated) Parmesan cheese

Freshly ground black pepper to taste

Preheat the oven to 325 degrees. To prepare the croutons, combine the olive oil and garlic in a blender or food processor and strain through a sieve; discard any remaining solid pieces of garlic. Place the diced bread in a mixing bowl and drizzle the strained oil over the bread. Toss to coat evenly and transfer to a baking sheet. Bake the croutons in the oven until golden brown and crisp, about 10 minutes. Shake the baking sheet after 5 minutes and watch the croutons carefully because they can scorch or burn quickly.

To prepare the dressing, place the oil and garlic in a blender or food processor and blend together. Strain through a sieve into a mixing bowl, pressing down to extract all the liquid. Add the egg yolks to the bowl and whisk together. Rinse the anchovies under cold running water for 30 seconds, finely mince, and add to the bowl. Add the mustard, lemon juice, sherry vinegar, cheese, and pepper, and whisk until emulsified. Whisk again before dressing the greens.

Place the romaine leaves in a mixing bowl and toss with the desired amount of dressing. Add a little of the grated Parmesan and the croutons, and toss to coat lightly. Divide between 4 serving plates and garnish with the remaining Parmesan and freshly ground pepper.

Pollo en Escabeche
Pickled Chicken Salad in Aromatic Spices

Most Americans think of pickles as vegetable garnish for sandwiches or burgers, but pickling in a spicy, aromatic brine (known as *en escabeche* in Spanish) was another essential method of preserving meat, fish, seafood, and vegetables in the days before refrigeration and canning. The pickling brine always contains salt as well as acid in the form of vinegar or citrus juice, which chemically "cooks" and preserves the ingredients.

The technique has been used for centuries, especially in the Mediterranean region. You often see this method of "cooking" used in the wonderful *tapas* dishes of Spain. The Spanish in turn brought this technique to the New World—the Latin American seafood ceviches are examples of this exchange of culinary ideas. Ceviches use citrus juice to pickle fish and shellfish; citrus fruit was introduced to the Americas by the Spanish.

This recipe makes a very refreshing salad for a hot summer day, and an ideal picnic or buffet item. Make sure that the vegetables don't get overcooked in the pickling brine, which can cause them to become too soggy. Note that the chicken should be marinated overnight. The pickled vegetables can be made up to one week ahead.

Yield: 4 servings

Marinade

2 teaspoons black peppercorns	½ teaspoon cumin seeds	1 teaspoon salt
½ teaspoon allspice berries	4 teaspoons dried Mexican oregano	2 tablespoons unseasoned rice wine vinegar
½ teaspoon cloves	24 cloves garlic, roasted (page 192) and minced to a paste	

2 boneless, skinless chicken breasts (about 8 ounces each)

Pickling Liquid

8 cups (2 quarts) unseasoned rice wine vinegar	2 teaspoons fennel seeds	2 cloves
4 cups (1 quart) water	1 tablespoon coriander seeds	1 cup sugar
8 serrano chiles, with seeds, thinly sliced into rings	1 teaspoon allspice berries	1 cup packed fresh cilantro leaves
1 teaspoon fresh thyme leaves	1 tablespoon star anise	
	1 cinnamon stick	

Vegetables

2 red bell peppers, seeded and cut into ¼-inch rings	2 yellow bell peppers, seeded and cut into ¼-inch rings	2 poblano chiles, seeded and cut into ¼-inch rings
		6 cloves garlic, sliced
Salt to taste	8 ounces mixed baby greens, such as arugula, mizuna, frisée, mustard greens, red leaf lettuce (about 8 cups)	12 fresh cilantro sprigs

To prepare the marinade, grind the pepper, allspice, cloves, cumin, and oregano in a spice grinder or blender to a fine powder. Transfer to a mixing bowl, add the garlic, salt, and vinegar, and mix well. Rub the chicken breasts with the marinade, cover with plastic wrap, and let sit overnight in the refrigerator.

Place all of the Pickling Liquid ingredients, except the cilantro, in a saucepan and bring to a simmer. Reduce the liquid over medium-high heat by one-third. Remove from the heat, add the cilantro, and let steep for 20 minutes. Strain into a clean pan and return to a simmer.

Cook the bell peppers, poblano chiles, and garlic in the Pickling Liquid until just tender, about 8 to 10 minutes. Transfer to a mixing bowl when cooked, cover with some of the Pickling Liquid, and allow to cool to room temperature.

Meanwhile, preheat the oven to 325 degrees. Season the marinated chicken with salt, place on a baking sheet or in an ovenproof dish, and roast for about 8 to 10 minutes, until cooked through. Let cool and cut into thin strips.

To serve, place a bed of baby greens on each serving plate. Top with the pickled vegetables and arrange the sliced chicken alongside the vegetables, on top of the greens. Garnish with the cilantro sprigs. ❧

OPPOSITE PAGE *Wild Forest Mushroom and Seared Scallop Salad*

Ensalada de Espinaca y Piñon
Salad of Young Spinach and Abiquiu Greens with Pine Nuts

Abiquiu (pronounced ABBEY-cue) is a spectacular area that lies an hour's drive north of Santa Fe. Here the Chama River winds its way, shimmering in the bright sunlight, through multicolored sandstone strata and past piñon-dotted, brick red- and tan-colored bluffs and outcroppings. These overlook a wide, cottonwood tree-covered valley south of the Ghost Ranch, made famous by Georgia O'Keeffe, who lived and painted here for more than fifty years. Her landscapes of the Abiquiu Valley perfectly capture the unique features and spirit of the land. This is also where our specialty produce grower, Elizabeth Berry, raises myriad heirloom, organic, and rare vegetables for Coyote Cafe. From corn, squash, beans, and chiles to eggplant, edible plants, and baby greens, Elizabeth truly nurtures all the produce she grows on her magnificent farm, situated by the river beneath towering vermillion cliffs.

This simple recipe works just fine if you prefer to use only spinach, rather than spinach and greens. Just be sure the greens are young and tender. The crisp, clean flavor and texture of the dressed greens contrasts tantalizingly with the rich toasted pine nuts. For a little extra pep, add some thinly sliced red serrano or red Fresno chile rings. Garlic Croutons (page 53) would also make a tasty, crunchy addition.

Yield: 4 servings

Dressing

½ cup extra virgin olive oil

2 teaspoons chopped lemon zest
2½ tablespoons fresh lemon juice

½ teaspoon salt

Salad

4 ounces baby spinach

4 ounces mixed Abiquiu greens, such as arugula, mizuna, baby red Chinese mustard greens, or red leaf lettuce (about 4 cups)

8 rings very thinly sliced onion
½ cup pine nuts, toasted (page 192)
Freshly ground black pepper to taste

Combine the dressing ingredients in a mixing bowl and whisk until emulsified. Whisk again before dressing the greens.

Place the spinach, greens, and onion in a mixing bowl. Toss with enough dressing to coat the leaves, and mix well. Transfer to serving plates and garnish with the pine nuts and pepper.

Ensalada Mixta en Naranja
Arugula and Orange Salad with Mixed Greens

The combination of orange and freshly ground pepper is a classic, especially in Spain, and in this recipe, we match orange with the peppery-flavored arugula. In addition to orange and black pepper, orange and chiles with fruity or smoky tones make a closely related pairing that also works well. For example, steamed tender Penn Cove mussels with a smoky chipotle chile broth spiced with fresh orange juice sounds pretty good to me right now!

Arugula is also known as rocket lettuce. It's especially favored in Italian communities because of its strong, cleansing flavor. It is becoming increasingly popular around the country, and several small produce farms in New Mexico now grow it. It has an aromatic, spicy flavor and a crisp texture; buy arugula without thick veins, which indicates older growth that will taste less peppery and have a less delicate texture. If necessary, you can substitute watercress or baby Chinese mustard greens. The addition of the maroon-colored radicchio in this recipe gives the salad another dimension in both texture and color. Navel oranges work best for sectioning because they are sweet and juicy, and tend to have less pith and membrane than other varieties.

This is another straightforward salad that pairs particularly well with barbecue or meat dishes, and tacos or enchiladas. A salad with light flavors like this one usually makes the best combination with more complex-flavored or rich dishes. As with other salads, here's one reminder: dress the salads at the last minute or the greens will get soggy and the vinegar may make the colors fade or change.

Yield: 4 servings

Dressing

½ cup fresh orange juice
¼ cup sherry vinegar

¼ cup honey
¾ cup walnut oil
2 teaspoons fresh lime juice

2 teaspoons salt
Freshly ground black pepper to taste

Salad

6 cups arugula
2 cups red oak leaf lettuce
1 cup radicchio

1 bulb fennel, sliced very finely
3 oranges, peeled and sectioned

¼ cup finely chopped red onion
16 fresh basil leaves

Chill 4 serving plates.

To prepare the dressing, mix together the orange juice, vinegar, and honey in a mixing bowl. Whisk in the oil and lime juice, season with salt and pepper, and reserve.

Place the arugula, red oak leaf lettuce, and radicchio in a separate mixing bowl. Add the fennel, orange sections, onion, and basil, and toss together. Stir the dressing, add just enough to thoroughly coat the greens, and divide between serving plates.

Salad of Smoked Duck Breast
with Mango Sauce and Field Greens

The technique of smoking meat in order to dry it was used by Native Americans to preserve game for the harsh, cold winters when meat was scarce. This traditional method was also familiar to the early European settlers. Many German and Central European immigrants who came to the United States in the mid-1800s to escape war, famine, and religious persecution settled in Texas near New Braunfels and Fredericksburg. They brought with them their heritage of smoking meat and sausage-making, and inspired one theory that credited them as the originators of barbecue.

Sun-drying meat, such as finely sliced jerky, works well, but substantial cuts need a more thorough method, such as smoking, to extract the moisture and kill all the bacteria. And, of course, smoking yields the by-product of added flavor. The process enhances the natural flavors and richness of duck particularly well. Cold-smoking, where the meat is smoked at a low temperature, ensures that the meat retains its texture and juiciness and does not dry out. I prefer to use fruit wood such as apple or cherry for smoking, because it is flavorful and non-resinous. Make sure the wood (or wood chips) is dried out or

aged, or the smoke will be acrid. Good-quality, small stainless steel stove-top smokers are available in well-stocked camping stores or through camping catalogs (such as REI's and L.L. Bean's), and they're worth the investment.

Peaches or nectarines can be substituted for the mangoes, and a blackberry sauce would also make an unusual alternative. You can use roasted duck or smoked quail if you prefer. For a vegetarian version, smoke a pound of meaty portobello mushrooms and substitute for the duck.

Yield: 4 servings

Marinade

1 tablespoon peeled and minced ginger	⅛ teaspoon salt	¼ cup peanut oil
2 cloves garlic, minced	¼ teaspoon ground chile caribe (red chile flakes)	

4 boneless, skinless duck breasts (about 4 ounces each)

Mango Sauce

½ cup peeled and diced mango	⅛ teaspoon salt	2 tablespoons olive oil
2 tablespoons unseasoned rice wine vinegar		
1 tablespoon fresh lime juice		

Salad

4 ounces mixed field greens, such as arugula, red oak leaf lettuce, mizuna, frisée, and radicchio (about 4 cups)	1 mango (about 8 ounces), peeled, pitted, and thinly sliced	1 red bell pepper, seeded and julienned

To prepare the marinade, thoroughly combine all the ingredients in a mixing bowl. Rub the duck breasts with the marinade and place the breasts in the bowl with the marinade. Cover and refrigerate overnight, or for at least 2 hours at room temperature.

In a smoker, or over a low fire covered with soaked wood chips on a barbecue grill, smoke the duck for about 1 hour until medium rare. Let cool and cut into thin slices.

To prepare the Mango Sauce, place the mango, vinegar, lime juice, and salt in a blender or food processor and blend together. With the blender running, slowly add the oil until it is thoroughly incorporated.

Place the greens in a mixing bowl and toss with the Mango Sauce. Transfer to serving plates and arrange the slices of duck breast, mango, and red bell pepper on top.

Garden Field Salad of Maple-Smoked Duck
Served with Andouille Sausage and Apple Cider-Glazed Shallot Vinaigrette

Andouille (ahn-DOO-ee), one of the famous foods of Louisiana, is smoked, spicy garlic sausage made from pork. It's a Cajun specialty and a primary ingredient in gumbo, but it originated (like a lot of other Cajun foods) in France. A good friend of mine from the San Francisco Bay Area, Bruce Aidells, markets a great andouille, available in many gourmet meat departments of grocery stores under the Aidells label. Paul Prudhomme also markets terrific andouille through his mail-order food company (see "Sources," page 199).

Many people don't associate Louisiana with Texas, but the two states are adjacent and southeastern Texas was settled in part by Louisianans. Both states share the rich culinary heritage of the Gulf Coast. There has always been a significant interchange of culinary ideas between Louisiana and Texas, and from there to the rest of the Southwest, and the use of chiles, spices, and seasonings is just one aspect the foods of these regions have in common. This recipe is my homage to Louisiana and its influence on Southwestern cuisine.

Use young, fresh shallots in this recipe as old ones tend to be bitter and too strongly flavored. A good-quality apple cider will also make a significant difference. You can substitute freshly smoked ham or smoked chicken for the duck, but taste it first to make sure it's moist and not over-salted.

Yield: 4 servings

Marinade

¼ **cup maple syrup**
¼ **cup apple cider**

½ **teaspoon ground canela or cinnamon**
½ **teaspoon ground allspice**

½ **teaspoon salt**

4 **boneless, skinless duck breasts (about 4 ounces each)**

Shallot Vinaigrette

1 **cup fresh unfiltered apple cider**
½ **stick canela or cinnamon**
1 **clove**
1 **allspice berry**

7 **shallots, minced and rinsed in cold water**
¼ **cup Spanish sherry vinegar**
½ **tablespoon good-quality Spanish fino sherry**

¼ **cup peanut oil**
⅛ **teaspoon salt**

Salad

4 **ounces andouille links**
2 **tablespoons sugar**
2 **teaspoons unsalted butter**

2 **Granny Smith apples, peeled, cored, and diced**
2 **cups cooked wild rice**
¼ **cup seeded and finely diced red bell pepper**

1 **scallion, finely diced**
2 **tablespoons chopped toasted pecans (page 192)**

To prepare the marinade, thoroughly combine all the ingredients together in a mixing bowl. Rub the duck breasts with the marinade, place the breasts in the mixing bowl with the marinade, cover and refrigerate overnight.

In a smoker, or over a low fire covered with soaked wood chips in a barbecue grill, smoke the duck for about 1 hour until medium rare. Let cool and cut into thin slices.

To prepare the vinaigrette, place the cider, canela, clove, and allspice in a saucepan, bring to a boil, and reduce the liquid by half, about 5 minutes. Let cool. Mix in the shallots, sherry vinegar, and sherry. Whisk in the oil, and season with salt.

Preheat the oven to 400 degrees. Place the andouille on a baking sheet and roast for 15 minutes. Reserve and keep warm.

In a sauté pan, caramelize the sugar by heating it over high heat until melted and golden brown. Melt the butter into the sugar and add the apples. Toss for 3 minutes, until the apples are coated with the sugar mixture. Transfer to a mixing bowl with the rice, bell pepper, scallion, and pecans. Toss together with half of the vinaigrette.

Arrange the rice salad on serving plates. Slice the andouille on the bias, and place together with the duck slices on and around the salad. Drizzle the remaining vinaigrette over the duck and salad.

Prairie Field Salad

with Native Goat Cheese Fritters and Apple-Cinnamon Oil

Goat cheese has become an increasingly fashionable ingredient in American cuisine during the last fifteen to twenty years, and every region has its own goat cheese producers. Goat cheese is another artifact of the Spanish culinary tradition. Goats and sheep were imported to the New World by the Spanish (along with chickens, pigs, cows, and horses), and herds were driven north from Mexico into the Southwest by early Spanish settlers. The livestock adapted well to the sparse high chaparral, and became invaluable for providing milk and cheese, meat, skins, and wool. After this, they were forever intertwined in the fabric of Southwestern history, providing the resources for woven art as well as yielding food. We take great pride in using New Mexican goat cheese at Coyote Cafe.

The animals were traded to the Navajo and other native groups of the Southwest, who became adept at breeding and raising them. They learned methods of weaving from the Spanish, and these methods can still be seen at Los Ojos in northern New Mexico, about ninety miles north of Santa Fe. Here, visitors are welcome at a traditional Hispanic weaving cooperative, Tierra Wools, where blankets, rugs, and other beautifully woven items are crafted, using the hand-dyed wool from historic breeds of sheep, such as the churros. Native Americans also claim a brilliant legacy of weaving that is one of the great artistic traditions of the continent. Only recently have these weavings been truly recognized for the masterpieces that they are.

One item that was very scarce in the early days of the Southwest was oil for cooking, but that's not the case today. In fact, flavored oils are fast becoming a popular culinary tool, and they can add a distinctive flavor and character to foods, just as the Apple-Cinnamon Oil does for this recipe. It's important to use a good-quality olive oil or a neutral oil such as canola, safflower, or grapeseed, and fresh aromatic herbs, spices, or other ingredients for flavoring.

Yield: 4 servings

Native Goat Cheese Fritters

4 ounces fresh goat cheese	2 tablespoons all-purpose flour	1 cup bread crumbs
1 tablespoon minced fresh basil	1 egg, beaten	

Apple-Cinnamon Oil

2 cups apple cider	1 tablespoon ground canela or	1 teaspoon ground allspice
1 tablespoon sherry vinegar	cinnamon	¼ cup canola oil

Salad

6 ounces mixed field greens, such as red oak leaf lettuce, arugula, frisée, and mizuna (about 6 cups)

In a mixing bowl, combine the goat cheese and basil. Form the mixture into 8 balls, about 1 tablespoon each. Lay the cheese balls on a plate, cover with plastic wrap, and freeze for 1 hour.

Preheat the oven to 350 degrees. Place the flour, egg, and bread crumbs in separate bowls. Remove the cheese balls from the freezer, roll first in the flour to coat, then the egg, and finally the bread crumbs. Place on a baking sheet and bake in the oven for 5 to 7 minutes or until the bread crumb coating is golden brown. Reserve the fritters, keeping warm.

Meanwhile, place the apple cider, sherry vinegar, canela, and allspice in a saucepan and reduce the liquid over high heat to 2 tablespoons. Strain into a mixing bowl, whisk in the oil until emulsified, and let cool to room temperature.

Place the greens in a mixing bowl and toss with the Apple-Cinnamon Oil. Place the tossed greens on serving plates, and place 2 warm fritters on top of the salads.

OPPOSITE PAGE *Sweet Clam Ensalada*

Wild Forest Mushroom and Seared Scallop Salad

with Asparagus, Chipotle Vinaigrette, and Grilled Jalapeño Corn Bread

The combination of fresh, briny, delicate seafood with earthy forest ingredients, such as mushrooms, is one of my favorites. Each adds greater definition to the other because they are so different. The forest and the sea are the two seminal partners of all life. Crab with mushroom gratin, fresh trout stuffed with wild mushrooms, and Maine lobster with truffles are other examples of these pairings that I am partial to. (I know I'm not alone!)

I'm always intrigued by the almost primordial appearance of asparagus; I picture it poking through the misty, dank swamps of the Jurassic or Cretaceous era, though in fact it favors sandy soil and chances are it's not ancient at all. Still, it reminds me of ancient forms of life like the horsetail.

Fresh wild mushrooms are now more accessible year-round since growers rapidly mastered the technique of domestically cultivating them. (Consequently, one might wonder at which point do cultivated wild mushrooms cease to be wild.) When you buy fresh mushrooms, make sure they are dry, not moist, and check them for mold or worm holes. To enhance the flavors of this dish, you can sprinkle a little mushroom powder (made from dried mushrooms ground in a spice mill) over the scallops before grilling them.

Yield: 4 servings • *Photo page 55*

Chipotle Vinaigrette

2 tablespoons canned chipotle chiles in adobo sauce, puréed	2 tablespoons sherry vinegar	Juice of ¼ lime (about ½ tablespoon)
¼ cup olive oil	Pinch of salt	

12 large scallops	4 ounces wild mushrooms, such as chanterelles, black trumpets, morels, or oyster mushrooms	1 red bell pepper, seeded and julienned
16 asparagus spears, pencil thin		4 ounces mixed baby field greens, such as red oak leaf lettuce, mizuna, arugula, and frisée (about 4 cups)
¼ cup canola or vegetable oil	2 cloves garlic, unpeeled	
4 corn tortillas, circle in center cut out to leave a 1-inch-wide "halo"	1 cup fresh corn kernels, roasted (page 192)	Jalapeño Corn Bread (page 19)

To prepare the Chipotle Vinaigrette, whisk together the puréed chipotle with the olive oil in a mixing bowl until emulsified. Then whisk in the vinegar, salt, and lime juice.

Place half of the vinaigrette in another mixing bowl, add the scallops, and cover. Marinate in the refrigerator for 1 hour.

Prepare the grill. Blanch the asparagus in boiling water for 30 seconds, and drain.

Heat the canola or vegetable oil in a heavy skillet and when hot (about 375 degrees), fry the tortilla rings until crisp, about 15 to 20 seconds. Remove and drain on paper towels. Add the mushrooms and garlic to the pan and sauté over medium-high heat for about 5 minutes, until the mushrooms are tender. Discard the garlic.

Remove the scallops from the marinade and grill to medium doneness, about 2 minutes per side.

To serve, fan the asparagus out on one side of each salad plate. Arrange the cooked mushrooms, roasted corn, and red bell pepper in the center of the plate. Place the greens in the center of the tortilla and place the circle next to the mushrooms. Place the scallops on top of the mushrooms and corn, and drizzle with the remaining Chipotle Vinaigrette. Cut 4 large triangles from the corn bread and stand one upright to the side of each salad.

Sweet Clam Ensalada

with Salsa Fresca, Seaweed and Frisée Salad, and Crispy Tortillas

The interior Southwest is not famous for its coastline. Most people's mental image of the Southwest is of cacti, cowboys, cattle, cookouts, and arid landscapes. However, Texas boasts a long and beautiful coastline and a great tradition of seafood. Indeed, as a modern element of Southwestern cuisine, seafood has been adopted from coastal Texan and Mexican cooking. Seafood combines well with Southwestern ingredients and, with modern shipping techniques, it's as fresh in the Southwest as anywhere else.

The Veracruz coast of eastern Mexico is notable for its rich bounty of seafood and extensive repertoire of seafood recipes. There you'll find mariscos (small shellfish dishes) offered on menus in most restaurants and seafood stands in the region. This salad is inspired by the Mexican marisco tradition.

Native Americans enjoyed a rich cultural heritage associated with seafood, especially in the Northwest, on the Eastern seaboard, and on the Gulf Coast. They harvested clams not only for food but for trade. Necklaces and trading beads (wampum) were made from the clam shells. Ironically enough, groups of the earliest European settlers on the East Coast starved to death instead of eating the rich bounty of strange-looking shellfish that they believed to be poisonous.

Premixed, packaged green or black seaweed can be bought in the refrigerated section of health food stores, or Japanese markets. For a Southwestern touch, sprinkle a little red chile powder over the tortillas.

Yield: 4 servings • *Photo page 60*

Clams

24 clams, in their shells	½ cup white wine 2 shallots, minced	2 sprigs fresh thyme

Salsa Fresca

2 tablespoons white onion, finely diced 8 Roma tomatoes (about 1 pound), diced	2 serrano chiles, minced, with seeds 2 tablespoons finely chopped fresh cilantro leaves 1 teaspoon sugar or to taste	¼ cup Mexican beer (such as Dos Equis) 1 teaspoon salt 1 tablespoon fresh lime juice

Dressing

1 cup unseasoned rice wine vinegar 1 tablespoon peanut oil	3 tablespoons sugar ½ teaspoon chile caribe (red chile flakes)	Pinch of salt

½ cup vegetable oil, for frying 4 corn tortillas, julienned Pinch of salt	Juice of ½ lime (about 1 tablespoon) 4 ounces frisée lettuce	4 ounces seasoned fresh green or black seaweed

To cook the clams, place them in a large saucepan with the wine, shallots, and thyme. Cover, bring to a simmer, and cook just until the clams open; discard any that remain closed. Remove from the heat and allow the clams to cool in the liquid. Remove the clams from the shells and dice.

To prepare the salsa, place the onion in a strainer, rinse under running hot water, and strain. Thoroughly combine the onion with the remaining salsa ingredients and the diced cooked clams in a mixing bowl. Add a little more sugar if the tomatoes are acidic, but make sure the salsa does not taste of sugar. Chill in the refrigerator for at least 30 minutes before serving to allow the flavors to combine.

To prepare the dressing, place all the ingredients together in a saucepan and reduce by half over high heat, stirring occasionally. Remove from the heat and let cool.

Heat the vegetable oil in a heavy sauté pan or skillet over high heat. Place the tortilla strips in the hot oil and fry for about 20 to 30 seconds, or until crisp. Remove and drain on paper towels, and sprinkle with the salt and lime juice.

Place the frisée in a mixing bowl and toss with the dressing. Place the salsa in the center of each serving plate and arrange the tossed frisée around it. Place the seaweed on top of the frisée and garnish with the fried tortilla strips. 🐾

TAMALES, EMPANADAS, & MORE

Tamales de Camarón
Shrimp Tamales Served with a Green Mole Sauce

Tamales de Venado
Texas Axis Venison Tamales Served with a Mole Sauce

Sweet White Corn and Wild Boar Bacon Tamales
with Fresh Apple Chutney

Wild Mushroom Tamales
with Roasted Tomatillo and Wild Mushroom Sauce

Tamales de Langosta y Salmón
Salmon and Lobster Tamales with a Smoked-Tomato and Jalapeño Sauce

Huitlacoche Tamales
with Tomatillo Verde Salsa and Huitlacoche Sauce

Layered Spicy Eggplant and Sweet Pepper Tostadas
with Aged Rio Grande Goat Cheese, Lemon Oil, and Fresh Herbs

Blue Crab Coyotas
Fried Blue Corn Turnovers with Fresh Texas Blue Crab and Avocado Salsa

Crab Enchiladas con Chile Amarillo
*Crab Rolled in Green Chile Corn Crepes with Blackened Yellow
Tomato Sauce and Pickled Carrot-Jicama Slaw*

Crispy Conejo Empanadas
with Yellow Mole and Tortilla Salad

Veracruz Tortas
of Fresh Lobster and Corn, Queso Fresco, Sweet Pepper Salsa, and Basil Oil

Barbecued Duck Crepes
Layered Corn Crepes with Roasted Duck, BBQ Sauce, and Corn-Chile Relish

For thousands of years, corn was the staff of life for the people of the Americas. In fact, the modern corn we know today took over five thousand years to develop. Originally a wild grass found in Central America called teosinte, corn was domesticated around 5500 BC. By about 500 BC, after five thousand years of genetic selection, these domesticated types of corn seeds and growing practices had spread to the Southwest, where corn cultivars were further developed for adaptation to local conditions. The Hopis, one of the most famous corn-based cultures, historically grew more than twenty varieties of corn.

Because of its nutritional value and central role in the diet, corn has also occupied a pivotal place in the belief system and ceremonial life of the Native Americans of the Southwest. The Hopis, for example, like earlier, successive Mesoamerican civilizations, believe that corn was a gift from the gods, and that it embodies the spirit of Mother Earth—"the giver of life." Corn dances are still held at the Indian pueblos, and prayers are offered to the spirit of the Corn Mother. Corn myths are handed down through the generations and festivals are held to celebrate its diversity as a food.

Corn, as a mainstay of the diet, led to a multiplicity of recipes. Southwestern cuisine has borrowed on the flexibility of corn to provide a foundation for other foods. Corn is a creative medium for using a staple ingredient in many ways—for breads, sauces, stews, and side dishes, as well as the items described in this chapter.

The arrival of Europeans in the region led to an expanded diet that included domesticated European varieties of vegetables and grains, especially wheat, and far less reliance on corn. However, in many parts of New Mexico where the Hispanic tradition remains strongest, and in Mexico, corn tortillas are still preferred to flour tortillas, and foods based on corn remain the most popular.

When you travel in Mexico, you'll find countless regional variations of the corn masa-based tamales, tacos, and enchiladas. Masa dough is made from soaked ground corn that is mixed with shortening—the same combination from which tortillas are made. Tamales might be cooked in corn husks, parchment paper, banana leaves, or hoja santa leaves; soft corn tacos may have all kinds of fillings, and likewise for enchiladas. At the stalls and tiny storefronts selling these inexpensive snack foods, you can see the corn masa dough sitting in buckets, tubs, bowls, or large

pans, waiting to be hand-patted or formed. The tortillas, quesadillas, tortas, and sopes (small boat-shaped masa shells) are then cooked on a griddle or comal.

The fillings or toppings range from the exotic—squash blossoms, tripe, pineapple-marinated pork, oysters, or ceviches—to the more common mushrooms, shredded pork, chicken or beef, grilled fish or seafood, cheese, and herbs. The best stands display an accompanying array of freshly made salsas, fresh and pickled chiles and vegetables, bowls of cooked beans and cremas, chopped herbs, and mounds of juicy lime wedges that you can add to taste. Sometimes, there's a choice of a dozen or more different toppings. One of the attractions of this style of eating is the freedom you have to flavor your own food to suit your palate.

The corn-based foods of this chapter are also an important part of New Mexican cuisine, reflecting the ties to its Mexican heritage. The main difference between the New Mexican and Mexican versions, in my opinion, is the flavor of the corn—it seems wonderfully rich and sweet in Mexico, with a denser, stronger flavor, and rather more delicate in the United States. The reason is that in Mexico, different varieties of corn are grown specifically for masa dough. These are older varieties that are less prodigious but more flavorful.

The recipes in this chapter are highly versatile and can be served as appetizers, sides, or as a main course. (The portions of these recipes can all be increased if you plan to use them as entrées.) In preparing these antojitos, it's easier to buy ready-made masa dough, which is available from a tortilla factory or a good Mexican market. However, the following recipes assume you don't have that convenience, and are based on dry packaged masa, which is available everywhere in the baking section of grocery stores.

Tamales de Camarón

Shrimp Tamales Served with a Green Mole Sauce

When I think of coastal Mexico, I visualize warm, tropical bays, sun-baked beaches, and small fishing villages with colorful boats bobbing on the tide. Mexico is surrounded by water—the Pacific Ocean, the Gulf of Mexico and the Caribbean, and the Gulf of California. The earliest civilizations were centered on the Gulf Coast. The ocean provided routes for trade and communication as well as livelihoods and sustenance; the diets of these societies relied heavily on seafood. Even when these civi-

lizations moved inland, seafood was still used extensively in pre-Columbian days (remember, there was no pork, beef, lamb, or chicken, which were all brought by the Spanish). Plenty of the catch was dried and shipped to the main population centers.

The dried shrimp used in this masa dough has been an important ingredient in Central American cooking for thousands of years. In the seafood stalls of most coastal regions of Mexico, you will see a large array of fresh and dried

fish, as well as shrimp that are fresh-dried with salt. They may be relatively expensive, but the flavor these shrimp give (in the case of this recipe, to the masa dough) is very intense. In southern Mexico, along the coastlines of Veracruz and Oaxaca, these dried shrimp are frequently used in brothy, picante soups. If you can't find the shrimp in a Latin market, oven-dried or plain shrimp shells will work well.

Yield: 6 tamales

Shrimp Butter

2 cups unsalted butter	3 cloves garlic, roasted (page192) and chopped	2 teaspoons dried Mexican oregano, toasted (page 192) and ground
3 ounces dried Mexican shrimp, or 8 ounces shrimp shells		

Shrimp Stock

18 extra-large shrimp (about 1 pound)	⅔ cup Fish Stock (page 193) or clam juice	1 white onion, diced
4 ounces dried Mexican shrimp	⅔ cup water	1 stalk celery, diced
	1 bunch fresh cilantro	1 carrot, diced

Marinade

½ cup olive oil	Zest of 1 lime	6 cilantro sprigs

2 cups Green Mole Sauce (recipe follows)

Masa

2 cups masa harina	½ teaspoon salt	2 tablespoons chopped fresh cilantro
1 teaspoon baking powder	2 tablespoons fresh corn kernels, roasted (page 192)	
2 teaspoons chile molido or other pure red chile powder		

7 large dried corn husks, soaked in hot water until pliable

To prepare the Shrimp Butter, melt the butter in a saucepan and add the shrimp, garlic, and oregano. Simmer over very low heat for 30 minutes; do not let the mixture brown. Transfer to a blender or food processor and purée. Strain through a fine sieve and allow to cool and solidify.

To prepare the Shrimp Stock, peel the shrimp, discarding the heads and reserving the shrimp. Place the shells and remaining stock ingredients in a saucepan and simmer for 30 minutes. Strain through a fine sieve, pressing down on the solids to extract all the liquid. Discard the solids.

For the marinade, combine the olive oil, lime zest, and cilantro in a bowl, and marinate the reserved peeled shrimp in it.

Prepare the Green Mole Sauce.

To prepare the Masa, whip the Shrimp Butter with the paddle attachment of an electric mixer until light and fluffy. Place the masa harina, baking powder, chile molido, and salt in a separate mixing bowl, and stir in ¾ cup of the Shrimp Stock. Add about 4 tablespoons of the masa mixture at a time into the Shrimp Butter, while beating at high speed. Continue to beat for 10 to 15 minutes, until light and fluffy. Fold in the corn and cilantro.

To prepare the tamales, first tear one of the corn husks into 12 narrow strips and reserve. Lay out one whole husk on a work surface, with the wider part facing you. With a spatula, take about 4 tablespoons of the prepared masa dough and spread in the middle of the corn husk to form (approximately) a 4-inch square, leaving a 1-inch border around the edges of the husk. Place 1 tablespoon of the green mole in the middle of the masa dough and top with 2 or 3 shrimp placed head to tail. Roll up the long side of the tamale in a tight cylinder, folding one side of the masa dough over the other, enclosing the filling. Twist the ends of the corn husk and secure each end with a reserved corn husk strip. Repeat for the remaining tamales.

Lay the tamales seam side down in a steamer and steam over simmering water for 15 to 20 minutes. Let rest, covered, for 10 minutes. Serve on a bed of the remaining green mole (about ¼ cup per plate); the mole should be warm but not hot.

Green Mole Sauce

Green mole (*mole verde*) is a traditional specialty of Oaxaca in southern Mexico; the following recipe is my version of this sauce. It is a light, delicate, and aromatic sauce that can also be served with pork, poultry, and seafood. The sauce should contain sweet and fragrant green leaves and hot green chiles. There are many variations; for example, you can use jalapeño chiles or green New Mexico chiles instead of the poblanos, other green lettuce instead of romaine, and mint, basil, chives, or parsley instead of the cilantro. Using a fresh or even dried hoja santa leaf (also known as the root beer plant because of its sassafras-like flavor) makes all the difference. Alternatively, for hoja santa use fresh licorice mint leaves, which are now available at good nurseries, or dried anise seed or fresh fennel tops. This sauce is traditionally made with duck fat, which you may wish to substitute for the peanut oil.

Yield: about 2 cups

3 tomatillos
½ cup Chicken Stock (page 193)
1 cup chopped romaine lettuce
¼ cup fresh cilantro leaves
1 large hoja santa leaf, or ¼ teaspoon anise seed, toasted (page 192) and ground

3 poblano chiles, roasted and peeled (page 192), seeded, and chopped
¼ teaspoon cumin seed, toasted and ground (page 192)
½ teaspoon coriander seed, toasted and ground (page 192)
¼ teaspoon salt

1 small corn tortilla, dried in the oven and chopped
1 tablespoon chopped fresh epazote (optional)
1 tablespoon peanut oil or duck fat

Husk the tomatillos, wash under hot water, and pat dry. Dry-roast in a skillet or under a broiler for about 4 or 5 minutes. Transfer to a blender or food processor and add the stock, romaine, cilantro, hoja santa, poblanos, cumin, coriander, salt, tortilla, and epazote, and purée.

Add the duck fat or oil to a large skillet and heat until almost smoking. Fry the sauce over high heat for about 4 or 5 minutes, stirring continuously. Strain the sauce and serve warm, not hot.

Sweet White Corn and Wild Boar
Bacon Tamales
with Fresh Apple Chutney

*W*ild boar bacon is a Southwestern specialty, although I read recently that debate is currently raging in England—well, perhaps "raging" is an overstatement—regarding whether to reintroduce the European version of the wild boar to woodlands and more remote public lands. Wild boar bacon has a less smoky flavor than regular bacon and is sweeter, more subtle in flavor, and less fatty. You may substitute a good smoked turkey, chicken, or ham if you prefer.

*W*hite corn tends to be sweeter than yellow because it contains more natural vegetable sugar. New hybrids of white corn also stay sweeter longer after they're picked because the sugar doesn't convert to starch as quickly. Two well-known sweet and flavorful varieties of white corn are Platinum Lady and Silver Queen. We grow these in New Mexico for cooking and for eating on the cob. Fresh corn on the cob is not commonly eaten in Europe because the older varieties of corn ("maize") grown there get dry and starchy quickly, and are used mostly for animal feed. For a sweeter tamale you can substitute apple cider, reduced by half, for the water in the masa recipe.

Yield: 8 tamales

Fresh Apple Chutney

½ tablespoon peanut oil
¼ onion, minced
1 teaspoon dried oregano
1 New Mexico or Anaheim green chile, roasted and peeled (page 192), seeded, and finely diced

1 tablespoon coarsely ground chile pasado, or 1 poblano chile, roasted and peeled (page 192), seeded, and finely diced
1 red Fresno chile or red jalapeño, seeded and minced

1 tablespooon sugar
2 tablespoons apple cider vinegar
¾ cup fresh apple cider, preferably unfiltered
1 large Granny Smith apple, peeled, cored, and diced

Masa

1½ cups masa harina
⅛ teaspoon baking powder
⅛ teaspoon ground cumin
⅛ teaspoon dried ground oregano

⅛ teaspoon salt
1 cup sweet white corn kernels, roasted (page 192)
6 ounces cooked wild boar bacon or regular bacon, diced

3 tablespoons melted unsalted butter
¾ cup water

10 large dried corn husks, soaked in hot water until pliable

To prepare the chutney, heat the peanut oil in a saucepan, and sauté the onion over medium heat until translucent, about 5 minutes. Add the oregano and stir to toast slightly. Stir in the green chile, chile pasado, Fresno chile, and sugar. Deglaze the pan with the vinegar and apple cider, and reduce the liquid by half. Add the apple and simmer for 5 minutes longer. The mixture should be fairly thick but the apple should not be too soft. Let cool.

To prepare the masa, place the masa harina, baking powder, cumin, oregano, and salt in a large mixing bowl. Add the corn, bacon, and butter and mix together. Stir in the water until incorporated. Divide the masa into 8 portions.

To prepare the tamales, first tear 2 of the corn husks into 8 narrow strips each and reserve. Lay out one whole husk on a work surface, with the wider part facing you. With a spatula, take a portion of the masa dough and spread in the middle of the corn husk to form (approximately) a 4-inch square, leaving a 1-inch border around the edges of the husk. Roll up the long side of the tamale in a tight cylinder, folding one side of the masa dough over the other. Twist the ends of the corn husk and secure each end with a reserved corn husk strip. Repeat for the remaining tamales.

Lay the tamales seam side down in a steamer and steam over simmering water for 20 to 25 minutes. Let rest, covered, for 5 to 10 minutes. Serve with the chutney.❧

OPPOSITE PAGE *Crab Enchiladas con Chile Amarillo*

Tamales de Langosta y Salmón

Salmon and Lobster Tamales with a Smoked-Tomato and Jalapeño Sauce

The same year we put this salmon and lobster tamale on our Indian Market Week menu, we prepared 1,200 of them at a single charity event hosted in Los Angeles by Wolfgang Puck to benefit Meals-on-Wheels. So don't be daunted by a recipe calling for a mere 6 tamales! With this recipe, it's important to spread the masa dough very thinly (no more than ¼ inch) because the seafood cooks quickly. If the dough is too thick, the seafood will be overcooked by the time the dough is cooked through.

This is one recipe that calls for the cooked tamale to be served out of the husk—this is an optional presentation, but it's important to eat the tamale with the sauce, which sometimes gets overlooked. The main thing is to be sure your guests do not try to eat the husk—some of ours have been known to try. You can substitute an equal amount of shrimp for the lobster, if you prefer, and you may use chipotle chiles in adobo sauce instead of the jalapeños in the sauce; this means that you don't have to smoke the tomatoes, because the chipotles will provide a smoky flavor. For an attractive presentation, use thin, festively colored curling ribbons to tie the tamales.

Yield: 6 tamales

Lobster Butter

2 cups unsalted butter
12 ounces lobster shells, crushed

6 cloves garlic, roasted (page 192)

4 teaspoons dried Mexican oregano, toasted (page 192) and ground

Filling

8 ounces salmon, cut into ¾-inch large dice
6 ounces uncooked lobster meat, cut into ¾-inch large dice

2 teaspoons seeded and diced red bell pepper
2 teaspoons seeded and diced yellow bell pepper
2 teaspoons seeded and diced poblano chile

1 teaspoon chopped fresh basil
1 teaspoon salt
Freshly ground black pepper to taste

2 cups Smoked-Tomato and Jalapeño Sauce (recipe follows)

Masa

2½ cups masa harina
½ cup Lobster Stock (page 194) or clam juice
1 teaspoon baking powder

1 teaspoon salt
2 tablespoons fresh corn kernels, roasted (page 192)

1 tablespoon seeded and diced red bell pepper
2 teaspoons chopped fresh basil

7 large dried corn husks, soaked in hot water until pliable

To prepare the Lobster Butter, melt the butter in a saucepan and add the lobster shells, garlic, and oregano. Simmer over very low heat for 30 minutes; do not let the mixture brown. Transfer to a blender or food processor and purée. Strain through a fine sieve and allow to cool and solidify.

Combine all the filling ingredients in a mixing bowl and reserve in the refrigerator. Prepare the sauce.

To prepare the Masa, whip the Lobster Butter with the paddle attachment of an electric mixer until light and fluffy. Place the masa harina, lobster stock, baking powder, and salt in a separate mixing bowl, and stir together. Add about 4 tablespoons of the masa mixture at a time to the butter, while mixing at a high speed. Continue to beat for 10 to 15 minutes, until light and fluffy. Fold in the corn, red bell pepper, and basil.

To prepare the tamales, first tear one of the corn husks into 12 narrow strips and reserve. Lay out one whole husk on a work surface, with the wider part facing you. With a spatula, take about 4 tablespoons of the prepared masa dough and spread in the middle of the corn husk to form (approximately) a 4-inch square, leaving a 1-inch border around the edges of the husk. Divide the filling and place in the middle of the masa dough. Roll up the long side of the tamale in a tight cylinder, folding one side of the masa dough over the other, enclosing the filling. Twist the ends of the corn husk and secure each end with a reserved corn husk strip. Repeat for the remaining tamales.

Lay the tamales seam side down in a steamer and steam over simmering water for 12 minutes. Do not overcook or the fish will become dry and crumbly. Let rest, covered, for 5 to 10 minutes. Open the husk and

Blue Crab Coyotas

Fried Blue Corn Turnovers with Fresh Texas Blue Crab and Avocado Salsa

When this item appeared on our first Indian Market menu, we were asked whether coyotas was a misprint or some fiendish made-up word. We explained that this is a recipe that Coyote, our resident quadruped, makes and that has been passed down through the generations. We also added that coyotas is a real Spanish word that refers to a version of an empanada, *a turnover that's usually baked or deep-fried (empanada means "cooked in pastry" in Spanish). Coyotas often contain pumpkin or sweet fillings, and are popular breakfast fare.*

These turnovers can be made ahead of time and reheated in a regular oven (reheating in a microwave will make the pastry too tough). They can be made into small bite-sized apertivos as a cocktail item, or used to accompany a gazpacho soup (page 47) or a smoked-tomato and jalapeño soup based on the sauce recipe (page 79). The flour is added along with the cornmeal to the dough because corn has a low gluten content and does not bind the pastry together on its own.

Yield: 4 to 6 servings (12 turnovers)

Dough

½ cup blue cornmeal	2 egg yolks	3 to 4 tablespoons water
1 cup all-purpose flour	¼ cup unsalted butter	
1 teaspoon salt	1 tablespoon cider vinegar	

Avocado Salsa (recipe follows)

Filling

1½ ounces bacon (about 3 slices), finely diced (optional)	1 tablespoon minced scallions, green parts only	½ tablespoon bacon fat (optional)
4 ounces blue crab meat or regular crab meat	2 tablespoons sour cream	Salt to taste

Egg Wash

1 egg	1 tablespoon water

4 cups (1 quart) vegetable or peanut oil, for deep-frying

To prepare the dough, sift the cornmeal and flour into a mixing bowl, add the salt, and blend in the egg yolks. Cream in the butter in tablespoon increments. Add the vinegar, then the water a little at a time, and mix just until a soft dough is formed; do not overmix. Chill the dough while making the salsa and filling.

Prepare the salsa.

For the filling, sauté the bacon in a skillet until browned and rendered of fat. Drain off the fat and reserve. Let the bacon cool. Transfer the bacon to a mixing bowl and add the crab meat, scallions, sour cream, and bacon fat. Stir until just blended and lightly season with salt.

To prepare the egg wash, whisk together the egg and water.

On a lightly floured work surface, roll out the dough to a thickness of ⅛ inch and cut into 12 circles about 3 inches across. Evenly divide the filling between the circles of dough, and brush egg wash around the circles' edges. Fold the dough over into half-moon shapes and using the tines of a fork dipped into flour, seal the turnovers tightly. Brush the turnovers with egg wash.

Heat the oil in a deep fryer or saucepan to 350 degrees. Deep-fry the turnovers for 3 to 4 minutes. Remove and drain on paper towels before transferring to serving plates. Serve with the salsa.

Avocado Salsa

Yield: about 2 cups

2 large avocados (about 1 pound), peeled, pitted, and chopped	3 tablespoons red onion, minced	2 teaspoons minced fresh cilantro
1 Roma tomato, diced	4 teaspoons minced serrano chile, with seeds	1½ teaspoons salt
		¼ cup fresh lime juice

Carefully fold all the ingredients together in a mixing bowl, guacamole-style.

OPPOSITE PAGE *Huitlacoche Tamales*

Veracruz Tortas

of Fresh Lobster and Corn, Queso Fresco, Sweet Pepper Salsa, and Basil Oil

Corn and lobster may seem like unlikely partners, but they have a natural propinquity. They're eaten together both in New England (where the traditional clambake includes lobster and corn on the cob as well as clams), and in the Mexican coastal regions of Veracruz and the Yucatán, where they're paired together in caldos (substantial soups) and in soft corn tacos filled with spiny lobster and chiles. Mexican lobster is also known in the United States as spiny lobster, a warm-water crustacean (unlike the cold-water Maine lobster).

In Mexico, a torta can either be a sandwich or layered tostadas—fried corn tortillas with an open-face topping, similar to Italian lasagna. This recipe refers to the latter style. You can substitute crab for the lobster, corn tortillas softened in hot oil for the flour tortillas or crepes, and a good fresh Parmesan for the queso fresco (which can be obtained from Paula Lambert's Mozzarella Co. in Dallas; see "Sources," page 199). Note that the basil oil takes about a week to marinate; however, you can buy a ready-made oil at gourmet and specialty stores. One really good brand, Consorzio, is marketed by Michael Ciorello's Tra Vigne restaurant in Napa Valley and sold by such specialty stores as Williams-Sonoma and Cost Plus.

Yield: 4 servings

Basil Oil

1 cup fresh sweet basil leaves (1 large bunch)	12 cloves (1 head) garlic, roasted (page 192)	3 cups virgin olive oil 1 tablespoon extra virgin olive oil
2 live Maine lobsters	4 flour tortillas	½ cup peanut oil

Filling

¼ cup olive oil 2 cups fresh corn kernels (from 3 ears) ½ cup roasted, peeled, seeded, and julienned red bell pepper (page 192)	½ cup roasted, peeled, seeded, and julienned yellow bell pepper (page 192) 4 scallions, minced 1 tablespoon chopped fresh basil 2 teaspoons cayenne powder	¼ teaspoon salt

¼ cup grated (or crumbled) queso fresco or jack cheese

To prepare the Basil Oil, place the basil in a jar or glass container large enough to hold the oil. Thread the garlic on a wooden skewer and place in the jar (this will keep the garlic suspended in the oil). Add the olive oils, seal tightly, and store in a cool, dark place for 1 week to fully blend the flavors. Basil Oil should be used within 3 to 6 months.

Bring a large stockpot of water to a boil. Blanch the lobsters for 5 minutes. Remove the lobsters from the water and shock in ice water until cool. Remove the tail and claw meat, cut into large pieces, and set aside (there should be about 1½ cups).

Cut out 2 circles, about 3 inches across, from the center of each tortilla. Heat the peanut oil in a sauté pan or skillet and when hot, fry the tortillas until crisp but not brown, about 15 to 20 seconds. Drain on paper towels and keep warm.

To prepare the filling, heat the olive oil in a sauté pan and sauté the corn over high heat for 2 minutes. Stir in the bell peppers and scallions, and cook for 1 minute longer. Stir in the reserved lobster meat, basil, cayenne, and salt, and toss to heat through. Remove from the heat.

To serve, place one fried tortilla on each plate, spread one-quarter of the lobster mixture over it, and put another tortilla on top to form a sandwich. Drizzle the basil oil around the plate. Repeat for the remaining tortas.

Barbecued Duck Crepes
Layered Corn Crepes with Roasted Duck, BBQ Sauce, and Corn-Chile Relish

This recipe was inspired by my friend Larry Forgione, a champion of American regional cuisine who owns An American Place on Park Avenue in New York City and The Beeckman Arms in Rhinebeck, (upstate) New York. Larry is also the creator and owner of American Spoon Foods, which is a wonderful product line of all-natural preserves, seasonings, and condiments, based in Michigan.

There is considerable regional variation in American barbecue sauces. Most are based on tomatoes or ketchup; in the Carolinas, they are mustard-based, thinner in texture, and spicier. In the Southwest, barbecue sauces usually contain molasses, brown sugar or sorghum syrup, and chiles, which makes them hotter and sweeter than Southern barbecue sauces, which are made with more vinegar. One of my favorite ready-made barbecue sauces is "Buckaroo," from Texas. Most commercial barbecue sauces are too sweet, not hot enough, and overpriced, so if you have the time, it's worth making your own. Most recipes for homemade barbecue sauce tend to be complicated, but you can adapt a store-bought version to taste by adding puréed roasted garlic, spices, chipotle chile purée, cider vinegar, and some drippings from the roasting pan. Strain, and ¡mira!

Yield: 8 servings

1 duck (4½ to 5 pounds)

2 cups hot and spicy barbecue sauce

Crepes

1 cup all-purpose flour
¾ cup cornmeal
1½ teaspoons salt
2 tablespoons chile molido or other pure red chile powder

3 eggs
1¼ cups half-and-half
1½ cups milk
½ cup melted unsalted butter

8 teaspoons clarified butter (page 192)
1 cup fresh cilantro leaves

6 ounces fresh goat cheese

4 cups Corn-Chile Relish (recipe follows)

Preheat the oven to 350 degrees. Place the duck in a roasting pan and roast in the oven for about 1½ hours, or until the juices run clear when the thigh is pierced. Remove, turn off oven, and let duck rest for at least 20 minutes. When cool enough, shred the meat from the carcass and toss with the barbecue sauce. Set aside.

To prepare the crepes, place the flour, cornmeal, salt, and chile molido in a large mixing bowl. In a separate mixing bowl, whisk together the eggs, half-and-half, and milk, and add to the flour mixture. Stir until smooth; the batter should be the consistency of heavy cream. Stir in the melted butter and strain into a clean bowl. Allow the batter to rest for 30 minutes.

Heat a nonstick or seasoned heavy cast-iron crepe pan or skillet and add 1 teaspoon of the clarified butter. Add enough batter to form a thin 6- to 7-inch-wide crepe. Cook the crepe over medium-high heat; just before turning, add 8 to 10 cilantro leaves. Lightly brown on both sides. Remove the crepe and keep warm, and repeat for the remaining crepes.

Preheat the oven again to 350 degrees. Lightly butter two 6-inch cake pans. Trim the crepes to fit the pans and place one in the bottom of each pan, cilantro side down. Spread one-quarter of the duck meat evenly over each crepe. Place another crepe over the duck meat in each pan, and spread the goat cheese over the crepe. Add another crepe to each cake pan and add the remaining duck. Top with the remaining crepes and cover with foil.

Bake in the oven for 25 minutes or until the crepes are hot in the center. Invert the crepes onto serving platters and let them cool slightly. Cut each cake into quarters and serve with the relish.❧

Corn-Chile Relish

Yield: about 4 cups

5 cups Brown Poultry Stock (page 193)

2 cups fresh corn kernels (about 3 ears)

2 serrano chiles, seeded and finely minced

½ cup seeded and diced red bell pepper

½ tablespoon fresh marjoram, finely chopped

½ teaspoon salt

2 teaspoons balsamic vinegar

1 tablespoon chopped fresh cilantro

1 tablespoon unsalted butter

8 sprigs fresh cilantro, for garnish

In a saucepan over high heat, reduce the stock to 2 cups. Add the corn, serranos, bell pepper, marjoram, and salt, and continue to reduce for 30 seconds. Remove from the heat. Add the balsamic vinegar and cilantro, whisk in the butter, and adjust the seasoning. Garnish relish with the cilantro sprigs (1 per portion).

APPETIZERS

Queso Fundido
Broiled Fresh Goat Cheese in a Poblano and Pumpkin Seed Sauce

Gallina Canyon Squash-Blossom Pudding
with Elizabeth's Ranch Arugula Salad

Blue Crab Cakes
Fresh Texas Blue Crab Sautéed in Sweet Butter
with Green Chile Chutney

Crepas de Elote con Salmón
Corn Crepes with Cured Salmon

Ostiones Yucateca
Fresh Pacific Oysters Cooked in a Spicy Black Pepper Sauce

Tortillas de Maíz
Griddle-Fried Fresh Corn Cakes
with Gulf Shrimp and Chipotle Butter

Fresh Washington Manila Clams
in a Spicy Broth of Smoked Chile,
Tomatoes, Orange Zest, and Roasted Garlic

Spicy Pacific Tartares
Tuna with Serrano-Cilantro Mayonnaise
and Salmon with Smoked Chiles

Barbecued Tamarind Baby Back Pork Ribs
Marinated Smoked Pork Ribs Finished in a Tamarind Glaze, Served with Mint-Tomatillo Chutney

Green Chiles Rellenos
Stuffed with Picadillo of BBQ Brisket

Sierra Blanca Lamb Tamale Tarts
with Achiote Masa, Pinto Beans, Garlic Custard, and Tomatillo-Chipotle Sauce

*A*ppetizers should stimulate the appetite and act as a curtain raiser for the main course of the meal. This is certainly the case in Southwestern cuisine, which features a strong tradition of satisfying and flavorful appetizers. This style is derived mainly from the Mexican and Latin American concept of snacks, and in turn, from the Spanish tapas, or small plates of tasty tidbits.

If you travel to Mexico today, you'll find snack foods sold at stands in the food markets, supermarkets, airports, railway stations, and just about any commercial area. In the coastal regions, the stands sell mariscos, or fish and seafood snacks. I enjoy visiting the food markets in Mexico and assuaging the inevitable hunger pangs that come with ogling chiles, fresh produce, and prepared foods like the juicy pork and pineapple taco pastore huraches (puréed bean and cheese long tostadas), or squash-blossom quesadillas. Sampling the snacks at these different stands is like eating an appetizer at several different restaurants, only much more convenient. These apertivos are real food, not just the pretzels, chips, popcorn, or nuts that are the familiar snack foods of North America.

This style of eating stems from the sociable nature of the Spanish and Mexican cultures. Bars, cafés, and snack stands are meeting places where people meet, sit and gossip, or tell stories over coffee or a beer and tapas or apertivos. Small food items are also convenient to keep at home for the inevitable visitors. Snacks can be prepared inexpensively and easily on a daily basis, although sometimes they are miniature versions of main courses.

The appetizers in this chapter reflect the philosophy of Southwestern food. They are satisfying, contain robust flavors, and are usually more complex than their European counterparts. They are meant to stand alone and not necessarily act as a prelude to a whole meal. They can be served on platters and shared, as well as served individually.

We've chosen appetizers that can be expanded into main meals, or adapted for picnics or brunches. You can make a meal by grouping some of these appetizers together (this is known as the menu "grazing" concept). I like this approach because it is less structured and lends itself to informality. Some of these appetizers may be familiar—like the Queso Fundido—while others, such as the oysters (Ostiones Yucateca) or the Squash-Blossom Pudding are more esoteric. For convenience, they're grouped here into three sections. The first couple of recipes are vegetarian; the next group is based on seafood; and the final group uses meat.

Queso Fundido

Broiled Fresh Goat Cheese in a Poblano and Pumpkin Seed Sauce

Queso Fundido ("melted cheese") is the Mexican equivalent of cheese fondue. It's usually made with a mozzarella-type of cheese that gets awfully stringy when melted, which can make eating it something of a test. Our version gets around this problem by using goat cheese, but as an alternative, you can substitute a mixture of cheeses such as Muenster, jack, and mozzarella, especially if you still crave the stringy effect. The boucheron called for in this recipe is a type of fresh, mild French log-style goat cheese, but you can use any kind of fresh goat cheese.

Pumpkin seeds, used for the pesto in this recipe, were grown by Native Americans and stored through the winter, along with dried pumpkin flesh. Pumpkin was an important crop and the seeds provided a good source of calories. They were also ground into flour and used for their oil. Buy hulled, unroasted, and unsalted pumpkin seeds, and make sure they're fresh because they can become rancid fairly rapidly. The best way to ensure their freshness is to buy them at a popular health food store that has a high turnover.

Yield: 6 servings

4 poblano chiles, roasted and peeled (page 192), seeded
¾ cup pumpkin seeds, toasted (page 192)
½ cup cilantro leaves
½ tablespoon salt
1½ tablespoons extra virgin olive oil
8 ounces boucheron goat cheese or fresh goat cheese
¾ cup pine nuts, lightly toasted (page 192), and coarsely chopped
Tortilla chips

Preheat the oven to 300 degrees. Place the roasted poblanos, pumpkin seeds, cilantro, and salt in a food processor or blender. Add the oil in a steady stream with the machine running until it reaches a puréed, pesto-like consistency.

Cut the cheese into 6 even slices. Roll them in the pine nuts, pressing the larger pieces into the sides of the cheese. Place each cheese slice in a small individual casserole dish, and spoon some of the pesto around.

Bake in the oven for 5 to 8 minutes, or until the cheese is warm and bubbly. Serve with warm tortilla chips. 🐷

Gallina Canyon Squash-Blossom Pudding

with Elizabeth's Ranch Arugula Salad

Squash blossoms have always been a feature of the Native American cuisine of the Southwest, and they were considered a particular delicacy by the Zuni tribe of western New Mexico. In fact, the Havasupai, who settled in the Grand Canyon area, and other Southwestern Native Americans made a squash-blossom pudding with immature corn, squash blossoms, and seasoning. The blossoms were boiled and mashed, added to the cooked corn, and then simmered until the mixture thickened. Squash blossoms are also a specialty at Coyote Cafe when they come into season, which is usually during June, and we stuff them with cheese and herbs, and use them in soups, quesadillas, and ravioli, as well as in this pudding recipe. This pudding is almost flanlike in consistency and also makes a great side for serving with grilled lamb.

Squash blossoms have a very delicate flavor, and are fragile. Our supplier, Elizabeth Berry, picks them early in the morning before the blossoms open, and delivers them, refrigerated, the same after-noon, carefully packed in trays covered with damp towels. Most people who grow squash in their gardens don't realize that the blossoms and stems are edible, which is a great shame. Male blossoms are preferred for picking because they grow larger than the female blossoms, and don't go on to form fruit. However, some male blossoms must be left for fertilization. Unfortunately, squash blossoms don't ship well, which is why you don't usually see them in stores.

Yield: 4 servings • *Photo page 100*

2 cups milk
¾ cup cornmeal
1 teaspoon seeded and diced red bell pepper
1 teaspoon seeded and diced yellow bell pepper

3 eggs, yolks and whites separated
10 squash blossoms, julienned
1 teaspoon chopped fresh thyme
1 teaspoon chopped fresh chives
⅔ cup fresh corn kernels (from 1 ear)

2 tablespoons unsalted butter, softened
4 teaspoons crumbled goat cheese

Tomato Vinaigrette

2 tablespoons olive oil
2 tablespoons sherry vinegar
1 tablespoon minced shallots

4 Roma tomatoes, oven roasted (page 192) and finely diced
1 tablespoon chopped fresh chives

⅛ teaspoon salt

Arugula Salad

2 ounces arugula (about 2 cups)

1 ounce frisée (about 1 cup)

Preheat the oven to 350 degrees. To prepare the pudding, bring the milk to a boil in a saucepan. Slowly stir in the cornmeal. Add the bell peppers, egg yolks, squash blossoms, thyme, chives, and corn. Set aside and let cool.

In a mixing bowl, whisk the egg whites until stiff peaks form. Fold the egg whites into the cooled batter in the saucepan.

Liberally butter four 6-ounce ramekins or pudding molds. Pour half of the batter into the ramekins. Add 1 teaspoon of the goat cheese to each ramekin. Then top with the remaining batter.

Place the ramekins in a water bath in the oven; the water should come about half-way up the sides of the ramekins when they are sitting in a baking pan. Bake the puddings for 20 minutes, uncovered, or until set.

Meanwhile, prepare the vinaigrette by thoroughly whisking all the ingredients together in a mixing bowl.

Remove the puddings from the oven and let cool slightly, about 5 minutes, before unmolding. Place in the center of each serving plate.

Toss the arugula and frisée with the vinaigrette and place the salad around the puddings.

Blue Crab Cakes

Fresh Texas Blue Crab Sautéed in Sweet Butter with Green Chile Chutney

Texas is the colorful home of the Red River, bluebonnets, yellow roses, and blue crabs. The fishing ports of Galveston and Corpus Christi are both situated on the long coastline that stretches for hundreds of miles from Louisiana to the Mexican border, and a huge amount of seafood passes through their wholesale markets. Much of the cuisine of southern Texas is based on fish and shellfish, and a good proportion of the seafood served in the Southwest, including landlocked states such as New Mexico, comes from Texas.

While crab meat can be used in many different ways, crab cakes are perennial favorites. It may sound obvious, but the best crab cakes are those composed of crab as the main ingredient. All too often, crab is regarded as an incidental and ends up dominated by filler ingredients. Cooking the crab cakes in clarified butter helps ensure they don't burn, but, even so, take care to sauté them slowly enough so they're well heated through. The green chile chutney gives the crab cakes a spicy New Mexico accent.

Yield: 4 servings

New Mexico Green Chile Chutney

- 2 tablespoons virgin olive oil
- 1 tablespoon minced white onion
- 2 cloves garlic, finely minced
- ½ tablespoon grated fresh ginger
- 6 New Mexico or Anaheim green chiles, roasted and peeled (page 192), seeded, and finely diced
- 6 jalapeño chiles, roasted and peeled (page 192), seeded, and finely diced
- ½ cup sugar
- ¾ teaspoon finely ground dried oregano
- ½ teaspoon ground cinnamon
- ½ teaspoon salt
- 1 cup cider vinegar

Crab Cakes

- 1 cup plus 2 tablespoons clarified butter
- ⅓ cup thinly sliced scallions (green part only)
- 1 pound blue crab meat
- 3 tablespoons fresh corn kernels, roasted (page 192)
- 2 tablespoons seeded and diced red bell pepper
- 2 tablespoons seeded and diced yellow bell pepper
- 1 egg, beaten
- 1 pound good-quality white loaf bread, crust removed
- 2 tablespoons heavy cream
- ½ tablespoon chopped fresh marjoram

To prepare the chutney, heat the oil in a stainless steel or other nonreactive saucepan and sauté the onion, garlic, and ginger for 5 minutes over medium heat. Add the chiles, sugar, oregano, cinnamon, and salt, and cook for 10 minutes longer, stirring to make sure the sugar is dissolved. Deglaze the pan with the vinegar and cook until thickened, about 10 minutes. Let cool.

To prepare the Crab Cakes, heat 2 tablespoons of the butter in a skillet and wilt the scallions over medium heat for 2 or 3 minutes. Remove the pan from the heat and let cool.

Carefully pick any shell from the crab meat, break up any large clumps, and place in a mixing bowl. Add the corn, bell peppers, beaten egg, and sautéed scallions and mix together. Set aside.

Place the bread in a food processor and pulse to make fine bread crumbs. Transfer half of the bread crumbs to a separate mixing bowl, add the cream and marjoram, and mix together thoroughly with a wooden spoon.

Form the crab mixture into 8 patties, about 2½ inches across and ¾ inch thick. Press each patty with the remaining bread crumbs to coat thoroughly, and refrigerate for about 1 hour.

Heat the remaining 1 cup of clarified butter in a heavy skillet, add the crab cakes, and cook for 3 or 4 minutes per side over medium-low heat until golden in color but not brown. Serve with the chutney.

Crepas de Elote con Salmón

Corn Crepes with Cured Salmon

The best-known and most famous cured fresh salmon is the Swedish gravlax, a classic recipe that uses fresh dill, salt, and sugar. In this version, we create Southwestern flavors by curing the salmon with pungent thyme and cilantro, fresh chile powder, and tequila.

Tequila is produced from the blue agave plant, which Mexican government regulations decree can be grown only in a specific area, contiguous to five states; most is grown in Jalisco, Nayarit, and Michoacan. Tequila is now immensely popular in the Southwest and enjoys the fastest-growing sales of all liquors nationwide. We stock more than twenty brands at Coyote Cafe. In her wonderful new book, ¡Tequila! (Ten Speed Press, 1995), my friend Lucinda Hutson describes all kinds of recipe applications for tequila, in addition to the best cocktails.

Most North American salmon is caught off the coast of Alaska and the Northwest, usually between the spring and fall. Before Europeans settled North America, Native Americans in the coastal Northwest fished for salmon with huge nets made from woven vines, and the fish were so abundant that they were scooped up by the thousands throughout the day and night while they were "running" to their breeding grounds. The Native Americans preserved whatever they couldn't eat by smoking, drying, and freezing, so they would have enough to last them through the winter.

Note: this recipe requires 3 to 4 days advance preparation.

Yield: 6 servings

Cured Salmon

- 2 pounds salmon, with skin
- 6 tablespoons sugar
- 6 tablespoons kosher salt
- ¼ cup chile molido or other pure red chile powder
- 1 teaspoon freshly ground black pepper, or to taste
- 3 tablespoons chopped fresh thyme
- ¼ cup chopped fresh cilantro
- 6 tablespoons (2 jiggers) tequila

Red Chile Crepes

- ¼ cup fresh corn kernels
- 1½ cups beer
- ¼ cup all-purpose flour
- ¼ cup cornmeal
- ¾ tablespoon paprika
- ¾ tablespoon cayenne chile powder
- 4 eggs
- ¼ cup canola oil

- 1 cup cooked black beans
- ½ teaspoon puréed canned chipotle chiles in adobo sauce
- 1 tablespoon chopped fresh cilantro
- ½ teaspoon salt
- ¾ cup Cucumber and Avocado Salsa (recipe follows)
- ½ red bell pepper, roasted and peeled (page 192), seeded, and julienned
- ½ poblano chile, roasted and peeled (page 192), seeded, and julienned
- ¼ cup sour cream
- 3 tablespoons salmon caviar, for garnish (optional)

Place the salmon skin side down in a shallow nonreactive pan. In a mixing bowl, combine the sugar, salt, chile molido, and black pepper. Spread the mixture evenly over the salmon and then sprinkle with the thyme and cilantro. Drizzle the tequila over the top, cover with plastic wrap, and refrigerate for 72 hours. Place an evenly resting, light weight on top of the salmon. Turn the salmon every 24 hours, discarding any accumulated liquid with each turn.

To prepare the crepes, purée corn kernels with beer. Combine puréed mixture with all the remaining crepe ingredients in a mixing bowl until smooth. Allow to set for 1 hour. Heat a small sauté pan and add a few drops of oil. Add just enough batter to cover the pan with a very thin layer, tilting the pan so the mixture spreads evenly. When cooked on one side, toss or turn with a spatula and cook on the other side. Repeat for the other 6 to 8 crepes, stacking the cooked crepes between sheets of waxed paper to keep them from sticking together.

Place the black beans, chipotle purée, cilantro, and salt into a food processor and purée. Lay the crepes out on a flat surface and spread each one with 2 tablespoons of the purée. Slice the salmon as thinly as possible on a sharp bias. Layer the slices evenly over the bean purée, using about 3½ ounces of salmon per crepe. Place 2 tablespoons of the salsa in a line across the bottom third of the crepe. Lay the roasted pepper strips next to the salsa and roll up the crepes as tightly as possible.

Evenly slice each crepe on a slight bias into 6 to 8 pieces. Garnish each slice with sour cream and caviar.

Cucumber and Avocado Salsa

Yield: about 1¼ cups

¼ cup diced and seeded cucumber

1 large avocado (about 8 ounces), peeled, pitted, and chopped

1 small Roma tomato, diced

1½ tablespoons red onion, minced

2 teaspoons minced serrano chile, with seeds

1 teaspoon minced fresh cilantro

¾ teaspoon salt

2 tablespoons fresh lime juice

Carefully fold all the ingredients together in a mixing bowl, guacamole-style.

Photo: Natt N. Dodge, Courtesy Museum of New Mexico.

Ostiones Yucateca

Fresh Pacific Oysters Cooked in a Spicy Black Pepper Sauce

In the Yucatán peninsula of Mexico, oysters, conch, and other shellfish are often simmered with black pepper, red chile, or spices. These antojitos are often served in cold sundae glasses in bars or at the marisco stands in markets, and taste wonderful with an ice-cold beer under the hot tropical sun.

Use large, plump oysters for this recipe, because the cooking process shrinks them by about half. Cold-water Washington State oysters that measure about 1½ inches long and ½ inch thick are among the best for this recipe; their texture holds up better to cooking than warm-water oysters.

Oysters were so plentiful in the early days of American colonization that they were a common part of the diets of the rich and poor alike. In the 1800s, oyster saloons, oyster bars, and oyster cellars flourished in most big cities on the East Coast. However, the demand was so intense that the supply began to seriously dwindle by the end of the century. Today, alas, there are very few safe oyster beds off the coast of North America.

For a variation, if you prefer, or if oysters are not in season, substitute the same amount of shrimp, scallops, or clams.

Yield: 4 servings

Pico de Gallo

1 tablespoon finely diced onion
1 cup diced Roma tomatoes
1 serrano chile, seeded and minced

1 tablespoon finely chopped fresh cilantro
1 teaspoon sugar, or to taste

2 tablespoons Mexican beer (such as Negra Modelo or Dos Equis)
1 teaspoon salt
Juice of ½ lime

---

12 large oysters
Clam juice (as needed)
¾ tablespoon freshly cracked black pepper

3 bay leaves
1 tablespoon extra virgin olive oil
2 teaspoons fresh lime juice
½ teaspoon sea salt

4 flour tortillas
Peanut or corn oil, for deep-frying

To prepare the Pico de Gallo, place the onion in a small strainer, rinse with hot water, and drain. Transfer to a mixing bowl, add the remaining salsa ingredients, and mix well. Let sit, refrigerated, for at least 30 minutes for the flavors to marry (the yield is about 1 cup).

Shuck the oysters by holding the hinged end of each shell toward you and inserting the tip of a knife into the hinge. Twist the knife to open the shell; run the knife tip along the inside edge of the top shell and sever the upper muscle. Then, run the knife under the oyster meat and sever the bottom muscle. Place ½ cup of their liquor (juice) in a saucepan; add a little clam juice, if necessary, to make ½ cup liquid. Add the pepper to the pan with the bay leaves. Bring the pan to a boil, reduce the heat to low, add the oysters, and poach lightly for 3 to 5 minutes, or until the oysters are just firm.

Remove the oysters with a slotted spoon and set aside in the refrigerator. Reduce the poaching liquid to ⅓ cup over high heat. Remove the liquid from the heat and chill in the refrigerator.

When the poaching liquid is cold, stir in the olive oil, lime juice, and salt. Pour the sauce over the chilled oysters and set aside.

Cut the flour tortillas into 3-inch wedges. Heat the oil in a saucepan until hot and fry the tortilla wedges until crisp.

Place the fried tortillas on a serving platter and top each wedge with 1 oyster and a dollop of the sauce. Garnish with the Pico de Gallo.

OPPOSITE PAGE *Gallina Canyon Squash-Blossom Pudding*

Tortillas de Maíz
Griddle-Fried Fresh Corn Cakes with Gulf Shrimp and Chipotle Butter

This appetizer is one of Coyote Cafe's best-known signature dishes, and it also makes a great breakfast or brunch dish. In addition to the tangy taste the buttermilk gives the batter, this recipe combines three of my favorite ingredients: shrimp, corn, and smoky chipotle chiles. Chipotles are the dried form of the fresh,

ripe jalapeño, slowly smoked over dried chile foliage or mesquite. They can be purchased either in dried form, in which case they need to be rehydrated in warm water (page 192), or canned in a spicy adobo sauce, a pickling liquid made with a base of tomatoes and vinegar.

Only use fresh, sweet corn—frozen just isn't as good and it doesn't work as well. The corn cakes are versatile and can be used in other ways; for example, layered with apple butter as a breakfast dish, or prepared as a side with quail, duck, or seafood dishes.

Yield: 6 servings

1 cup Pico de Gallo (page 101)

6½ tablespoons puréed chipotle chiles in adobo sauce

2 tablespoons water
30 large shrimp (about 1½ pounds), peeled and deveined

1 cup unsalted butter, softened

Corn Cakes

¾ cup all-purpose flour
½ cup coarse cornmeal
½ teaspoon baking powder
½ teaspoon baking soda
1 teaspoon salt

1 teaspoon sugar
1¼ cups buttermilk
2 tablespoons melted unsalted butter, cooled to room temperature

1 egg, beaten
1 cup fresh corn kernels (from 2 small ears)
2 scallions, chopped

3 tablespoons unsalted butter

2 scallions, finely chopped, for garnish

Prepare the Pico de Gallo.

In a mixing bowl, combine 2 tablespoons of the chipotle purée with the water. Add the shrimp and toss to thoroughly coat. Marinate for 30 minutes to 1 hour in the refrigerator.

In a small mixing bowl, stir together the 1 cup of softened butter with the remaining 4½ tablespoons of chipotle purée; use more or less chipotle, to taste. Set aside at room temperature.

To prepare the Corn Cakes, thoroughly combine the flour, cornmeal, baking powder, baking soda, salt, and sugar in a mixing bowl. In a separate large mixing bowl, whisk the buttermilk and melted butter together, then whisk in the egg. Gradually add the combined dry ingredients, stirring continuously until thoroughly incorporated. In a food processor, purée ½ cup of the corn kernels and fold into the batter. Then add the whole corn kernels and scallions, and mix together. Add a little more buttermilk if the batter is too thick. Set aside.

To cook the shrimp, heat the 3 tablespoons of butter on a griddle or in a skillet. Sauté the shrimp for 3 to 5 minutes over medium heat, turning once. Be careful not to overcook. Keep warm.

To cook the Corn Cakes, heat a nonstick pan over medium heat and ladle enough Corn Cake batter to make 3-inch cakes. Cook until golden brown, about 2½ minutes per side. Repeat for remaining cakes (there should be enough batter for 18 cakes).

Place 3 warm Corn Cakes on each serving plate. Place 5 shrimp on top of the cakes and spread the warm soft chipotle butter liberally over the shrimp. Spoon the Pico de Gallo next to the Corn Cakes and garnish with the scallions. 🦐

Fresh Washington Manila Clams

in a Spicy Broth of Smoked Chile, Tomatoes, Orange Zest, and Roasted Garlic

Clams were another type of shellfish that coastal Native Americans gathered in significant quantities. They are the easiest type of seafood to harvest, because they are found on shores and beaches at low tide. It was the Native Americans in the Northeast who taught European settlers the technique of clambakes.

Manila clams are small and sweet, and they're usually available year-round. Other similar clams suitable for this recipe are cherrystones or littlenecks. Clams should always be cooked or steamed just until they open; if they are overcooked, they will be hard and dry. Discard any shells that do not open, because this indicates that the clams were already dead, or filled with mud.

Be sure to use sweet oranges for this recipe, such as the navel, Valencia, or blood orange. When preparing the zest, be very careful that you leave all the bitter white pith behind.

Yield: 4 servings

1 tablespoon olive oil
1 tablespoon minced roasted garlic (page 192)
2 shallots, thinly sliced
4 pounds Manila clams (about 6 dozen)

1 cup clam juice
¼ cup chipotle chile purée (page 192)
4 Roma tomatoes, roasted (page 192), peeled, chopped
2 teaspoons brown sugar

¼ teaspoon salt
½ cup fresh orange juice
2 tablespoons orange zest
1 tablespoon chopped fresh marjoram
1 tablespoon extra virgin olive oil

In a large sauté pan or skillet, heat the olive oil and sauté the garlic and shallots for about 3 minutes over medium-low heat, being careful not to let them brown. Add the clams and stir. Add the clam juice, chipotle purée, tomatoes, sugar, and salt and cook over medium heat for 3 to 5 minutes, or just until all the clams have opened.

Remove the pan from the heat and stir in the orange juice, orange zest, marjoram, and extra virgin olive oil. To serve, ladle the clams and broth into serving bowls. 🐟

Spicy Pacific Tartares
Tuna with Serrano-Cilantro Mayonnaise and Salmon with Smoked Chiles

Tartares are believed to have originated in the Baltic region of central Europe, where a feature of the diet of the ruling medieval Tartars was raw, shredded meat. The classic tartare dish is made with beef and seasonings, but any raw meat or fish can be prepared in the same style.

It goes without saying that both fish used in this recipe must be of the latest vintage and highest quality (look for sashimi-quality tuna, preferably yellowfin). In fact, don't attempt this dish unless you are confident of the source and freshness of the fish. In the same vein, and to retain the firm texture of the fish, place a plastic chopping board in the refrigerator or freezer ahead of time so you're working with the fish on a cold surface (if you only have a wooden board, chill briefly or it might crack). While making the recipe, keep the fish in stainless steel bowls set over ice and water. Remember, it's important to keep everything chilled.

Each of the mayonnaise recipes given below makes about 2 cups. However, although you need only about ¼ cup of each, they cannot be feasibly made in smaller quantities. They will keep in the refrigerator for up to a week. You can serve the tartares with corn or flour chips, on croutons, or stuffed in jalapeños, if you prefer.

Yield: 4 servings

Serrano-Cilantro Mayonnaise

10 serrano chiles, roasted (page 192), with seeds	1 tablespoon fresh lime juice	1½ cups peanut oil
1 egg plus 1 egg yolk	1 tablespoon fresh cilantro leaves	
	½ tablespoon salt	

Chipotle Mayonnaise

1 egg plus 1 egg yolk	¼ cup chipotle chile purée (page 192)	1½ cups peanut oil
1 tablespoon fresh lemon juice	1 clove garlic	

8 ounces fresh tuna, minced	1 small loaf Green and Red Chile Brioche (page 20) or plain brioche, sliced and toasted	Lime wedges, for garnish
8 ounces fresh salmon, minced		

To prepare the Serrano-Cilantro Mayonnaise, let the roasted serranos cool completely (otherwise the mayonnaise will separate). Transfer to a blender or food processor, add the egg, egg yolk, lime juice, cilantro, and salt, and purée until smooth. With the machine running, pour in the oil in a slow and steady stream until completely absorbed and thick. Keep chilled.

To prepare the Chipotle Mayonnaise, place the egg, egg yolk, lemon juice, chipotle purée, and garlic in a blender or food processor and purée until smooth. With the machine running, pour in the oil in a slow and steady stream until completely absorbed and thick. Keep chilled.

In separate bowls, thoroughly combine the tuna with ¼ cup of the Serrano-Cilantro Mayonnaise, and the salmon with the ¼ cup of the Chipotle Mayonnaise. Divide each tartare evenly between serving plates, keeping them separate. Serve immediately with the toasted brioche and lime wedges.

OPPOSITE PAGE *Sierra Blanca Lamb Tamale Tart*

Barbecued Tamarind Baby Back Pork Ribs

Marinated Smoked Pork Ribs Finished in a Tamarind Glaze, and Served with Mint-Tomatillo Chutney

If there's one given in the restaurant business, it's that every meat-eater loves ribs. Good ribs must be marinated and cooked slowly, either in the oven or on the grill so they stay moist. If they're roasted in the oven, then they should be finished on the grill so they have a distinctive, smoky flavor. If ribs are cooked over too high a heat, they'll dry out, and if they are glazed too early or brushed with a barbecue sauce over a hot flame, the sugar will burn, so take care to use low heat. Another given in the restaurant business is

that no one likes dry, burned ribs.

This recipe matches chipotle chiles and tamarind in a barbecue glaze. At Coyote Cafe, we also pair these two ingredients in a shrimp appetizer, which shows how versatile this combination can be. The tamarind tree is native to subtropical India and Southeast Asia, and it is also grown throughout southern Mexico. It produces long pods that contain seeds and pulp, which are boiled down into a sweet-and-sour flavored syrup or paste. You can buy tamarind paste from Asian

or Latin markets, which makes it a lot easier than processing fresh tamarind. Tamarind is used, among many applications, as a flavoring in Worcestershire sauce and some cola drinks.

The chutney makes a refreshing counterpoint to the smoky, heavy, complex flavors of the ribs. If you prefer, you can make this recipe with beef short ribs, which take about twice as long to cook.

Yield: 4 servings

Marinade

2 cups olive oil	12 cloves garlic, chopped	4 teaspoons sugar
1 cup fresh lime juice	3 tablespoons chile caribe (dried red chile flakes)	

2 racks baby back pork ribs (about 2 to 3 pounds)

2 cups Mint-Tomatillo Chutney (recipe follows)

Tamarind Glaze

1 cup (8 ounces) tamarind paste	1 clove garlic, roasted (page 192)	3 teaspoons adobo sauce (from the canned chipotles)
1½ cups water	2 canned chipotle chiles in adobo sauce	Juice of ½ lime
½ cup brown sugar		

Mix all the marinade ingredients together in a large mixing bowl. Place the ribs in a nonreactive pan. Pour the marinade over the ribs and make sure they are thoroughly coated. Let marinate overnight in the refrigerator.

Remove the ribs from the refrigerator and allow to come to room temperature, about 20 minutes. Reserve the marinade. Meanwhile, preheat the oven to 200 degrees.

Place the ribs in a roasting pan, cover with foil, and cook in the oven for 1½ hours, or until it is tender but still firm.

Meanwhile, prepare the chutney.

Prepare the grill. Transfer the roasted ribs to the grill and cook for 45 minutes to 1 hour, turning and brushing with the reserved marinade as they cook.

To prepare the glaze, bring the tamarind paste and water to a boil in a saucepan. Strain through a sieve into a clean saucepan, and reduce the liquid over medium heat to 3 cups. Let cool slightly and transfer to a food processor.

Add the sugar, garlic, chipotles, and adobo sauce. Add the lime juice and adjust the sugar and chile to taste. Keep warm.

During the final 10 minutes of grilling the ribs, brush on the tamarind glaze, turning the ribs often so the glaze does not burn.

Serve a half-rack of ribs per person with the chutney and the warm Tamarind Glaze on the side.

Mint-Tomatillo Chutney

Yield: about 2½ cups

1 tablespoon peanut oil
2 shallots, finely minced
12 tomatillos (about 14 ounces), husked, rinsed, and diced

½ cup sugar
1½ tablespoons chile caribe (dried red chile flakes)
¼ cup cider vinegar

⅔ cup chopped fresh mint
1 teaspoon salt
2 teaspoons fresh lime juice

Heat the peanut oil in a nonreactive sauté pan or skillet and sauté the shallots over medium heat for about 3 minutes, until translucent. Add the tomatillos, sugar, and chile caribe, and sauté for 3 minutes longer, until the tomatillos are just tender. Deglaze the pan with the vinegar and reduce the liquid for about 3 to 5 minutes, until the ingredients have thickened. Remove from the heat and let cool slightly. Fold in the mint, salt, and lime juice. Let cool.

Green Chiles Rellenos
Stuffed with Picadillo of BBQ Brisket

Brisket is a tough cut of beef from the breast area beneath the ribs that absorbs a lot of flavors when it is barbecued, braised, or cooked slowly with other ingredients. In Texas and the Southwest it's regarded as the classic meat for barbecue, and it makes a great filling for tacos, enchiladas, or tostadas. Brisket is also the cut from which corned beef is made.

At Coyote Cafe, we slowly smoke our brisket for up to twenty-four hours to tenderize it, render its fat, and maximize its flavor. To make this recipe at home, you can either buy ready-smoked brisket from a source that sells barbecued meat or you can cover fresh store-bought brisket with barbecue sauce, wrap it in foil and slowly cook it in a 250-degree oven for 8 to 12 hours.

In Mexico, chiles rellenos, or stuffed chiles, are usually made with poblano chiles. Poblanos vary in heat, but are never scorching. You can also use New Mexico or Anaheim green chiles, but I urge you to avoid substituting bell peppers for this recipe if at all possible; they are not used this way in authentic Southwestern cooking because of their green, grassy, unripe flavors. Buy fresh, firm poblano chiles and roast them quickly or the texture of the flesh will become weak.

Yield: 6 servings

Smoked Tomato and Jalapeño Sauce (page 79)

Filling

12 ounces beef brisket, barbecued or cooked, shredded

4 canned chipotle chiles in adobo sauce, minced

4 teaspoons adobo sauce (from the can of chipotles)

2 Roma tomatoes, blackened (page 192) and chopped

½ large red bell pepper, roasted and peeled (page 192), seeded, and diced

1 poblano chile, roasted and peeled (page 192), seeded, and diced

2 teaspoons capers

3 tablespoons cooked black beans (page 192), puréed

½ cup currants or raisins, plumped in warm water

¼ cup sliced almonds, toasted

⅓ cup barbecue sauce of your choice

½ teaspoon ground cinnamon

1½ tablespoons chopped fresh cilantro leaves

6 poblano chiles, or green New Mexico chiles, roasted and peeled (page 192), stems left intact

3 eggs, beaten

3 tablespoons milk

½ cup all-purpose flour

¾ to 1 cup blue cornmeal or yellow cornmeal

Peanut oil, for deep-frying

Prepare the Smoked Tomato and Jalapeño Sauce and keep warm.

In a large mixing bowl, thoroughly combine the filling ingredients and adjust the seasoning.

Carefully make an incision the length of each roasted poblano chile and remove the seeds and internal ribs. Spoon the filling into the chiles; do not overstuff.

Mix the eggs and milk together to form an egg wash. Dredge the chiles in the flour, shaking off the excess. Then dip them into the egg wash, briefly let any excess liquid drain, and finally, coat in the cornmeal.

Heat the peanut oil in a deep fryer to 350 degrees. Gently lower the chiles into the oil and deep-fry for 6 to 8 minutes, until golden and crisp. Serve with the Smoked Tomato and Jalapeño Sauce.

Sierra Blanca Lamb Tamale Tarts

with Achiote Masa, Pinto Beans, Garlic Custard, and Tomatillo-Chipotle Sauce

This recipe is inspired by a signature dish of my Texan friend and colleague Stephan Pyles. You can find the original recipe (which uses Gulf crab meat rather than lamb) in his excellent cookbook, The New Texas Cuisine (Doubleday, 1993). This book is required reading for anyone curious about the historical origins of Texas food or fascinated with the way in which classic recipes can be adapted imaginatively with European techniques. Stephan hails from Big Spring, in West Texas, and his cooking is a good example of the evolving living traditions of Southwestern cooking. You can sample it at Stephan's new Dallas restaurant, Star Canyon.

This recipe combines the rustic combination of corn masa and beans with a silky garlic custard and slowly braised, tender lamb. The smoky tomatillo sauce brings the whole dish together with its intriguing range of flavors.

Yield: 4 servings • *Photo page 105*

Masa

1 cup masa harina	1 teaspoon ground cumin	2 tablespoons achiote paste
2 tablespoons yellow cornmeal	1 teaspoon salt	¼ cup water
⅛ teaspoon cayenne chile powder	3 tablespoons melted unsalted butter	

1 cup cooked pinto beans	2 tablespoons pinto bean cooking liquid, or water	½ teaspoon salt

Garlic Custard

1½ cups heavy cream	2 egg yolks	⅛ teaspoon freshly ground black pepper
1½ tablespoons puréed roasted garlic (page 192)	1 teaspoon salt	

Tomatillo-Chipotle Sauce (recipe follows)	1⅓ cups cooked, shredded lamb meat, preferably braised leg	

To prepare the masa dough, combine the masa harina, cornmeal, cayenne, cumin, and salt in a mixing bowl. Stir in the melted butter and achiote paste and mix until smooth. Add the water and mix thoroughly. Set aside.

Purée together the cooked beans, bean liquid, and salt, and set aside. Whisk all the Garlic Custard ingredients together in a mixing bowl.

Prepare the Tomatillo-Chipotle Sauce and keep warm.

To prepare the tamale tarts, lightly grease four 2- or 3-inch molds, or use a nonstick molds. Press ¼ cup of the masa dough into the base and around the sides of each mold and spread 1 tablespoon of the pinto beans over the masa to cover. Add ⅓ cup of the lamb to each mold, spreading it evenly, and then pour the garlic custard on top, spreading it out to the sides of each mold. Cover the molds with plastic wrap.

Prepare a steamer, or use a vegetable basket in a pan of simmering water. Steam the tamale tarts for 20 minutes. Serve hot with the Tomatillo-Chipotle Sauce.

Tomatillo-Chipotle Sauce

Yield: about 2 cups

1 pound tomatillos (about 15), blackened (page 192) and coarsely chopped	½ teaspoon sugar	2 tablespoons adobo sauce (from the can of chipotles)
1 large clove garlic, roasted (page 192)	½ teaspoon salt	⅓ cup chopped fresh cilantro leaves
	4 canned chipotle chiles in adobo sauce	

Place the tomatillos, garlic, sugar, and salt in a food processor or blender. Blend until puréed. Add the chipotles, adobo sauce, and cilantro leaves and blend again until smooth. Transfer to a saucepan and warm through.

POULTRY & FOWL

Sautéed Breast of Chicken
Stuffed with Texas Wild Boar Ham, Fontina Cheese, and Wild Sage, and Served with Black Beans and Baby Squash

Grilled "Rocky" Free-Range Chicken Breast
with a Roasted Chile Poblano-Corn Sauce

Adobe-Style Range Chicken
with Red Chile Jus, Roasted Summer Vegetables, Painted Pony Beans, and Mesilla Valley Pecans

Pollo Huitlacoche
Free-Range Chicken Breast Stuffed with Goat Cheese and Corn, with Huitlacoche Sauce, Fresh Corn Tamales, and Field Greens

Roast Chicken Picadillo
with Quinoa Grain Salad, Olives, and Caperberries

Pato en Parrilla
Pecan-Grilled Maple Duck with Velarde Apricot Chutney

Cordoníz Asado con Relleno de Chorizo
Roasted Fresh Quail with Blue Corn-Chorizo Stuffing

Acoma Pueblo Quail
with Chicken-Apple Sausage Stuffing and Cider Glaze, Crispy Carrot Hash, and Angel Fire Potatoes

Squab con Chile Rojo
with Purée of Potato and Wild Mushroom, Red Chile-Squash Blossom Sauce, and Crispy Squab Livers

A well-roasted bird says it all—juicy, crisp-skinned, and fragrant, it is just light enough to go with red or white wine. Poultry and game, from a small duck to a hearty turkey, mild poussin, or gamey grouse, are definitely my favorite meats, whether roasted, pan-fried, grilled, or sautéed. I'm particularly fond of the wild, herbaceous tones and succulent texture of game birds. In fact, I've been accused of consuming enough quail to sprout pin feathers from my eyebrows!

Poultry and fowl are becoming increasingly popular as more and more people are eating less red meat and seeking healthier alternatives. At Coyote Cafe, we have seen a particularly strong demand for free-range and organically raised birds during recent years.

Birds were revered in the early Mesoamerican societies (primarily because they could fly), and were assigned magical powers as the messengers between Man and the Gods. This largely explains why bird motifs frequently appear on pottery, weavings, baskets, petroglyphs, musical instruments, and sculptures throughout Central and South America, as well as in the North American Southwest. The affluent elite of Mesoamerican cultures such as the Toltecs and Aztecs dined on turkey and quail cooked with pipián sauces and chiles. Bernal Diaz, who accompanied Cortés during the conquest of Mexico, confirmed this, writing that all types of wild fowl and game were cooked in Emperor Montezuma's court.

Game birds, especially quail, wild turkey, and duck, were previously a common feature of the Southwestern landscape, and were hunted for meat by the Navajo and other Native Americans. However, as the livestock that the Spanish introduced to the Southwest began to deplete the grasslands and woodlands of the region, and as the human population increasingly intruded on the natural habitat of game birds, their numbers steadily declined. In certain areas, however, they still continue to thrive; in Texas, especially, quail, dove, turkey, duck, and pheasant are all hunted enthusiastically in the fall. While camping out in the Sonoran desert of southern Arizona in the spring, when the wild flowers create a magical colored carpet, you can see and hear the prolific flocks of dove and quail scurrying and diving into the brush.

In Navajo mythology, the turkey symbolizes friendship and is regarded as a provider of seeds. In fact, these birds are also represented in the fall Corn Dances held by the Pueblo Indians. Wild turkey is native to the New World, and the birds were domesticated long before the Spanish reached Mexico. The Spanish quickly took to turkey as well and brought it back to Europe, where the meat proved popular and became commonplace as early as the sixteenth century. Wild turkey, of course, was brought by the Indians to the original Thanksgiving feasts of the Plymouth Colony in the 1620s, leading Benjamin Franklin to later muse on the bird's credentials as a more appropriate symbol for the American nation than the eagle.

Bobwhite or blue quail are also native to the Southwest and other regions of North America; they are of the same general order as European quail, but are not directly related. The term "bobwhite" refers to the birds' soft, musical call, and they can typically be heard as well as seen scuttling though the low brush of the Southwest—they fly only in brief spurts and for short distances. Duck were domesticated in Central and South America at least as early as the Chinese were raising them, and both wild and domesticated duck such as the canvasback and mallard were used in pre-Columbian times as a source of meat by Native Americans of the Southwest.

Today's chicken does not originate in Kentucky or Boston as fast-food fans might think. It was originally domesticated from wild jungle fowl for ceremonial purposes in the Indian subcontinent about four thousand years ago. Their culinary use spread to China, but it was only in medieval times that chicken became common in Europe. Most of the chicken available today comes from the large-scale commercial poultry production that began in the United States during the 1800s. Inexpensive, mass-produced chicken lacks the texture and taste of the free-range birds, and I strongly recommend using the more naturally raised chickens whenever you have the choice, even if they are more expensive. They have greater freedom of movement and a more varied diet, and they don't contain the levels of hormones and antibiotics that the commercially raised birds are fed.

When preparing game birds, always check for the small pin feathers around the wing tips, and pull them out by hand if necessary. You might also need to check for lead gunshot—your teeth will thank you later! Poultry and fowl should be brought to room temperature (between 60 and 75 degrees) before cooking, but be careful not to let them sit unrefrigerated any longer than necessary. This procedure ensures even and thorough cooking results in a shorter cooking time. This is particularly important for game birds, which have little or no internal fat. The shorter the cooking time, the less dried out the meat will be. Leaving strips of bacon over the birds while they roast and frequent basting will also help to keep them moist.

Sautéed Breast of Chicken

Stuffed with Texas Wild Boar Ham, Fontina Cheese, and Wild Sage, and Served with Black Beans and Baby Squash

Statistics indicate that the chicken population is probably greater than the human population—another reason to be grateful for our opposable thumbs (and all the better to hold chicken legs with). Chicken is an important part of Southwestern and Mexican cuisines, but it was not always so; Columbus introduced the domesticated chicken to the New World, although in Mexico the indigenous turkey, or guajalote, *continues to rival it in popularity.*

This recipe is a Southwestern twist on the Italian dish, saltimbocca, *a specialty of the Rome region made with sage-sprinkled veal wrapped with prosciutto. In fact, you can substitute prosciutto or a good Smithfield ham for the wild boar ham in this recipe. The creamy, semifirm Italian fontina cheese makes the best stuffing, but a mild Swiss or Muenster cheese would also work well. Make sure the stuffing is cold, or it might leak out during the cooking process; securing with a toothpick also helps to avoid this. It's best to* use large chicken breasts for this recipe. *Wild sage is used by the Navajo and other Native Americans of the Southwest for medicinal as well as culinary purposes. Sage tea does wonders for sore throats and indigestion, and smudge sticks made with sage are popular in the Southwest for their cleansing and protective properties. Native Americans also use sage for sweat-lodge healing ceremonies. Serve this dish with cooked black beans and sautéed squash.*

Yield: 4 servings

Marinade

3 tablespoons olive oil
2 cloves garlic, crushed

2 tablespoons coarsely chopped fresh rosemary
2 tablespoons coarsely chopped fresh thyme

2 tablespoons coarsely chopped fresh sage

4 single chicken breasts, skin and wing joint still attached (about 12 ounces each), pre-cut, or cut from 2 chickens (about 3½ pounds each)

1 cup Smoked Tomato and Jalapeño Sauce (page 79)

Stuffing

5 ounces fontina cheese, grated (about 1 cup)

4 ounces wild boar ham or smoked proscuitto, thinly sliced and finely chopped

2 tablespoons finely chopped fresh sage
Freshly ground black pepper to taste

4 tablespoons olive oil

Combine all the marinade ingredients in a large mixing bowl. Add the chicken and let marinate for at least 1 hour (or, preferably, up to 6 hours) in the refrigerator.

Prepare the Smoked Tomato and Jalapeño Sauce.

Remove the chicken from the marinade, and with your fingers, loosen the skin from the chicken meat to form a pocket, taking care to leave the skin attached and not rip it. Bring to room temperature while preparing the stuffing.

Combine all the stuffing ingredients in a mixing bowl. Place the mixture in the refrigerator to chill for 30 minutes. Then stuff about ¼ cup of the mixture into the pockets between the skin and the meat of each chicken breast; do not overstuff. Secure with toothpicks if necessary.

Preheat the oven to 325 degrees. Heat the olive oil in a nonstick pan or skillet and sauté the stuffed breasts, skin side down, over medium heat for about 6 minutes, or until golden brown.

Transfer the chicken, skin side up, to a roasting pan and cook in the preheated oven for 10 to 12 minutes or until tender and cooked through.

Ladle ¼ cup sauce onto each serving plate, add the chicken and serve with cooked black beans and sautéed baby squash. ❧

Grilled "Rocky" Free-Range Chicken Breast
with a Roasted Chile Poblano-Corn Sauce

This is a straightforward recipe that also makes a terrific brunch dish. The marinade tenderizes and flavors the meat with its crisp, green, refreshing ingredients.

There's some confusion over the identity of the poblano chile. For example, in parts of California this dark green, thick-fleshed chile is referred to as a "pasilla." In actuality, the pasilla is a dried chilaca chile (also known as chile negro). As the name suggests, poblano chiles originated in the Puebla region of Mexico, to the southeast of Mexico City. They are probably the antecedent of bell peppers that were developed in Europe after the early explorers took back seeds of various chiles. When they are dried, poblanos are known as either ancho or mulato chiles; both exhibit an interesting range of complex flavor characteristics.

I prefer to use soft Oaxacan cheese for the sauce, but if you don't live in Southern Mexico or have a source for it, the semisoft, mild but tangy Danish smoked Havarti is a good alternative.

Corn and chile have a natural affinity that has been harnessed for many centuries in Mesoamerica and by Native Americans of the Southwest, especially in hearty stews. In fact, you can make this recipe into a soup by leaving out the cheese. The sauce also makes a great accompaniment for scrambled eggs or crab. As an option, you can also serve this dish with mustard greens, which add a peppery dimension.

Yield: 4 servings

Marinade

2 cloves garlic, crushed
1 bunch cilantro

½ bunch Italian parsley
5 scallions
3 serrano chiles, chopped, with
  seeds

1 cup olive oil

4 single chicken breasts, skin and wing joint still attached (about 12 ounces each), pre-cut, or cut from
  2 chickens (about 3½ pounds each)

Sauce

1 tablespoon unsalted butter
2 tablespoons finely chopped onion
3 ears fresh corn, husked
½ cup water
¼ cup heavy cream

1 poblano chile, seeded and diced
2 tablespoons grated smoked
  Havarti or smoked Cheddar
  cheese

Salt and freshly ground black
  pepper to taste
1 tablespoon chopped fresh basil

Place all the marinade ingredients in a blender and purée until smooth. Transfer the marinade to a large mixing bowl, add the chicken, and coat thoroughly. Let marinate for 6 to 8 hours in the refrigerator.

Prepare the grill. Remove the chicken from the marinade, scrape off any excess marinade, and bring to room temperature. Grill over medium-low heat for 6 to 8 minutes per side, turning often.

Meanwhile, to prepare the sauce, heat the butter in a sauté pan or skillet and sauté the onion over medium heat for 3 to 5 minutes, or until translucent.

Cut the corn kernels from the cob (there should be about 1½ to 2 cups) and set aside. Scrape the cobs with the back of a knife to extract the corn germ and "milk" and reserve. Add the corn kernels and water to the pan with the onions and cook for 2 minutes longer, or until the corn begins to soften.

Add the cream, corn germ, and "milk," and simmer for 1 minute longer. Add the poblano chile and stir in the cheese, in small increments, adding just enough to achieve a thick, saucelike consistency. Be careful not to add too much cheese at a time or the sauce will become stringy. Season with salt and pepper and remove the pan from the heat. Stir in the basil.

Ladle the sauce onto the serving plates and place the chicken on top of the sauce.

Adobe-Style Range Chicken

with Red Chile Jus, Roasted Summer Vegetables, Painted Pony Beans, and Mesilla Valley Pecans

It's important to buy large chickens (between 4 and 5 pounds) for this recipe, because smaller birds will fall apart during the braising process. Free-range chickens are older than the commercially raised type when they're butchered, which gives them a firmer texture and more flavor. However, even with free-range chicken that's labeled as free of additives you run the risk of getting one that has been fed grain treated with herbicides or pesticides at some point. So, your best bet is to find free-range chicken that's raised organically. Fortunately, the supply is gradually increasing.

This recipe follows the fricasee technique—sautéeing in butter or oil and then stewing or braising with vegetables. "Adobe-style" refers to the horno ovens introduced by the Spanish that were readily adopted by Native Americans, especially by the Pueblo Indians of the Rio Grande Valley. These ovens are still made from adobe bricks, a traditional Southwestern building material made from a mixture of local red clay, earth, and straw.

Yield: 4 servings

Painted Pony Beans

½ cup dried pony beans (large pinto beans)

Picante Dried Red Chile Rub

2 tablespoons chile caribe (dried red chile flakes)
1 tablespoon dried oregano

¾ cup chile molido or other pure red chile powder
1 tablespoon sugar

1 teaspoon salt

2 chickens (4 to 5 pounds each)
¼ cup peanut oil
1 red bell pepper, seeded and chopped
1 yellow bell pepper, seeded and chopped

1 poblano chile, seeded and chopped
2 ears corn, shucked and cut into 1½-inch rounds
1 white onion, chopped

¼ cup chipotle chile purée (page 192)
3 cups Chicken Stock (page 192)
¾ cup pecan halves, toasted (page 192)

To prepare the beans, carefully sort through them and remove any foreign objects. Rinse in a sieve and soak overnight. Drain and rinse the beans, place in a saucepan, and add enough water to cover the beans by at least 2 or 3 inches. Bring the water to a boil and cook the beans for 2 hours, adding more water as necessary.

To prepare the rub, place the chile caribe and oregano in a dry skillet and toast over medium heat for 2 minutes, until fragrant. Transfer to a spice grinder and pulse until smooth. Place in a bowl and combine thoroughly with the chile molido, sugar, and salt.

Cut up the chickens into pieces (each portion should include a half breast, leg, thigh, and wing). Coat the chicken with the rub.

Preheat the oven to 350 degrees. Heat the peanut oil in a heavy skillet and sear the chicken over high heat until brown on all sides, about 10 minutes. Transfer the chicken to a large casserole or oven-proof dish. Add the bell peppers, poblano, rounds of corn, onion, chile purée, stock, and cooked beans, and bring to a boil on top of the stove. Transfer to the oven and braise for 45 minutes.

To serve, place the chicken on warm plates and spoon the vegetables over. Ladle some of the sauce around the chicken and sprinkle with the toasted pecans. 🪶

Pollo Huitlacoche

Free-Range Chicken Breast Stuffed with Goat Cheese and Corn, with Huitlacoche Sauce, Fresh Corn Tamales, and Field Greens

Huitlacoche is the mysterious black, rich fungus that grows on fresh corn. Because they are from the same plant, it is no surprise that its flavor complements fresh corn so wonderfully. Huitlacoche has many uses in Mexican cuisine, including in sauces, soups, and fillings for tamales and quesadillas. It is also used to stuff beef fillets. The first time I ate this heady combination was at a rather hard-to-find restaurant called Isadora in Mexico City (at least, my taxi

driver had a hard time finding it), but the detours we took were worth it in the end.

Plain corn tamales must be made with fresh young, sweet corn, and their delicate, subtle flavor is best brought out by steaming them at the last minute, because they don't hold together as well as flavored tamales. Because these tamales are made with fresh rather than dried corn husks, it's important to buy good-quality, large corn cobs with attractive husks.

Stuffing meat with cheese in this style is a French tradition; in this recipe, you can use cream cheese instead of fresh goat cheese if you prefer, or a herbed or peppered goat cheese, or boursin (goat cheese flavored with garlic). Salt the vegetables to be used for the stuffing before sautéeing them and gently squeeze out any excess moisture so that the stuffing does not become too watery.

Yield: 4 servings

Tamales

5 ears fresh corn, husks reserved	½ tablespoon sugar	¼ teaspoon baking powder
⅓ cup cornmeal, preferably stone-ground	1 egg plus 1 egg white	2 tablespoons unsalted butter, softened
	¼ teaspoon salt	
4 free-range chicken breasts with skin (about 2 pounds)	Salt and freshly ground black pepper to taste	2 tablespoons peanut oil

Goat Cheese Stuffing

¼ cup fresh goat cheese	½ cup fresh corn kernels, roasted (page 192)	1 poblano chile, roasted and peeled (page 192), seeded, and diced
1 tablespoon minced fresh basil	¼ teaspoon salt	

Huitlacoche Sauce

1 cup fresh corn kernels	½ tablespoon toasted and ground oregano (page 192)	1 tablespoon salt
2 cups huitlacoche		Juice of 1 lime
½ cup Vegetable Stock (page 193) or water	½ tablespoon toasted and ground cumin (page 192)	2 tablespoons chipotle chile purée (page 192)
2 tablespoons chopped fresh cilantro	1 tablespoon ground dried green chile	
1 tablespoon unsalted butter	1 tablespoon water	¼ teaspoon salt
6 ounces red or green chard		

To prepare the tamales, cut a thin layer of the kernels from the cobs with a sharp knife. Purée the kernels in a blender or food processor. Transfer to the bowl of an electric mixer fitted with a paddle attachment. Scrape the corn cobs with the back of a knife to extract the corn germ and "milk" and add to the bowl, along with the cornmeal, sugar, egg, egg white, salt, and baking powder. Add the butter a little at a time and beat until smooth.

Set 4 of the large outer corn husks aside. Pick out 4 of the smaller, inner husks and set aside. Tear 8 thin strips from the remaining husk. Lay out one large whole husk on a work surface, the wider part facing you. With a spatula, take one-quarter of the filling and spread in the middle of the corn husk, leaving a 1-inch border around the edges of the husk. Lay a small inner husk on top, and fold its edges over the filling so that it is completely covered. Fold the edges of the large husk over the smaller one, roll tightly, and secure each end with 2 of the thin strips. Lay the tamales seam side down in a steamer and steam over simmering water for about 30 minutes. Let rest, covered for 5 minutes.

Meanwhile, preheat the oven to 350 degrees. Season the chicken with salt and pepper. Heat the peanut oil in a large sauté pan or skillet and sear the chicken over medium-high heat for 2 to 3 minutes on each side.

Remove from the heat and allow the breasts to cool.

With your fingers, loosen the skin from the chicken meat to form a pocket, taking care to leave the skin attached. Thoroughly mix all the goat cheese stuffing ingredients together in a mixing bowl. Stuff this mixture into the pockets between the skin and the meat of the chicken breasts, being careful not to overstuff. Secure with toothpicks if necessary. Transfer to a roasting pan and roast in the oven for 25 to 30 minutes. Keep hot.

To prepare the Huitlacoche Sauce, place the corn, huitlacoche, and stock in a saucepan and bring to a boil. Reduce the heat to a simmer and cook for 20 minutes, stirring occasionally. Add the cilantro, oregano, cumin, green chile, and salt. Remove from the heat and pour half of the mixture into a food processor or blender and purée. Return to the pan (off the heat) and stir in the lime juice and chipotle purée.

In a sauté pan, melt the butter, add the chard, water, and salt, and sauté over medium-high heat, while stirring, until the chard wilts, about 2 minutes. Drain, and divide the wilted chard between 4 serving plates. Place the chicken on top of the wilted chard. Ladle ¼ cup of the Huitlacoche Sauce on top and serve the tamales at the side.❧

Roast Chicken Picadillo

with Quinoa Grain Salad, Olives, and Caperberries

Picadillo is a Spanish dish that originated in Moorish North Africa centuries ago. Typically, it contains ground meat, garlic, onions, tomatoes, and spices, as well as raisins and almonds. There are many regional variations on this basic theme, and when the Spanish brought picadillo to Mexico, chiles soon became an essential ingredient. It is a popular dish around Puebla, in southeast-central Mexico, and in San Miguel, which lies in the colonial heartland of north-central Mexico. Picadillo is particu-larly associated with festivals and special occasions. It's also used as a stuffing for chiles and poultry, and is commonly served with rice and beans. This is our adaptation.

Quinoa (pronounced "KEEN -wah") is a high-protein grain that is quickly becoming popular in the United States. It's now grown commercially in southern Colorado and has long been adapted to high altitudes. In its native Andes region of South America it was a staple for the Incas, who consumed the plant's leaves and seeds. Combined with potatoes, quinoa provided the Incas with the essentials for a nutritionally balanced diet. It can be used in recipes in place of rice or couscous, it makes a good brunch item, and is good eaten cold. When cooking quinoa, it's helpful to know that it expands to four or five times its uncooked volume.

This picadillo recipe can also be made with tuna, swordfish, pork, or game birds such as pheasant.

Yield: 4 servings

Toasted Cumin and Black Pepper Rub

¼ cup cumin seeds	1 tablespoon black peppercorns	½ teaspoon sugar
2 tablespoons dried oregano	¼ teaspoon salt	

4 chicken breasts (about 7 or 8 ounces each)	2 tablespoons peanut oil

Quinoa Salad

1 teaspoon peanut oil	½ cup pine nuts	3 tablespoons olive oil
1 cup quinoa	½ cup chopped scallions	2 tablespoons julienned fresh basil
2 cups water	3 tablespoons balsamic vinegar	⅛ teaspoon salt

Picadillo

2 tablespoons olive oil	1 poblano chile, seeded and julienned	½ cup sliced capers
2 cloves garlic, minced	2 Roma tomatoes, julienned	1 teaspoon ground cinnamon
1 red bell pepper, seeded and julienned	1 red onion, julienned	1 tablespoon water
1 yellow bell pepper, seeded and julienned	½ cup Kalamata black olives, pitted and sliced	1 tablespoon chopped fresh parsley

To prepare the rub, place all the ingredients in a dry skillet and toast over medium heat for 2 minutes, until fragrant. Transfer to a spice grinder and pulse until smooth.

Preheat the oven to 350 degrees. Thoroughly coat the chicken with the rub. In a sauté pan or skillet, heat the peanut oil and sear the chicken on both sides over medium-high heat until browned, about 3 to 5 minutes per side. Transfer to a roasting pan and roast in the oven for 20 minutes.

To cook the quinoa, heat the peanut oil in a saucepan, add the quinoa and stir for 1 minute over medium heat. Add the water and bring to a boil. Cover the pan, reduce the heat to a simmer and cook for 15 minutes. Transfer to a large mixing bowl and allow to cool. Add the pine nuts, scallions, balsamic vinegar, olive oil, basil, and salt, and toss together to thoroughly combine.

To prepare the Picadillo, heat the olive oil in a sauté pan or skillet over medium-high heat and sauté the garlic, bell peppers, and poblano chile for 3 minutes. Stir in the tomatoes, onion, olives, capers, cinnamon, and water, and cook for 5 minutes longer. Remove from the heat and add the parsley.

To serve, place the chicken breasts on the center of each serving plate. Spoon the Picadillo over the chicken and serve with the Quinoa Salad.

OPPOSITE PAGE **Roast Chicken Picadillo**

Pato en Parrilla
Pecan-Grilled Maple Duck with Velarde Apricot Chutney

When Spanish settlers first came north to New Mexico, they settled in some of the high fertile valleys close to the Rio Grande. They brought livestock, seeds, and fruit trees of European heritage with them, and subsequent generations of these orchards are still thriving in northern New Mexico communities, such as Velarde and Dixon. In these microclimates, a difference in elevation of one thousand feet can mean the growing season varies by several weeks; the valleys support temperate conditions in stark contrast to some areas of the surrounding environment. These valleys are heavily dependent on the runoff from the mountain snows which is diverted through the man-made acequias or irrigation ditches. Soft fruit, such as apricots, plums, apples, pears, and chiles, grow here in abundance, and during the summer and earingly fall, roadside produce stands selling them (as well as chile ristras and wreaths) are a hallmark of the region.

Fruit and nut woods are the best for grilling. We use aged pecan wood from the Mesilla Valley in southern New Mexico for all our grilling at Coyote Cafe; once a year an eighteen-wheeler drops off thirty or so cords of aged (year-old) wood. Unaged green wood of whatever variety (including evergreen woods such as pine, fir, or piñon) is unsuitable for grilling because it's too resinous and smoky, and cooks unevenly. A good method of gathering grilling wood is to ask orchard-owners whether you can purchase their fruit-wood prunings during late fall, or in early spring, and then age it at home. An alternative to fruit or nut woods, such as pecan or hickory, is to buy aromatic wood chips and soak them before adding to the grill.

You may want to serve this dish with sweet potatoes and rice.

Yield: 4 servings

Marinade

5 tablespoons maple syrup
3 cups fresh orange juice
Juice of 1 lime

1½ tablespoons chipotle chile purée (page 192)
1 teaspoon ground cinnamon
1 teaspoon salt

Pinch of ground cloves
1 teaspoon freshly ground black pepper

4 single duck breasts, cut from a 4½- to 5-pound duck, with first wing bone attached

Velarde Apricot Chutney

1 teaspoon olive oil
½ cup diced onion
1 teaspoon chile caribe (dried red chile flakes)

1¾ cups pitted and diced fresh apricots
¼ cup sugar
½ cup unseasoned rice vinegar

1 teaspoon seeded and minced habanero chile
1 tablespoon roasted, peeled, seeded, and diced red bell pepper (page 192)

Mix all the marinade ingredients together in a large nonreactive bowl. Place the duck in the mixture and coat thoroughly. Place in the refrigerator and let marinate overnight.

To prepare the chutney, heat the olive oil in a sauté pan or skillet, and sauté the onions and chile caribe over medium heat for 2 to 3 minutes. Add the apricots and stir in the sugar until dissolved. Add the vinegar and reduce the liquid by three-quarters, until the liquid thickens slightly. Remove from the heat and stir in the habanero chile and red bell pepper. Refrigerate until needed.

Prepare the grill. Remove the duck from the marinade and reserve the marinade. Grill the duck for 3 to 6 minutes per side for medium rare, turning frequently as the marinade will have a tendency to burn.

Meanwhile, place the reserved marinade in a nonreactive saucepan and reduce to a glazelike consistency over medium-low heat for 6 or 7 minutes, skimming the foam as it rises. Brush over the duck during the last few minutes of cooking.

Serve the duck with the chutney to the side. ➤🐖

Cordoníz Asado con Relleno de Chorizo
Roasted Fresh Quail with Blue Corn-Chorizo Stuffing

The blue corn gives this stuffing a different, festive appearance. It's a combination I've adapted from a recipe created by my friend Stephan Pyles, celebrated chef and owner of Star Canyon in Dallas, and it makes a wonderful fall or holiday season dressing for chicken, turkey, game hen, or dove. It also goes well with fresh clams or oysters—just spoon the stuffing into their open shells and bake in a hot oven.

Chorizo originated in Spain as a garlic and smoked pork hard sausage. It was brought to Mexico, where it was transformed into a spicy, coarsely ground pork sausage, usually in crumbled or patty form rather than in a casing. In this recipe, the pork should contain enough fat (approximately 25%, or add fresh fatback if needed) to keep the chorizo from drying out and becoming tough. For the same reason, be sure to add enough water to allow the chorizo to cook ade-

quately before it browns. Chorizo makes a great side for brunch with eggs, or you can use it in enchiladas, quesadillas, or tacos, so don't be afraid to whip up a whole batch; you can always freeze any leftovers.

Although it's a popular hunting bird, I always think it's a lot easier to buy quail in the store than to pick out all that buckshot with your teeth! I recommend you serve this dish with asparagus or haricots verts.

Yield: 4 servings

Marinade

½ cup olive oil
3 sprigs fresh thyme, coarsely chopped

2 sprigs fresh rosemary, coarsely chopped
2 teaspoons ground cinnamon

1 teaspoon ground allspice
8 black peppercorns, cracked

8 quail (about 4 ounces each)

Stuffing

2½ tablespoons unsalted butter
1 teaspoon minced garlic
½ cup diced onion
½ cup diced celery

1 cup peeled, cored, and diced apple
1 teaspoon minced fresh thyme
2 teaspoons minced fresh marjoram
14 ounces blue corn bread (page 18)

1 egg
1 cup Chicken Stock (page 193)
8 ounces chorizo, cooked and drained

Sauce

1 tablespoon unsalted butter
5 shallots, minced
½ green apple, peeled, cored, and chopped

¾ cup apple cider
2 cups Brown Poultry Stock (page 193)
1 sprig fresh thyme

1 bay leaf
Salt and freshly ground pepper to taste

Glaze

3 cups apple cider
1 tablespoon brown sugar
1 cinnamon stick

2 tablespoons puréed ancho chile (page192)
2 tablespoons puréed guajillo chile (page 192)

Freshly ground black pepper to taste

½ cup clarified butter (page 192)

Place the marinade ingredients in a large mixing bowl and combine. Add the quail and marinate overnight in the refrigerator.

To make the stuffing, heat the butter in a sauté pan or skillet and sauté the garlic over medium heat for 2 to 3 minutes. Add the onion, celery, and apple and cook for 3 to 5 minutes, or until translucent. Add the thyme and marjoram and remove the pan from the heat.

Crumble the corn bread into a bowl. Pour the stuffing mixture over the corn bread and set aside to cool. When cool, mix in the egg, chicken stock, and chorizo, and thoroughly incorporate. Set aside.

To prepare the sauce, heat the butter in a sauté pan or skillet and sauté the shallots and apple over medium-high heat until well browned. Deglaze with the cider and reduce the liquid by half. Add the stock, thyme, and bay leaf, and reduce to 1 cup. Season with salt and pepper, strain, and keep warm.

To prepare the glaze, heat the cider, brown sugar, and cinnamon in a saucepan over medium-high heat and reduce by three-quarters. Add the ancho and guajillo chile purées and continue cooking until a glazelike consistency is achieved. Stir in the pepper and keep warm.

Preheat the oven to 325 degrees. Remove the quail from the marinade and stuff the cavities with the stuffing. Heat the clarified butter in a large skillet and sear the quail over medium heat until golden, about 2 to 3 minutes. Transfer to a roasting pan. Insert a meat thermometer, making sure it doesn't touch the bone, and cook in the oven for 12 to 15 minutes, or until an internal temperature of 125 degrees is reached. (If you are using a more sensitive, professional-quality thermometer, insert it during the last few minutes of cooking time.) Brush the glaze over the quail during the last minutes of roasting.

Ladle the sauce onto serving plates and place the quail on the sauce.

Acoma Pueblo Quail

with Chicken-Apple Sausage Stuffing and Cider Glaze, Crispy Carrot Hash, and Angel Fire Potatoes

Quail is a game bird that's indigenous to the Southwest, especially in the lowlands of West Texas, in New Mexico, and south into the Sonoran desert of southern Arizona and northern Mexico. In fact, the quail motif is depicted on some of the ancient Mimbres pottery from that region, from around the eleventh century. Acoma (known as "Sky City" because of its isolated location atop a precipitous mesa to the west of Albuquerque) is famous for its modern pueblo pottery that is characterized by black-and-white animal motifs, including quail, and geometric fine-line painting. This distinctive work can be viewed at stalls on Santa Fe's Plaza during Indian Market Week.

Potatoes were first cultivated in the high Andes by the Incas of Peru, who grew more than two thousand varieties. The Incas also genetically selected certain types of potatoes for their different characteristics. Angel Fire, in northern New Mexico, lies at an altitude of over nine thousand feet, and provides a natural setting for the more than fifty varieties of potatoes that are now grown on farms there. These farms utilize the same fields that nineteenth-century silver miners tended for food, and that lay fallow until just a decade ago. Potatoes need frost to "set," after which they can be harvested. If the ground temperature gets too warm, they can become starchy. Frost and moderate temperatures are two things potato farmers can be sure of in Angel Fire, with its altitude and proximity to Mount Wheeler, the highest peak in New Mexico.

Yield: 4 servings

Chicken-Apple Sausage Stuffing

1½ tablespoons olive oil
1 pound ground chicken breast
4 ounces ground fatback
¼ small white onion, minced
2 cloves garlic, minced
2 serrano chiles, minced, with seeds

2 Granny Smith apples, peeled, cored, and diced
2 tablespoons cider vinegar
1 cup apple cider, preferably unfiltered

1 cup herbed bread crumbs (store bought)
2 teaspoons chopped fresh marjoram
⅛ teaspoon salt

8 quail (about 4 ounces each)
½ cup peanut oil

1¼ pounds Angel Fire (or other variety) fingerling potatoes

Carrot Hash

3 tablespoons olive oil
2 large carrots, diced (about 2 cups)
3 small potatoes, diced (about 1 cup)

1 onion, diced (about 1 cup)
1 tablespoon minced fresh basil
¼ teaspoon cayenne chile powder

½ teaspoon salt
1 teaspoon freshly ground black pepper

¼ cup olive oil
8 shallots, minced (about ⅔ cup)

1 tablespoon minced fresh marjoram
¼ teaspoon salt

Cider Glaze

1 cup Chicken Stock (page 193)
1 cup apple cider, preferably unfiltered
½ Granny Smith apple, peeled, cored, and chopped
½ teaspoon minced garlic

¼ teaspoon brown sugar
⅛ teaspoon ground cinnamon
½ teaspoon maple syrup
½ teaspoon Jack Daniels whiskey
Pinch of ground allspice

¾ teaspoon unsalted butter, softened (optional)
⅛ teaspoon salt

To prepare the stuffing, heat the olive oil in a sauté pan or skillet, add the ground chicken and fatback, and cook for about 5 minutes over medium heat, stirring until it begins to brown. Stir in the onion, garlic, and serranos, and cook for about 3 minutes longer, until lightly browned. Stir in the apples, vinegar, and cider, and cook for 5 minutes. Fold in the bread crumbs, marjoram, and salt and immediately remove from the heat. The stuffing should be fairly dry and formed together (not loose or grainy).

Preheat the oven to 350 degrees. When the stuffing has cooled, stuff the quail. Heat the peanut oil in a sauté pan or skillet, and sear the quail on all sides over medium-high heat, about 5 minutes. Put the quail in a roasting pan and roast in the oven for 20 to 30 minutes.

Meanwhile, cook the fingerling potatoes in boiling water for 20 minutes, or until just tender but not soft. Remove from the water and allow to cool.

To prepare the Carrot Hash, heat the olive oil in a heavy sauté pan or skillet and when hot, sauté the carrots and diced potatoes for 5 to 8 minutes over high heat, stirring constantly. Reduce the heat to medium, add the onion, and cook for 3 minutes longer. Stir in the basil, cayenne powder, salt and pepper, and remove from the heat. Keep warm.

When the fingerling potatoes have cooled, slice them into ¼-inch-thick rounds. In a sauté pan or skillet, heat the olive oil and sauté the shallots for 3 minutes over medium-low heat, until translucent but not brown. Stir in the fingerling potato slices and sauté for 5 minutes. Stir in the marjoram and salt, and keep warm.

To prepare the Cider Glaze, heat the stock in a saucepan over medium-high heat and reduce to ½ cup. Add the apple cider and reduce again to ½ cup. Transfer to a food processor or blender and add the apple, garlic, sugar, cinnamon, maple syrup, whiskey, and allspice. Purée and strain into a clean pan. Whisk in the butter, if desired, and season with salt.

To serve, place the Carrot Hash in a circle at the center of each serving plate. Place 2 quail in the center of the hash and arrange the potatoes around the quail. Pour the glaze over the quail, and serve.

Squab con Chile Rojo

with Purée of Potato and Wild Mushroom, Red Chile-Squash Blossom Sauce, and Crispy Squab Livers

Squab is another name for young, tender domesticated pigeon. It has dark, rich meat that tastes a little like mild veal liver, and its medium to strong flavors can successfully balance assertive Southwestern sauces. However, this is probably not the reason squab was considered a special delicacy during the Victorian era in Britain!

Puréed potatoes and flavored mashed potatoes have come into vogue lately. One reason for this is that they are such a good medium for playing with interesting flavors, such as roasted garlic, herbs or herb oil, olives, horseradish, chile purées, and even truffles or truffle oil. Any of these ingredients make mashed potatoes a lot healthier than the tradi-

tional butter or cream. As a child I had more fun than you could imagine, mashing up potatoes with milk, butter, salt, and pepper. Perhaps that's why I'm still partial to them.

Be sure to cook the squab only to medium rare, or the meat will dry out, toughen up, and taste overly strong.

Yield: 4 servings

Picante Dried Red Chile Rub

2 tablespoons chile caribe (dried red chile flakes)	1 tablespoon dried oregano ¾ cup chile molido or other pure red chile powder	1 tablespoon sugar 1 teaspoon salt

4 boneless squab (about 1 pound each)

Potatoes

2½ pounds baking potatoes, peeled and chopped	⅛ teaspoon salt 2 tablespoons unsalted butter	2 tablespoons minced shallots 6 ounces mushrooms, sliced

Sauce

4 cups (1 quart) Dark Poultry Stock (page 193) ¼ cup chipotle chile purée (page 192)	2 tablespoons chile molido or other pure red chile powder 4 squash blossoms, julienned	⅛ teaspoon salt

Squab Livers

1 tablespoon all-purpose flour ½ teaspoon ground cumin	½ teaspoon cayenne chile powder ¼ teaspoon ground cinnamon	4 squab livers ¼ cup peanut oil

To prepare the rub, place the chile caribe and oregano in a dry skillet and toast over medium heat for 2 minutes until fragrant. Transfer to a spice grinder and pulse until smooth. Place in a bowl and combine thoroughly with the chile powder, sugar, and salt.

Thoroughly coat the squab with the rub, and refrigerate for 2 hours to absorb the flavors.

Prepare the grill. To prepare the potatoes, bring a large pot of salted water to a boil, and cook the potatoes for 20 to 25 minutes, until tender. Drain the potatoes and mash by hand until smooth. In a sauté pan, heat the butter and sauté the shallots and mushrooms over medium heat for 5 minutes. Fold into the potato purée and season to taste. Keep warm.

Grill the squab to medium rare, about 15 minutes.

Meanwhile, for the sauce, reduce the stock, chipotle purée, and chile molido in a saucepan over high heat to 1 cup. Add the squash blossoms and salt, and keep warm.

For the squab livers, combine the flour, cumin, cayenne, and cinnamon together in a bowl. Dredge the livers in the spiced flour mixture and coat thoroughly. Heat the peanut oil in a sauté pan and sauté the livers over high heat until crisp, about 1 or 2 minutes.

To serve, cut the squab in half. Divide the potatoes among the serving plates and lean each squab half against the potatoes. Divide the sauce among the plates, pouring it around the squab and potatoes. Garnish with the crispy squab livers.

OPPOSITE PAGE *Squab con Chile Rojo*

FISH & SEAFOOD

Atún Verde en Parrilla
Grilled Fresh Tuna with Tomatillo Salsa and Spicy Green Rice

Paillard of Fresh California Salmon
with Chipotle Crema and Squash Salsa

Salmón a la Parrilla
with Pecan-Grilled Sweet Green Scallions and Corn-Red Pepper Salsa

Blue Corn-Crusted Salmon
with Elizabeth's Haricots Verts, Chanterelles, and Basil Oil

Grilled Gulf Snapper
with Savory Stew of White Beans, Sun-Dried and Oven-Roasted Tomatoes, with Lemon Zest and Fresh Parsley

Piñon-Crusted Fresh Halibut
with a Red Chile Shrimp Sauce

Pan-Seared Nambé Trout
Crusted with Sunflower Seeds and Stuffed with Crab Slaw

Poblano Lobster Rellenos
with Roasted Sweet Corn Salsa and Manchamantel Sauce

Sweet Lobster and Mango Marengo
on Yucatán Black Bean Cakes with Cucumber Salad

Grilled Brochette of Fresh Eastern Sea Scallops
on a Serrano-Cucumber-Avocado Salsa

Paillard of Fresh California Salmon
with Chipotle Crema and Squash Salsa

Once upon a time, when the tallest structures in the Northwest were totem poles, long before the Seattle Space Needle towered over the region's premier city, there were more than one hundred varieties of North American salmon in the surrounding rivers. Although the Native Americans of the Northwest caught them in prolific numbers, the Indians' belief system led to selective harvesting, for fear of angering the salmon spirit and driving the fish from their waters forever. The salmon were still so plentiful that the tribes of the region had to spend very few hours securing other forms of sustenance; they were able to devote a majority of their time to creating great art and holding festivals. Most of this art—giant totem poles, masks, bent wood boxes, and bark blankets—was carved out of cedar wood.

Like oysters, salmon was so common in colonial times (and into the twentieth century) that it was not regarded as the luxury it has become today. As in Europe, all the major rivers of the United States once were spawning grounds for salmon, but the clean, oxygenated water that the fish require has rapidly dwindled. Even in the Northwest, relatively healthy rivers support a fraction of the salmon they did at the turn of the century. Other significant factors that contribute to the salmon population's decline have been the scale of river damming and the sheer volume of deep-sea fishing. Restrictions on the commercial fishing season have been introduced in an attempt to replenish depleted stocks.

Yield: 6 servings

Chipotle Crema

2 cups heavy cream
2 tablespoons buttermilk

1 clove garlic, roasted (page 192) and peeled

2 tablespoons canned chipotle chiles in adobo sauce

Squash Salsa

⅔ cup unseasoned rice wine vinegar
⅓ cup sugar
1 small zucchini, finely diced
1 small yellow squash, finely diced
1 small carrot, finely diced
2 tomatillos, husked, rinsed, and finely diced

¼ small red onion, finely diced
4 oven-dried tomatoes or sun-dried tomatoes packed in oil, finely diced
5 serrano chiles, with seeds, minced
1 teaspoon finely chopped fresh marjoram

1½ tablespoons minced fresh chives
1½ tablespoons finely chopped fresh basil
⅔ cup extra virgin olive oil
Salt and freshly ground pepper to taste

6 salmon steaks (6 to 7 ounces each)

2 teaspoons sea salt

4 sprigs fresh cilantro, for garnish (optional)

To prepare the Chipotle Crema, heat the cream in a saucepan to about 160 degrees while stirring. Stir in the buttermilk and remove from the heat. Cover with cheesecloth and allow to sit overnight at room temperature. The next day the crema should have the consistency of loose sour cream. Cover with plastic wrap and refrigerate.

Place the crema, garlic, and chipotles in a blender and purée until smooth. Keep at room temperature, covered, until ready to serve.

To prepare the salsa, place the vinegar and sugar in a saucepan and bring to a vigorous simmer. Stir in the zucchini, yellow squash, carrot, tomatillos, onion, tomatoes, and chiles, and cook for 1 or 2 minutes. Remove from the heat and let cool slightly, about 5 minutes. Stir in the marjoram, chives, basil, and olive oil, and season with salt and pepper.

Season the salmon with the sea salt. Heat a dry nonstick pan, and when very hot, add the salmon. Sear over medium-high heat for 2 to 3 minutes on each side, or until medium-brown on the outside, but still rare to medium rare in the center.

To serve, place a pool of the crema in the center of each serving plate. Center the salmon on the crema and spoon the salsa over the fish. Garnish with cilantro sprigs, if desired.

Salmón a la Parrilla

with Pecan-Grilled Sweet Green Scallions and Corn-Red Pepper Salsa

In Mexico, cebollitos would take the place of the green scallions in this recipe. These small onions are sweeter than our scallions, and they have a larger bulb at their base. They are always on the menu in taquerias or storefronts selling pollo asado, where you can order them as a side. They're brushed with oil, sprinkled with salt, grilled, and then given a spritz of fresh lime juice and a dash of chile powder. At Coyote Cafe, we often hear our guests remark how pleasantly

surprised they are by the sweet, smoky flavor of grilled scallions if they've never tried them before. Soaking them in water for 30 minutes helps prevent the fragile green tops from burning. They make a wonderful side dish with quesadillas or tacos, or served with steaks and grilled meat or fish.

The Corn-Red Pepper Salsa proves that the natural affinity of corn and chiles also extends to bell peppers, which are the mildest chiles of all. You can use

fresh red New Mexico or Anaheim chiles if you prefer a more picante-style salsa, or you can roast the bell peppers (at the same time as the scallions) for a smokier flavor.

This is a versatile dish: you can substitute halibut, sea bass, John Dory, shrimp, or scallops for the salmon, or you could use chicken breasts or pork loin.

Yield: 4 servings

Corn-Red Pepper Salsa

2 cups fresh corn kernels (about 3 ears)
¼ cup water
1 tablespoon peanut oil
½ cup julienned white onion

5 red Fresno or red jalapeño chiles, roasted and peeled (page 192), seeded, and julienned
5 green jalapeño chiles, roasted and peeled (page 192), seeded, and julienned

1 cup fresh cilantro leaves
1 tablespoon toasted and ground coriander seed (page 192)
¼ teaspoon salt

¼ cup olive oil
1 tablespoon fresh lime juice
12 scallions

4 salmon fillets (about 6 to 7 ounces each)
1 teaspoon sea salt

Freshly ground black pepper to taste

To prepare the salsa, place the corn kernels in a sauté pan, add the water, and cook for 2 to 3 minutes over medium heat, or until tender and the water has just evaporated. Transfer to a mixing bowl. Heat the peanut oil in a sauté pan and sauté the onion over medium heat for about 8 minutes, or until slightly browned. Add to the mixing bowl along with the roasted chiles, cilantro, coriander, and salt, and thoroughly combine. Set aside.

Place the olive oil and lime juice in a small bowl, and marinate the scallions while preparing the grill (preferably using pecan wood or wood chips, or fruit wood).

Season the salmon with the sea salt and pepper. Grill the salmon for 2 to 3 minutes per side; it should be rare to medium rare inside. Grill the scallions until just wilted. Arrange 3 scallions in a triangle on each plate and place the salmon on top. Serve with the salsa.

Blue Corn-Crusted Salmon

with Elizabeth's Haricots Verts, Chanterelles, and Basil Oil

It has been estimated that three-quarters of the diet of the coastal Northwest Native Americans consisted of seafood, and of this, three-quarters was salmon. With this natural abundance from the water, together with the bounty from the rainforests, it is little wonder that the type of farming and agriculture developed in the Southwest was unnecessary in the Northwest. Corn, which was traded throughout most of North America, was not in evidence in any part of the Northwest. However, in this recipe, we combine these two historic American Indian foods—salmon and corn. Dusting the salmon with seasoned coarse blue cornmeal and then searing and baking it provides wonderful contrasts in color, texture, and flavor. The pink salmon and the blue-gray crust make a visually striking presentation on the plate. Of course, the recipe works exactly the same with yellow cornmeal, but the color contrast is more subdued.

Haricots verts, the long, slender green beans usually associated with French cuisine, are actually native to the New World. The word haricot is derived from the Nahuatl (Aztec) word for the bean, ayacotl. In this recipe, you can substitute sea bass, halibut, or char for the salmon. You'll need to make the Basil Oil one week ahead of time, or buy it pre-made.

Yield: 4 servings

Basil Oil (page 89)

6 tomatoes, cut in half and seeded

2 teaspoons salt

Blue Corn Crust

½ cup coarse blue cornmeal
⅛ teaspoon salt

⅛ teaspoon freshly ground black pepper

Cilantro Pesto

6 tablespoons pine nuts, toasted (page 192)
6 poblano chiles, roasted and peeled (page 192), seeded

1 small clove garlic
4 to 6 tablespoons virgin olive oil
¾ cup fresh cilantro leaves (about 1 bunch)

Sea salt to taste
Juice of 1 or 2 limes

4 ounces haricots verts
4 salmon fillets (about 6 to 7 ounces each)

¼ cup peanut oil
4 tablespoons unsalted butter

4 chanterelle mushrooms, quartered (about ½ cup)

Prepare the Basil Oil.

Preheat the oven to 275 degrees. Place the tomatoes on a baking sheet and sprinkle with the salt. Place in the oven for about 3 to 3½ hours. Remove from the oven, and set aside.

For the crust, mix the blue cornmeal with the salt and pepper in a mixing bowl, and set aside.

To prepare the Cilantro Pesto, place the pine nuts, poblano chiles, garlic, olive oil, and cilantro in a food processor and pulse into a coarsely textured paste. Add the salt and lime juice to taste, and set aside.

Blanch the haricots verts in boiling salted water for 3 minutes. Remove and immediately shock in ice water. When cool, drain and set aside.

Preheat the oven to 350 degrees.

Dredge the salmon in the Blue Corn Crust. Heat the peanut oil in a sauté pan or skillet, and when hot, sear the salmon for 1 minute per side. Place in a single layer in a baking dish or on a baking sheet and finish in the oven for 10 to 15 minutes.

Meanwhile, heat the butter in a sauté pan and sauté the mushrooms until cooked through. Cut the reserved oven-dried tomatoes in half and add to the pan, together with the reserved blanched haricots verts. Sauté briefly until warmed through.

To serve, place the sautéed mushroom mixture in the center of 4 serving plates, and top with the salmon. Drizzle the Basil Oil over the salmon and add 1 heaping tablespoon of the Cilantro Pesto on top of each fillet.

Grilled Gulf Snapper

with Savory Stew of White Beans, Sun-Dried and Oven-Roasted Tomatoes, with Lemon Zest and Fresh Parsley

There are several varieties of Gulf snapper. The best known and most popular of them is the subtly flavored red snapper (known as rouget in Louisiana and huachinango in Mexico). Rockfish, tilefish, and imported John Dory are often erroneously marketed as red snapper or snapper, so it helps to know the difference or to have a fishmonger that you can trust to steer you right. Sea bass is the best substitute for snapper in this recipe.

Again, I firmly believe that the fresh, delicate flavor of fish is best complemented by light sauces rather than traditional heavy sauces, such as beurre blanc, béarnaise, béchamel, or hollandaise. In this recipe, the beans and vegetables are the sauce, and the vibrant flavors of this combination makes an oil- or butter-based sauce for the fish redundant. Besides, vegetable sauces are healthier and more nutritionally correct.

Oven-roasting is a simple and inexpensive home technique that takes 4 to 6 hours, using a very low oven setting (see "Basic Techniques and Recipes," page 192).

Yield: 4 servings

Marinade

1 tablespoon chopped fresh parsley
1 tablespoon minced garlic

½ teaspoon seeded and minced serrano chile

2 tablespoons seeded and minced red bell pepper
2 tablespoons olive oil

4 snapper fillets (about 6 ounces each)

2 tablespoons olive oil
2 tablespoons minced shallots
2 cups cooked white beans (page 192)
½ cup sun-dried tomatoes (packed in oil and drained)

½ cup oven-roasted tomatoes (page 192)
2 tablespoons chipotle chile purée (page 192)
¼ cup fresh lemon juice
2 tablespoons lemon zest

¼ cup chopped fresh parsley
1 tablespoon minced fresh marjoram
4 sprigs fresh parsley, for garnish

To prepare the marinade, thoroughly combine the parsley, garlic, serrano chile, bell pepper, and olive oil in a large mixing bowl. Place the snapper into the marinade and let marinate for about 1 hour, turning from time to time.

Meanwhile, heat the olive oil in a sauté pan or skillet and sweat the shallots over medium heat, about 2 minutes. Add the cooked beans, sun-dried and oven-roasted tomatoes, and chile purée, and sauté for 10 minutes longer. Add 1 to 2 tablespoons of water if the mixture becomes dry. Remove from the heat and stir in the lemon juice, zest, chopped parsley, and marjoram. Set aside.

Prepare the grill.

Remove the snapper from the marinade and grill for 3 or 4 minutes on the first side and 2 to 3 minutes on the second side. To serve, place the bean mixture in the center of each serving plate and place the grilled snapper on top. Garnish with the fresh parsley.

Piñon-Crusted Fresh Halibut
with a Red Chile Shrimp Sauce

The unlikely pairing of flavors from the deep sea and the high desert come together in this recipe. The delicate halibut is an ocean-bottom flatfish that dwells in the cold waters of the North Pacific and the North Atlantic. It is a mild-flavored, firm-fleshed fish with attractive, bright white flesh. You can substitute cod, char, skate, or salmon for the halibut in this recipe.

The combination of piñon (pine) nuts, tortillas, and bread crumbs results in a uniquely rich crust that ideally complements the fish's texture. At the same time, the flavor of the crust is not too pervasive or dominant. Crusting fish or seafood with seeds or nuts is a popular technique, from nouvelle cuisine to Asian cooking. The traditional method of dipping the fish in an egg batter, rolling it in fine bread crumbs, and then deep-frying it is an early version of crusting, albeit a high-calorie one.

Pecans, pine nuts, peanuts, macadamias, and cashews are all popular nuts these days for crusting meat or fish, and pine nuts are one of the richest because of their high oil content. They also contain the highest percentage of protein—more than 51 percent. The bread crumbs and ground tortillas should be fresh, and the best method of ensuring this is to dry out a fresh loaf and fresh tortillas in a low oven.

Yield: 4 servings

Red Chile Shrimp Sauce

2 tablespoons peanut oil
2 tablespoons finely chopped onion
2 tablespoons finely chopped carrot
2 tablespoons finely chopped celery
¼ cup brandy
¼ cup tomato purée

4 cups Shrimp Stock (page 68), Lobster Stock (page 194), or Fish Stock (page 194)
½ cup heavy cream
2 tablespoons olive oil
8 ounces fresh shrimp, peeled, deveined, and finely chopped

2 tablespoons minced shallots
2 tablespoons canned chipotle chile in adobo sauce
Salt and freshly ground black pepper to taste

Piñon Crust

3 corn tortillas
½ cup pine nuts

¾ cup fresh bread crumbs
2 tablespoons minced fresh thyme

Pinch of salt

4 halibut fillets (about 6 ounces each)

Salt and freshly ground black pepper to taste
1 cup all-purpose flour

3 eggs, whisked
¼ cup peanut oil

To prepare the sauce, heat the peanut oil in a saucepan and sauté the onion, carrot, and celery over medium-low heat for 5 minutes. Raise the heat to medium-high, carefully add the brandy, and ignite. When the alcohol has burned off, add the tomato purée and cook for 5 minutes. Add the stock and reduce the liquid by half. Add the cream and heat through; remove from the heat and set aside.

Heat the olive oil in a separate pan and sauté the shrimp and shallots over medium-high heat until the shrimp is cooked through. Add the chipotles and stir to combine. Add the vegetable-cream mixture, combine thoroughly, and season with salt and pepper. Keep warm.

Preheat the oven to 350 degrees.

To prepare the crust, tear the tortillas into irregular pieces and place in a food processor together with the pine nuts, bread crumbs, thyme, and salt. Pulse until thoroughly combined and finely textured, and set aside.

Season the halibut with salt and pepper and dredge in the flour. Dip in the whisked eggs, and then coat with the Piñon Crust mixture.

Heat the peanut oil in a large sauté pan or skillet and sauté the crusted halibut over medium heat until the crust is lightly browned. Remove the halibut and transfer to an ovenproof dish. Bake in the oven for 5 to 10 minutes.

Transfer the halibut to serving plates and spoon the reserved sauce around the fillets.

Pan-Seared Nambé Trout
Crusted with Sunflower Seeds and Stuffed with Crab Slaw

Nambé is the site of a northern New Mexico pueblo on the Rio Grande River, about twenty-five miles north of Santa Fe. It's famous for lending its name to Nambé Ware—attractive, durable kitchenware made from silver alloy—and features some lovely waterfalls that are worth visiting.

The Rio Grande, as it rushes over its shallow gravel bed in this part of northern New Mexico, is the perfect setting for a relaxed afternoon of trout fishing while sitting beneath a shady,

aromatic cottonwood tree. Trout is a fresh-water fish related to the salmon, and it, too, has suffered a severe decrease in population over the last 150 years because of overfishing and water pollution. Before this, the beautiful native rainbow trout was abundant in the fast-flowing mountain rivers of the Southwest.

Many other types of trout, notably the European brown trout and the brook trout, have been introduced to the United States with the purpose of replenishing the diminished stocks. Ironi-

cally, the American rainbow trout has been exported to stock the rivers of a great many other countries, to the extent that it is universally recognized and enjoyed for its delicate white flesh.

Sunflowers are native to North America and were gathered by Plains Indians in particular, who dried them for sustenance during the winter and made pemmican with them. This recipe demonstrates that seeds can be used for crusting in the same way nuts are.

Yield: 4 servings

Crab Filling

1½ tablespoons seeded and minced serrano chiles	1 small red bell pepper, seeded and finely diced	1 tablespoon chopped fresh basil
3 tablespoons minced scallions	Juice of ½ lime	1 tablespoon chopped fresh cilantro
	8 ounces lump crab meat	2 tablespoons mayonnaise
		1 teaspoon salt

Sunflower Seed Crust

3 corn tortillas	1 tablespoon minced fresh lemon thyme or thyme	2 tablespoons crushed red chile flakes (chile caribe)
¾ cup sunflower seeds		½ teaspoon salt
¼ cup bread crumbs		

Beurre Blanc

1½ cups white wine	20 black peppercorns	Salt and freshly ground black pepper to taste
2 shallots, minced	1 cup butter cut into cubes	
2 bay leaves	1 tablespoon minced fresh marjoram leaves	

4 fresh boneless trout, about 10 ounces each, cleaned	2 eggs	2 tablespoons clarified butter (page 192) or peanut oil
½ cup all-purpose flour	2 tablespoons water	

To prepare the Crab Filling, thoroughly combine the serrano chiles, scallions, bell pepper, lime juice, crab meat, basil, cilantro, mayonnaise, and salt in a mixing bowl and set aside.

To prepare the crust, tear the tortillas into irregular pieces and place in a food processor together with the sunflower seeds, bread crumbs, thyme, chile, and salt. Pulse until thoroughly combined and finely textured, and set aside.

To prepare the Beurre Blanc, combine the wine, shallots, bay leaves, and black peppercorns in a saucepan, and reduce over medium-high heat until ¼ cup remains. Reduce the heat to medium, stir in the butter, a little at a time, until emulsified. Remove the pan from the heat and strain into a clean saucepan. Add the marjoram leaves and season with salt and pepper to taste. Keep warm.

Dredge the trout on both sides in the flour. Whisk together the eggs and water and brush the trout with the egg wash. Cover the trout with the prepared crust and stuff the internal cavity with the crab filling, deepening the cavity with a knife if necessary.

Heat the clarified butter in a nonstick skillet over medium heat. Sauté the trout on both sides until golden brown and the filling is warmed through, about 8 to 10 minutes, turning to cook evenly.

Place the trout in the center of each serving plate and spoon the Beurre Blanc around it or to one side. Serve immediately.

OPPOSITE PAGE *Sweet Lobster and Mango Marengo*

Poblano Lobster Rellenos

with Roasted Sweet Corn Salsa and Manchamantel Sauce

The word relleno *means "stuffed" and usually refers to dishes in which chiles are stuffed and then cooked. In the United States, most people associate chiles rellenos with the infamous combination plate and anemic canned chiles stuffed with tasteless, processed cheese that are then battered and deep-fried. This is far from the case in Mexico, where chiles rellenos originated and where this classic dish has countless regional variations and is prepared in many different forms for special occasions and feast days.*

The thick-fleshed, medium-hot green poblano chile is the preferred stuffing chile, and fillings range from fresh melted regional cheeses to beans, vegetables, seafood, meat and game. One of the classic Mexican rellenos is chile nogada, *a traditional fall holiday dish created by the Augustine nuns of Puebla to commemorate the occasion of the visit by Don Augustin de Iturbide, who was briefly the Mexican Emperor following the War of Independence in the early nineteenth century. The dish features the patriotic colors of the Mexican flag (provided by the green chile, walnut-white cream sauce, and brilliant red pomegranate garnish), with a rich filling of pork and fruit.*

This healthful recipe makes a great main course for lunch or dinner, especially in summer when corn and lobster are in their prime.*

Yield: 4 servings

Roasted Sweet Corn Salsa

1½ cups fresh corn kernels (about 2 ears)
1 tablespoon plus ¼ cup olive oil
2 ounces wild mushrooms, julienned

1 large poblano chile, roasted and peeled (page 192), seeded, and finely diced
3 cloves garlic, roasted (page 192), and mashed to a paste
2 tablespoons chipotle chile purée (page 192)

1 tablespoon minced fresh marjoram
1 tablespoon sherry vinegar
Juice of ½ lime
¼ teaspoon kosher salt

Manchamantel Sauce

5 dried ancho chiles
2 dried New Mexico red chiles
2 cups hot water
1 Roma tomato, roasted (page 192)
1 clove garlic, roasted (page 192)
⅔ cup peeled, cored, and chopped pineapple

1 small ripe banana, peeled and chopped
½ Granny Smith apple, peeled, cored, and chopped
½ teaspoon ground canela or cinnamon
1 tablespoon cider vinegar

Small pinch of ground cloves
⅛ teaspoon ground allspice
½ teaspoon salt
½ tablespoon brown sugar
1½ cups pineapple juice

4 live lobsters (about 2 pounds each)

4 poblano chiles, roasted and peeled (page 192), with stem intact

To prepare the salsa, dry-roast the corn kernels in a single layer in a hot, dry skillet over medium-high heat for about 10 minutes, shaking frequently. Remove from the heat and transfer to a mixing bowl. Heat 1 tablespoon of the olive oil in a sauté pan or skillet and sauté the mushrooms until just tender. Add to the mixing bowl and let cool. Add the poblano, garlic, chipotle purée, marjoram, sherry vinegar, lime juice, kosher salt, and remaining olive oil to the bowl, thoroughly combine, and set aside.

To prepare the Manchamentel Sauce, rehydrate the ancho and New Mexico chiles in the water for 20 to 30 minutes, or until soft. Drain the chiles, and transfer to a blender or food processor. Add the tomato, garlic, pineapple, banana, apple, canela, cider vinegar, cloves, allspice, salt, sugar, and pineapple juice and purée until smooth.

Bring a large stockpot of salted water to a boil and cook the lobsters for 5 to 6 minutes. Remove and immediately shock in a bowl of ice water. When cool, split the lobsters in half, remove the lobster meat from the shell and claws, and dice. Add to the salsa and combine.

Preheat the oven to 350 degrees.

With a knife, make a slit down one side of each poblano and carefully extract the seeds. Gently stuff the poblanos with the salsa mixture, closing the slit and returning the poblanos to their original shape.

Place the stuffed poblanos on a lightly oiled baking sheet and bake in the preheated oven for 15 minutes, until hot. Remove from the oven.

Spoon ¼ cup of the Manchamantel Sauce in the center of each serving plate (serve the remaining sauce in a bowl or sauce boat on the side.) Place the hot stuffed poblanos on top of the sauce and serve.

Sweet Lobster and Mango Marengo
on Yucatán Black Bean Cakes with Cucumber Salad

As the song goes, "These are a few of my favorite things." Lobster paired with mango would certainly have to be included on my list of favorites, whether cold or hot, in a sauce or salsa, or combined in a salad. The tropical flavors of the lobster and mango are heightened by the black beans, which are used extensively in the Yucatán peninsula and throughout southern Mexico, Central America, and the Caribbean.

I first encountered black beans on my early travels to Guatemala. There, black beans are ubiquitous in their pairings with eggs, tortillas, and rice. I sometimes ate black beans for breakfast, lunch, and dinner (no exaggeration!). They might, however, have been refried with a little mint or epazote for variety. In contrast, you never see pinto beans in those more tropical regions, probably because the locals appreciate the deeper, richer flavor of black beans.

Black beans first came into vogue in the United States in the late 1970s, which happily, was a time when I was beginning to experiment with flavors and ingredients of the Southwest and Latin America. In 1979, James Beard wrote a glowing review of my Black Bean Soup, which he tasted at my first restaurant in Berkeley, the Fourth Street Grill. Ever since, black beans have occupied a special place in my heart.

Yield: 4 servings • *Photo page 141*

Cucumber Salad

1 cucumber (about 8 ounces), peeled, seeded, and thinly sliced on the bias
½ cup julienned red onion

½ red bell pepper, seeded and julienned
½ yellow bell pepper, seeded and julienned
¼ cup unseasoned rice wine vinegar

½ teaspoon freshly ground black pepper
1 teaspoon sugar
Salt to taste

4 lobsters (about 2 pounds each)

Black Bean Cakes

⅓ cup all-purpose flour
¼ cup yellow cornmeal
¼ teaspoon baking powder
¼ teaspoon baking soda
¼ teaspoon ground cumin
1 teaspoon salt
½ teaspoon sugar

½ cup cooked black beans (page 192), puréed
⅓ cup black bean cooking liquid
1 small egg, beaten
1 tablespoon chipotle chile purée (page 192), or Coyote Cafe Howlin' Hot Sauce (or another habanero chile sauce)
¼ cup finely diced scallions

1 teaspoon minced fresh oregano
1 tablespoon melted unsalted butter
¼ cup buttermilk

2 tablespoons plus ¼ cup peanut oil
6 shallots, minced

½ yellow bell pepper, seeded and diced
½ red bell pepper, seeded and diced

1 mango, peeled, pitted, and diced
1 teaspoon salt

Thoroughly combine all the Cucumber Salad ingredients in a mixing bowl, toss well, and refrigerate until ready to serve.

Bring a large stockpot of salted water to a boil and cook the lobsters for 5 to 6 minutes. Remove and immediately shock in a bowl of ice water. When cool, split the lobster in half and remove the meat from the shell and claws, reserving the shells. Dice the lobster meat and set aside.

To prepare the Black Bean Cakes, sift together the flour, cornmeal, baking powder, baking soda, cumin, salt, and sugar into a large mixing bowl. Make a well in the center, add the puréed beans, bean liquid, egg, chipotle purée, scallions, oregano, butter, and buttermilk, and stir together thoroughly, until well incorporated.

Heat 1 tablespoon of the peanut oil in a nonstick sauté pan or griddle over medium heat. Place about 2 to 2½ tablespoons of the bean cake mixture into the pan, and form into a cake. Repeat for 3 more cakes and sauté for 3 to 4 minutes per side until the cakes are set and firm, and a little brown. Remove and drain the cakes on paper towels. Add another tablespoon of oil to the sauté pan and repeat this process for the remaining 4 bean cakes. Keep warm.

Preheat the oven to 350 degrees.

Heat the remaining peanut oil in a sauté pan or skillet and sauté the reserved lobster meat with the shallots and bell peppers for 3 minutes. Remove the pan from the heat and gently stir in the mango and salt. Spoon the lobster-mango mixture back into the lobster shells and place the filled shells on a baking sheet. Place in the preheated oven for 1 or 2 minutes to heat through.

To serve, place 2 bean cakes on each serving plate. Set a filled lobster shell next to the cakes and serve with the Cucumber Salad.

Grilled Brochette of Fresh Eastern Sea Scallops
on a Serrano-Cucumber-Avocado Salsa

Scallops, like lobster and other types of shellfish, are dense and rich and call for accompaniments with light tones and contrasting flavors. This recipe is a good example of how such a combination can also prove complementary, and the same principle would apply if you substituted shrimp, sea bass, or monkfish for the scallops.

Buy scallops that are hard and a little sticky rather than soft and watery, which indicates they have been sitting around in liquid to preserve them. Never buy them in pre-packaged plastic or if they smell of ammonia, and don't be afraid to ask how old the scallops are.

The salsa in this recipe is a spicy variation of guacamole. Use a darker, bumpy-skinned Haas avocado, which has a rich and buttery texture. The larger, lighter-skinned Fuerte avocado is more watery and less intensely flavored.

Yield: 4 servings

16 to 20 large fresh sea scallops
½ cup olive oil

Red Chile Rice

4 tablespoons unsalted butter
1 large clove garlic, minced
½ cup minced onion
2 cups long-grain rice
4½ cups water

Zest of 1 lime
6 sprigs fresh cilantro

1 teaspoon toasted and ground dried Mexican oregano (page 192)
1 tablespoon minced fresh marjoram
1½ teaspoons salt

1 teaspoon toasted and ground cumin seeds (page 192)
⅓ cup chile molido powder or other pure red chile powder

Serrano-Cucumber-Avocado Salsa

1 small cucumber, peeled, seeded, and diced
1 ripe avocado, peeled, pitted, and diced
2 teaspoons diced serrano chile, with seeds
8 to 10 peeled and seeded orange segments, diced

2 teaspoons minced scallion, green part only
2 teaspoons finely chopped fresh cilantro
1 teaspoon chopped hoja santa (optional)
3 tablespoons fresh lime juice

1 tablespoon unseasoned rice wine vinegar
1 tablespoon extra virgin olive oil
½ teaspoon salt
Freshly ground black pepper to taste

Green Chile-Apple Glaze

1 poblano chile, roasted and peeled (page 192), seeded
1 or 2 serrano chiles, seeded and coarsely chopped (optional)

3 cups unfiltered apple cider
1 teaspoon fresh lime juice

Freshly ground black pepper to taste

Pre-soak 4 wooden skewers in water. To prepare the brochettes, place 4 or 5 scallops on each skewer (depending on the size of the scallops). Place the olive oil, lime zest, and cilantro in a shallow platter or bowl, mix together, and add the scallop skewers. Marinate for 30 minutes to 1 hour, refrigerated.

To prepare the Red Chile Rice, heat the butter in a large sauté pan or skillet, and sauté the garlic and onion over medium heat for 6 to 8 minutes, until soft. Add the rice, water, oregano, marjoram, salt, cumin, and chile molido and bring to a boil. Cook for 2 minutes and then reduce the heat to low. Cover and simmer for 20 to 25 minutes, just until the water has evaporated.

Gently stir the cooked rice with a wooden spoon to fluff, and add a little butter if desired. The rice can be kept warm and reserved up to 2 hours.

Meanwhile, place all the salsa ingredients together in a nonreactive mixing bowl and combine, stirring as little as possible. Adjust the seasonings and keep chilled until serving.

Prepare the grill, preferably using pecan or fruit wood, or wood chips.

To prepare the glaze, combine the chiles and apple cider in a blender or food processor and purée until smooth. Transfer to a nonreactive saucepan and reduce over medium-high heat until a light syrupy glaze consistency is achieved. Add the lime juice and pepper, and keep warm.

Grill the brochettes on the hot grill for about 3 minutes per side, or until they have visible grill marks but are still translucent in the center. Brush with the glaze for the last few moments of cooking.

Serve each brochette on a bed of the salsa, with the Red Chile Rice. Serve the remaining glaze on the side (in a sauce boat, if desired).

Photo: Cross Studio, Courtesy Museum of New Mexico.

MEATS & GAME

Bistec de New York en Parrilla
Pecan-Grilled Aged New York Steak Served with Tobacco Onion Rings

Pan-Fried Dry-Aged Ribeye Steak
with Bricklayers Salsa and Oven-Roasted New Potatoes

Grilled Beef Tenderloin
with Serrano-Blackened Tomato Butter, Roasted-Garlic Mashed Potatoes, and Caramelized Onion Toasts

Lomo de Puerco
Pan-Roasted Pork Loin Stuffed with Wild Cherries and Ancho Chiles

Tenderloin of Pork
with Roasted-Tomatillo and Wild Mushroom Sauce

Stuffed Loin of Pork
with Fig and Thyme Stuffing and Green Chile-Apple Chutney

Cordero Yucatán
Roasted Lamb Yucatán-Style with Cinnamon Rice

Roasted Rack of Lamb
with Pecan Crust and Roasted Corn Salsa

Grilled Local Lamb T-Bones
with Chorizo-White Bean Stew and Fresh Mint

Texas Axis Venison
with Wild Chokecherry-Ancho Chile Sauce

Blackfoot Buffalo Ribeye
with Wild Mushrooms, Green Onions, Applewood-Smoked Bacon, and Cheyenne Batter Bread

Besides Ben & Jerry's or Häagen-Dazs ice cream, the real value of cattle probably lies in their meat and leather. It's hard to imagine a world today without hamburgers, steaks, barbecue, and beef franks. In former times, before the mechanical revolution, cattle and oxen had been used as draft animals in Europe, pulling plows and carts as well as providing dairy products to make cheeses, and meat. They were too valuable as a source of energy and strength to be eaten on a large scale, and there were no open grasslands or ranches on which to pasture them. Consequently, beef was a luxury that only the wealthy could afford, except perhaps when the animals met with an accident or fell victim to old age.

The development of animal husbandry in the New World brought unprecedented abundance and destruction simultaneously. Domesticated livestock were first introduced onto the Caribbean island of Santo Domingo, where Columbus had initially landed and which was the first large Spanish settlement in the New World. Like other Caribbean islands, the ecological system was delicately balanced after thousands of years of trial and error. On Santo Domingo, the Taino Indians had developed a constant and abundant food supply,

and practiced a mound system of agriculture. Inside these 4- or 5-foot-high mounds, they grew root vegetables and starches, such as manioc and cassava, which provided the mainstay of their diet. On the outside of the mounds they grew beans, chiles, and leafy vegetables. Soon, the newly introduced livestock destroyed this delicately balanced system. The pigs rooted into the mounds and the cattle ate the leafy vegetables. Soil erosion followed, and in the absence of any natural predators, the animals multiplied unchecked and the compounded results were disastrous.

Livestock was next imported into Mexico, where it proliferated to such an extent that by the 1580s, the glut of beef resulted in the meat of whole slaughtered cows being given away in the great square (now the Zócalo) of Mexico City. The demand remained strong for salted beef, used by the seaborne adventurers during the age of exploration, as well as for leather, popular both with the settlers in the New World and the Spanish market back home. Unfortunately, the same pattern of destruction that had occurred in Santo Domingo was experienced in Mexico, with massive deforestation, overgrazing, and soil erosion. As cattle were driven northward and huge ranches were estab-

lished in Sonora, Chihuahua, and Monterrey in conjunction with the expansion of the Spanish settlement of Mexico, so the grasslands were overgrazed and the landscape changed forever. Mexico (not the United States) was where the cowboy culture originated—including the hats, boots, spurs, and horses, and even the guitars, songs, and tradition of the barbecue.

The Spanish next brought cattle to the Southwest, and New Mexico and Texas became major grazing lands. (The Mexican-American War of 1848 was fought in part over these grasslands.) Before the Western range was largely enclosed by barbed wire in the 1880s, huge herds of wild cattle were rounded up in the historic cattle drives. They were transported from the Western trailheads by the railroads to the enormous stockyards of Chicago and Kansas City, where the beef was later shipped East. Many of these trailheads became sizeable towns and later, major cities of the Southwest. However, along with the growth came conflict. The Range Wars of the latter half of the nineteenth century ensued over water and cattle, as the homesteaders, who wanted to enclose land as small farms, battled cattlemen who wanted to keep the land as open range.

Pigs, sheep, and goats were also imported into Mexico by the Spanish. Pork became a favorite in Mexican cooking, especially in the north, but it has always played a secondary role, compared to beef, in Southwestern cuisine. Pork was also the source of lard, which became the standard cooking fat as oils were scarce. (Spain had prevented the export of olive trees to the New World to maintain a monopoly of the olive oil trade.)

Sheep are raised in the mountain grasslands of the Southwest, and are particularly valued for their wool; for centuries, weaving has been a traditional craft of both the Native American (especially Navajo) and Hispanic communities. The hybrid, grain-fed lamb available today may be available year-round and it may be more tender than the traditional range-raised breeds, but, for the most part, it's also less lean and flavorful.

Before the introduction of this domesticated livestock, wild game animals were the main source of meat and protein in North America and in the Southwest (the land where the deer and the antelope truly play, not to mention the elk). The immense buffalo herds that once roamed the Great Plains ranged as far west as eastern New Mexico, where Las Vegas, New Mexico, stands today. It has been estimated that up to sixty million head populated North America before Europeans arrived. By 1895, however, only one thousand survived the systematic slaughter at the hands of American hunters and skinners. They narrowly avoided extinction, and over 130,000 buffalo are now raised on more than one thousand ranches across the United States. Buffalo meat has only one-third of the cholesterol content of chicken, and too often people assume that buffalo, elk and venison are "unhealthy" red meats. In fact, I prefer them because they contain no hormones or steroids and are "naturally" fed.

Bistec de New York en Parrilla
Pecan-Grilled Aged New York Steak Served with Tobacco Onion Rings

New York steak is also known as Kansas City steak, shell steak, or strip steak, depending on which part of the United States you're in. Paradoxically, the term is rarely used in New York itself. The cut comes from the short loin, or the underdeveloped top loin muscle that is consequently one of the most tender sections of the steer.

The sign of any good steak is evenly patterned marbling, or white lines of fat, which indicate the animal has been regularly grain-fed. When grain-feeding has occurred only at the end of the fattening process, the white marbling is unevenly distributed, and a higher proportion ends up around the edges. It is the marbling or fat content that makes the steak more moist, tender, and flavorful. Unfortunately, it also makes the steak less healthful to eat, so it's best to limit it to special occasions or to consume it in very small quantities, as the Japanese do.

Some of the most tender beef I've ever tasted comes from Japan. Kobe cattle are massaged with sake and enjoy a pampered diet that includes beer. This special treatment makes the steak meat very tender and tasty, but also very expensive. Even more rich tasting and expensive (up to $150 per pound) is Matsutake beef, another exclusive grade of beef that is usually sliced thinly for sukiyaki. It has such a rich texture that it too can be eaten only in small quantities, like foie gras, for example.

Yield: 4 servings

Serrano Chile Butter

- 8 tablespoons unsalted butter, at room temperature
- 4 or 5 serrano chiles, roasted (page 192) and minced, with seeds intact and blackened skin left on
- ½ tablespoon minced scallion
- 1 tablespoon finely chopped fresh cilantro
- ½ teaspoon finely chopped fresh Italian parsley
- 1 teaspoon fresh lime juice
- ⅔ teaspoon salt
- Freshly ground black pepper to taste

- 4 dry-aged New York steaks (10 to 12 ounces each)
- Salt and freshly ground black pepper to taste

Tobacco Onion Rings

- 5 cups peanut oil, for frying
- 1 cup all-purpose flour
- ½ tablespoon cayenne chile powder
- 1½ tablespoons chile molido or other pure red chile powder
- ⅓ teaspoon salt
- Freshly ground black pepper to taste
- 1 cup buttermilk
- 1 large white onion, thinly sliced into rings

To prepare the serrano butter, beat all the ingredients together in a mixing bowl until smooth. Using plastic wrap or parchment paper, roll the butter into a cylinder about 1½ inches across; reserve, refrigerated. When ready to serve, slice the cylinder into 4 pieces.

Prepare the grill, using pecan wood or soaked pecan wood chips. Season the steaks with salt and pepper and grill for 5 to 7 minutes per side for medium rare.

Meanwhile, prepare the onion rings. Heat the peanut oil to 375 degrees in a deep fryer or deep, heavy skillet. In a mixing bowl, combine the flour, cayenne, chile molido, salt, and pepper together. Place the buttermilk in a separate bowl. Dip the sliced onions in the buttermilk to moisten, draining off the excess. Then dip the onions into the seasoned flour, thoroughly coating and shaking off the excess.

Place the coated onion rings into the hot oil and fry until golden brown, about 2 to 3 minutes. Remove from the skillet and drain on paper towels to absorb the excess oil. Season with salt to taste while they are still hot.

Place the hot steaks on serving plates and top each with a slice of the serrano butter. Serve with the onion rings.

Pan-Fried Dry-Aged Ribeye Steak
with Bricklayers Salsa and Oven-Roasted New Potatoes

Ribeye, or prime rib steak, is a tender, juicy cut of beef that comes from inside the ribs, between the short loin and chuck. This is the cut that we use at Coyote Cafe for our trademark grilled Cowboy Steak. Ribeye steaks are often boneless, but for both looks and flavor, I think they are best left on the bone, which also makes them great for grilling. Of all cuts of steak, I prefer the flavor of ribeye; it dry-ages well because its outside layer of fat helps prevent spoilage.

The dry-aging process develops the tenderness and flavor of beef. This is due to aerobic bacteria (that need oxygen) and the anaerobic variety (that don't) gradually breaking down the internal tissue while the meat's overall firmness is maintained. Dry-aging must be done with meat that still has its bone and that contains some fat, in temperatures ranging from above-freezing to 40 degrees F., and in humidity of about 55 percent. In former days, all great butcher stores had a dry-aging meat locker, and you still see displays in some butcher's windows in New York, for example. Next time you're in a well-known steak house that advertises dry-aged beef, create a minor stir and ask to see their meat locker.

Never buy meat in plastic wrapping, because it traps the juices and prevents the anaerobic bacteria from working. You end up with mushy, soggy meat that has little flavor.

The strong, assertive salsa is inspired by a recipe of my friend Patricia Quintana, an authority on Mexican food and author of several wonderful cookbooks on the subject, including The Taste of Mexico (Stewart, Tabori & Chang, 1986).

Yield: 4 servings

Bricklayers Salsa

1 ounce dried arból chiles (about 40), stemmed, seeded, toasted, and rehydrated (page 192)	1 teaspoon minced roasted garlic (page 192)	¼ teaspoon toasted and ground dried Mexican oregano (page 192)
4 cups Roma tomatoes, blackened (page 192)	¼ teaspoon toasted and ground cumin (page 192)	¼ teaspoon salt

12 medium-sized new potatoes, quartered	¼ cup olive oil	Freshly ground black pepper to taste
	1 teaspoon salt	

¼ cup peanut oil	4 dry-aged ribeye steaks, with bone (about 16 ounces each)	Salt and freshly ground black pepper to taste

Preheat the oven to 350 degrees.

To prepare the salsa, purée the rehydrated chiles in a blender with just enough of the reserved rehydrating liquid to make puréeing possible (if this liquid tastes bitter, use plain water). Add the tomatoes, garlic, cumin, oregano, and salt, and purée together. Set aside.

Toss the potatoes in the olive oil, place on a baking sheet or in a roasting pan, and season with salt and pepper. Roast in the oven for 12 to 15 minutes, stirring occasionally. Pierce with a fork to test for doneness and roast for 5 more minutes, if necessary.

Meanwhile, to cook 1 or 2 steaks at a time, heat about 1 or 2 tablespoons of the peanut oil, or just enough to prevent each steak from sticking to the pan, in a heavy cast-iron skillet over medium-high heat. Season the steaks with salt and pepper and cook the steaks for 5 to 7 minutes per side for medium rare, turning often. Reduce the heat to medium after a few minutes.

Serve the steaks with the salsa and roasted new potatoes.

Grilled Beef Tenderloin

with Serrano-Blackened Tomato Butter, Roasted-Garlic Mashed Potatoes, and Caramelized Onion Toasts

Tenderloin is the name given to the long, internal muscle in the short loin that is also marketed as filet mignon, tournedos, and chateaubriand. It's a boneless cut and has little or no fat, and is sometimes sold as part of a porterhouse steak. Tenderloin is aptly named, since it's the most tender beef cut of all. However, it also contains the least natural flavor unless it is dry-aged properly. Although the most used and most highly developed muscles of cattle—the neck and legs, which are used for grazing, moving, and supporting—have the toughest texture, long, slow cooking techniques, such as braising, make them among the most flavorful. They are also the best choices for stocks and sauces.

In this recipe, the grilled steak is matched with roasted, smoky, caramelized ingredients that evoke range cooking over campfires. These earthy flavors also form the backbone of rustic Mexican food. The natural fructose of the vegetables becomes caramelized with the roasting process, bringing out their full sweetness and giving them a less sharp and more rounded flavor than other cooking techniques. The effect of smoke and fire is further enriched by retaining the blackened skin of the chiles. The chile rub we use in this recipe is effectively a dry marinade, and the technique creates a flavorful crust that enhances the texture of the meat.

Yield: 4 servings

Serrano-Blackened Tomato Butter

4 Roma tomatoes, blackened (page 192)

½ cup unsalted butter, softened
2 serrano chiles, blackened (page 192), seeded, with skin left on

⅛ teaspoon salt

Caramelized Onion Toasts

2 tablespoons peanut oil
1 white onion, diced (about 1 cup)

½ tablespoon sugar
1 tablespoon sherry vinegar

4 slices French bread

Red Chile Rub

2 tablespoons chile caribe (dried red chile flakes)
1 tablespoon dried oregano

½ cup chile molido or other pure red chile powder
1 tablespoon sugar

1 teaspoon salt

4 beef tenderloin fillets (about 8 ounces each), at room temperature

Roasted-Garlic Mashed Potatoes

2 pounds russet potatoes, peeled and diced

1 tablespoon minced roasted garlic (page 192)
2 tablespoons unsalted butter

¼ cup heavy cream
Pinch of salt

To prepare the butter, gently squeeze the blackened tomatoes to drain off most of their liquid. Keep their skin on and put them in a mixing bowl. Add the butter, serranos, and salt and whip together until smooth. Set aside.

To prepare the onion toasts, heat the peanut oil in a sauté pan or skillet and sauté the onions with the sugar over medium-high heat until brown. Add the vinegar and deglaze the pan. When ready to serve, toast the bread and spread the onion mixture on top.

To prepare the chile rub, place the chile caribe and oregano in a dry skillet and toast over medium heat for 2 minutes, until fragrant. Transfer to a spice grinder and pulse until smooth. Place in a bowl and combine thoroughly with the chile molido, sugar, and salt. Set aside.

Prepare the grill.

Meanwhile, bring a large saucepan of water to a boil. Add the potatoes, reduce the heat but maintain a high simmer and cook until tender, about 20 minutes. Drain and transfer the potatoes to a large bowl. Add the garlic, butter, cream, and salt, and mash until smooth. Adjust seasoning to taste. Dredge the beef tenderloin fillets in the chile rub. Slowly grill the fillets, turning often, about 4 or 5 minutes per side for medium rare.

Serve the tenderloin fillets with the mashed potatoes. Place approximately 1 tablespoon of butter on top of each fillet, serving the remaining butter on the side, and top with the onion toasts.

OPPOSITE PAGE *Stuffed Loin of Pork*

Lomo de Puerco
Pan-Roasted Pork Loin Stuffed with Wild Cherries and Ancho Chiles

Pork and fruit are a classic combination, as all lovers of applesauce with roasted pork will attest. In Southeast Asia, pork satays are matched with pineapple; in Central America, pork is paired with fruity mole sauces; and in Brazil, roasted pork is served with orange, rum, and cloves. In this recipe, we combine pork with dried cherries and ancho chiles. Anchos are dried poblanos, replete with rich, dried fruit tones and mild, sweet heat, so they perfectly complement the intense dried cherries.

Many of the meat recipes in this chapter call for marinades. There are several reasons to marinate meat. First, the acids in the marinade, whether vinegar, citrus juice, or wine, tenderize and break down the meat tissue. Because of this, take care not to leave meat in a marinade for too long. Marinades made with strong or assertive ingredients can restore taste to many meats with neutral or minimal flavor. Another reason to marinate meat is to retain or provide natural moisture; new breeding programs have made meat much leaner, and after marinating, the cooked cut of meat is much less likely to dry out and become tough. Note that this recipe calls for the pork to be marinated for three days (smaller cuts can be marinated for much shorter periods). If you wish, you may serve this dish with steamed asparagus or spaghetti squash.

Yield: 4 servings

Pork Marinade (page 158)

1½ pounds trimmed pork loin, fat and silver skin removed

Wild Cherry Stuffing

1 pound pitted fresh wild cherries or regular cherries, or 8 ounces dried cherries
Zest of ¼ orange (about 2 teaspoons)
½ tablespoon unsalted butter
¾ cup diced onion

2 tablespoons bourbon
3½ cups Pork Stock or Veal Stock (page 194)
1 tablespoon rehydrated and puréed ancho chiles (page 192)
2 cloves garlic, roasted (page 192)
¼ teaspoon ground anise

1 teaspoon chopped fresh thyme
1 teaspoon ground cinnamon
½ teaspoon seeded and minced habanero chile
¼ cup pine nuts, toasted (page 192)
Salt and freshly ground black pepper to taste

½ cup clarified butter (page 192)

¼ cup Pickapeppa Sauce (optional)

Freshly ground black pepper to taste

Sauce

2 teaspoons unsalted butter
4 shallots, minced
⅔ cup bourbon
2 cups water or reserved cherry rehydrating liquid

2 tablespoons pitted fresh wild cherries, or 1 tablespoon rehydrated cherries (page 192)
3 cups Pork Stock (page 193)
1 sprig fresh thyme

2 bay leaves
½ teaspoon seeded and minced habanero chile

Prepare the marinade. Add the pork loin to the marinade, making sure it is covered by the liquid on all sides. Cover the bowl and refrigerate for at least 2 days (preferably 3 days).

To make the stuffing, cook the cherries in an inch or so of water in a heavy saucepan and stew down to about 1 cup.

Wrap the orange zest in cheese cloth and blanch in boiling water for 2 or 3 seconds. Drain and reserve.

Heat the butter in a sauté pan or skillet and sauté the onion over medium heat for 2 or 3 minutes. Add the bourbon, deglaze the pan, and reduce the liquid over medium heat by about one-third. Add the stock and ancho chile purée, and reduce the liquid to ⅓ cup.

Place one-quarter of the cooked or softened cherries in a blender with the roasted garlic and just enough water (or rehydrating liquid) to make puréeing possible.

Stir the cherry-garlic purée into the onion mixture and add the remaining three-quarters of the cherries, the anise, thyme, cinnamon, and blanched orange zest. Add the habanero chile and mix together. Remove from the heat and allow to cool thoroughly. Stir in the toasted pine nuts just before stuffing and season to taste with salt and pepper.

Remove the pork loin from the marinade, pat dry, and butterfly (almost cut through, down the middle into two halves, folded out to resemble a butterfly shape). Pound the butterflied loin lightly with a mallet to achieve an even thinness.

Stuff the pork loin and roll it tightly into a cylinder. Tie tightly with butcher's twine at 1½- to 2-inch intervals. Preheat the oven to 325 degrees. Let the loin sit until it reaches room temperature.

In a sauté pan or skillet, heat the clarified butter and sear the loin over medium-high heat for about 7 to 8 minutes, or until browned on all sides. Transfer to a roasting pan. Insert a meat thermometer and roast in the oven for 20 to 25 minutes, or until an internal temperature of 125 degrees is reached, for medium rare to medium. (If you are using a more sensitive, professional-quality thermometer, insert it during the last few minutes of cooking time.) During the last few minutes of cooking, brush the loin lightly with the Pickapeppa Sauce and black pepper to taste. Remove from the oven and let rest for 5 to 8 minutes.

Meanwhile, prepare the sauce. In a sauté pan or skillet, heat the butter and caramelize the shallots over medium heat, about 3 to 4 minutes. Deglaze with the bourbon and reduce the liquid by two-thirds, about 4 to 5 minutes. Add the water, cherries, stock, thyme, and bay leaves, and reduce slowly by half over low heat. Add the habanero chile, adjust the seasonings, and strain.

Ladle 3 or 4 tablespoons of the warm sauce on each serving plate. Remove the twine from the resting loin and cut into 8 to 12 equal slices. Serve 2 or 3 slices per serving on top of the sauce.

Tenderloin of Pork
with Roasted-Tomatillo and Wild Mushroom Sauce

This recipe combines a wet marinade and a dry spice rub that give the cooked pork an intense, satisfyingly complex flavor and a subtle crust that contrasts with the texture of the meat. It is an unfortunate result of domestication and farm raising that most commercial meat has less flavor. One of the primary reasons is that the animals are not free to graze in their natural environment, where wild plants with their trace elements contribute more flavor to the meat. One of the best examples of the difference that a natural diet can make is the famous jabugo *hams of Southwest Spain. The rich, oily meat and very intense flavor is the result of the pigs' foraging for wild acorns, and the result is one of the most flavorful hams in the world.*

Filé powder, a spice contained in the rub, is made from ground, dried sassafras leaves (because of its flavor, sassafras is also known as "the root beer plant"). Filé is best known as a seasoning and thickener in gumbo, the Creole dish from Louisiana.

If desired, you may serve the pork loin with wilted chard and mustard greens.

Yield: 4 servings

Pork Marinade

6 cups water
1½ cups sugar
¼ cup salt
1 tablespoon dried thyme
½ tablespoon ground cumin

1 tablespoon crushed bay leaf
1 teaspoon crushed black pepper
1 teaspoon toasted and ground dried Mexican oregano (page 192)

3 tablespoons chile caribe (dried red chile flakes)
4 allspice berries
4 cloves
1 stick cinnamon

1½ pounds trimmed pork tenderloin, fat and silver skin removed

2 cups Roasted Tomatillo and Wild Mushroom Sauce (page 75)

Dry Spice Rub

1½ tablespoons filé powder
1½ tablespoons mushroom powder

3 tablespoons freshly ground black pepper
2 tablespoons chile molido (or other pure red chile powder)

Zest of 3 lemons, minced (about 1½ tablespoons)

½ cup clarified butter (page 192)

Mix together all the marinade ingredients in a mixing bowl. Add the pork loin to the marinade, making sure it is covered by the liquid on all sides. Cover the bowl and refrigerate overnight.

Prepare the tomatillo-mushroom sauce. Warm through in a saucepan when ready to serve the pork.

To prepare the spice rub, thoroughly combine all the ingredients together in a mixing bowl.

Remove the tenderloin from the marinade, pat dry, and lightly dredge in the spice rub. Let the loin sit until it reaches room temperature.

Preheat the oven to 325 degrees. Heat the clarified butter in a sauté pan or skillet, and sear the tenderloin over medium heat for about 3 or 4 minutes or until browned, turning often.

Transfer to a roasting pan and cook in the oven for 6 to 8 minutes for medium doneness. Remove from the oven and allow the tenderloin to rest for 5 to 8 minutes.

Slice the tenderloin on a bias (at a slight angle) and serve on the warm sauce.

Stuffed Loin of Pork
with Fig and Thyme Stuffing and Green Chile-Apple Chutney

This is another recipe that matches the sweetness of pork with fruit. In this case, it's with the figs in the stuffing, and the apple in the chutney. An alternative fruit stuffing that goes well with pork is prunes soaked in Armagnac; you could also use raisins, dried plums, or dried peaches. Dried apricots would be good,

too, but sometimes they are only available sulphurated—you can tell by their bright color. The pairing of dried fruit with pork (as well as duck) is a strong tradition in Eastern European cuisines.

The combination of figs and thyme is distinctively Mediterranean, and a tradition of Provence in particular, where fresh

figs are cooked with honey and thyme. The chile chutney gives this recipe a Southwestern twist. If desired, serve with wilted spinach and Roasted-Garlic Mashed Potatoes (page 154).

Yield: 4 servings • *Photo page 155*

Pork Marinade

6 cups water	1 tablespoon crushed bay leaf	4 allspice berries
½ cup sugar	1 teaspoon crushed black pepper	½ tablespoon juniper berries, crushed
1 tablespoon salt	1 teaspoon toasted and ground dried Mexican oregano (page 192)	3 cloves
1 tablespoon dried thyme	3 tablespoons chile caribe (dried red chile flakes)	1 stick cinnamon
1 tablespoon fennel seeds		
½ tablespoon ground cumin		

1½ pounds trimmed center-cut pork loin, fat and silver skin removed

Fig and Thyme Stuffing

8 ounces dried figs	1 small clove garlic, roasted (page 192)	Zest of 2 lemons
½ cup pitted black olives	2 dried ancho chiles, toasted and rehydrated (page 192)	½ tablespoon freshly ground black pepper
½ tablespoon chopped fresh lemon thyme, or regular thyme	1 tablespoon lemon oil or extra virgin olive oil	
1½ tablespoons chopped fresh Italian parsley		

Green Chile-Apple Chutney

2 tablespoons unsalted butter	4 New Mexico or Anaheim green chiles, roasted and peeled (page 192), seeded, and diced	1 cup apple cider
½ white onion, diced	¼ cup sugar	1 tablespoon dried marjoram
4 Granny Smith apples, peeled, cored, and diced		¼ cup pine nuts, toasted (page 192), optional

3 tablespoons peanut oil

Mix together all the marinade ingredients in a mixing bowl. Add the pork loin to the marinade, making sure it is covered by the liquid on all sides. Cover the bowl and refrigerate for at least 24 hours.

Place all the stuffing ingredients in a food processor, blend to a paste, and set aside.

To prepare the chutney, heat the butter in a heavy saucepan, add the onion, cover, and sauté over medium-high heat for about 3 minutes, until soft. Reduce the heat to low and remove the lid. Add the apples, chiles, and sugar, and cook uncovered for 10 minutes longer.

Meanwhile, in another saucepan reduce the apple cider to ¼ cup. Add to the chile-apple mixture together with the marjoram and pine nuts if desired. Remove from the heat and allow to cool.

Remove the pork loin from the marinade, pat dry, and butterfly (see page 156). Stuff the pork and roll it tightly into a cylinder. Tie the meat with butcher's twine, at 1½- to 2-inch intervals. Let the loin sit until it reaches room temperature.

Preheat the oven to 325 degrees.

Heat the peanut oil in a skillet and sear the stuffed loin over medium-high heat for about 7 to 8 minutes, turning to brown on all sides. Transfer to a roasting pan and cook in the oven for about 25 minutes for medium doneness. Remove from the oven and let rest for 5 to 8 minutes.

Remove the twine from the resting pork loin and cut into 8 equal slices. Serve 2 slices per serving with the chutney. ❧

Photo: Courtesy Museum of New Mexico.

Cordero Yucatán
Roasted Lamb Yucatán-Style with Cinnamon Rice

Each region of Mexico has its own pastes, sauces, and rubs, such as the Oaxacan moles and pipiáns from Puebla. Mérida, the capital of the Yucatán, has its own specialty: recados. These are very dense, red or green oily spice pastes with earthy, pungent aromas, set out all through the food markets in huge, brightly colored plastic basins, and sold in plastic bags or colorful plastic tubs. Recados are made with ingredients such as red annatto seeds, saffron, allspice, cumin, oregano, roasted garlic, and chiles. Recados are used as basic seasonings, stuffings, and also as meat rubs. Black recados are made with blackened chiles and wood ashes. You can see cooked meats rubbed with these recados in the markets of the Yucatán. I figure Mérida is a little out of your way, so this recado recipe is my easier, contemporary version.

The cinnamon and raisins give the rice sweetness without the addition of sugar, and the rice counterbalances the lamb's spicyness. An optional side dish with this recipe is grilled prickly pear cactus. To prepare, remove any needles from the pads with thick gloves and a paring knife, wash under water, and brush with olive oil. Grill whole pads for about 5 minutes until tender. (The grilled pads can also be puréed for other uses.)

This recipe takes 2 days to prepare; making the Lamb Stock takes about 7 hours in all, and the lamb should marinate overnight.

Yield: 6 to 8 servings

Recado Marinade

6 cloves garlic, lightly crushed and peeled
½ cup olive oil
1½ tablespoons cumin seeds

1 tablespoon black peppercorns
¼ cup dried Mexican oregano
3 tablespoons dried thyme

½ teaspoon salt
4 dried chipotle chiles, broken

6 cups Lamb Stock (page 193)

1 boneless leg of lamb, about 4 to 5 pounds

Cinnamon Rice

4 tablespoons unsalted butter
½ cup finely diced carrot
½ cup finely diced celery

½ cup finely diced onion
2 cups long-grain rice
2 teaspoons salt

4 teaspoons ground cinnamon
½ cup raisins
3 cups water

To prepare the marinade, place the garlic in a small skillet. Add the olive oil and heat over medium-low heat for about 5 minutes. Remove the skillet from the heat and let the garlic oil steep for 30 minutes. Discard the garlic, and set the oil aside.

In a separate skillet, toast the cumin, peppercorns, oregano, and thyme over medium heat. Stir frequently and remove from the heat when the mixture becomes aromatic and before it starts to smoke. Add the salt and chipotles, transfer to a spice mill or blender, and grind to a fine powder.

Prepare the stock.

With a boning knife, carefully trim all the fat and outside membranes from the leg of lamb right down to the red meat. Rub the lamb with the garlic oil and then with the powdered ingredients. Cover and place in the refrigerator to marinate for several hours, or preferably overnight.

Remove the lamb from the marinade and bring to room temperature (about 4 hours before cooking).

Preheat the oven to 350 degrees. Place the lamb on a rack in a shallow roasting pan. Insert a meat thermometer and cook in the oven for 1 hour, or until the meat reaches an internal temperature of 120 degrees. (If using a more sensitive, professional-quality thermometer, insert it during the last few minutes of cooking time.) Increase the oven temperature to 450 degrees for 5 to 10 minutes to brown the exterior, or until the lamb has an internal temperature of 130 degrees. Remove the lamb from the oven and let it rest for 10 minutes before carving.

While the lamb is roasting, prepare the Cinnamon Rice. Heat the butter in a large saucepan and sauté the vegetables over medium-high heat for 3 to 5 minutes, until translucent. Add the rice and heat until warmed through, about 2 minutes. Add the salt, cinnamon, raisins, and water, and bring to a boil. Cover the pan, reduce the heat to a simmer, and cook for 10 to 15 minutes, stirring occasionally, or until the water has evaporated. Allow the rice to rest for 3 to 5 minutes and fluff up before serving with a wooden spoon.

To prepare the sauce, pour off the lamb fat from the roasting pan into a saucepan, and add the Lamb Stock. Reduce over high heat, stirring occasionally, until the liquid is reduced by two-thirds; adjust the seasoning.

Carve the lamb, spoon the sauce over, and serve with the rice.

Roasted Rack of Lamb
with Pecan Crust and Roasted Corn Salsa

At Coyote Cafe, we generally use range-raised native New Mexican lamb, which has a strong herbaceous flavor, often with nutty tones, and a good texture. In the past, we've also used churro lamb, a rare, historic breed originally from Spain and introduced to the New World by the Spanish. Churros are famous for their fine, strong wool, and they have a darker meat and a robust,

almost gamey flavor. Crusting meat and fish has become popular in recent years, and using ingredients such as nuts, seeds, or ground tortillas, for example, provides contrasting texture as well as enhanced flavor. Pecans are a major crop in New Mexico, and their richness and crunch compare with the complex flavors and tenderness of the lamb.

The corn salsa is one of my favorites. It combines the smoky tones of the chipotle chiles, roasted corn, garlic, and poblano chiles, with the flavorful sun-dried tomatoes and earthy wild mushrooms. The complex flavors of this salsa act as an intriguing counterpoint to the lamb.

Yield: 4 servings

Marinade

½ cup Dijon-style mustard
2 tablespoons honey

3 tablespoons molasses
4 cloves garlic, minced

2 racks of lamb (about 1½ pounds each), trimmed of all fat and sinew

Roasted Corn Salsa

2 tablespoons extra virgin olive oil
1 cup diced morels, chanterelles, or other wild mushrooms
3 cups fresh corn kernels, roasted (page 192)
¼ cup sun-dried tomatoes (packed in oil and drained)

1 large poblano chile, roasted and peeled (page 192), seeded, and diced
1 large red bell pepper, roasted and peeled (page 192), seeded, and diced
2 teaspoons finely chopped fresh marjoram

1 clove garlic, roasted (page192), peeled, and minced
1 teaspoon adobo sauce (from canned chipotle chiles in adobo sauce)
½ teaspoon sherry vinegar
1 teaspoon fresh lime juice

Pecan Crust

½ cup finely chopped pecans

½ cup fresh bread crumbs

1½ teaspoons chopped fresh marjoram

Combine all the marinade ingredients in a small mixing bowl. Rub the lamb with the marinade, cover, and refrigerate, preferably overnight.

Remove the lamb from the marinade and bring to room temperature (about 4 hours before cooking) in a roasting pan. Reserve the remaining marinade. Preheat the oven to 400 degrees.

Meanwhile, prepare the salsa. Heat 1 tablespoon of the olive oil in a large sauté pan or skillet and sauté the wild mushrooms over medium-high heat for 3 or 4 minutes, until they develop a nutty color. Remove from the heat and let cool. Transfer to a large mixing bowl, combine with the remaining oil and salsa ingredients, and adjust the seasoning.

Roast the lamb in the oven for 8 minutes. Remove from the oven and let the lamb rest for 10 minutes. Reduce the oven to 325 degrees.

Combine all the Pecan Crust ingredients together in a small mixing bowl. Brush the lamb with the remaining marinade and then dredge in the Pecan Crust. Insert a meat thermometer and return the lamb to the oven and roast for an additional 6 to 8 minutes, or until it reaches an internal temperature of 125 degrees. (If using a more sensitive, professional-quality thermometer, insert it during the last few minutes of cooking time.)

Remove the lamb from the oven and let rest for 5 minutes before slicing. Serve on a bed of the salsa.

Grilled Local Lamb T-Bones

with Chorizo-White Bean Stew and Fresh Mint

T-bones are a favorite of any meat lover. The cut comes from a cross-section of the loin bone that includes both loin and tenderloin meat. Another type of lamb chop, the shoulder cut, is not as tender and is best when marinated. The T-bones should not be cut too thin—they should be at least 1½ inches thick.

With this recipe, as with most of the recipes in this chapter, it's important to bring the lamb to room temperature before cooking it. Grilling or pan-roasting chilled meat over too hot a fire will shrink it, make it tough, and leave it too rare and cold on the inside.

If you have the time and inclination, you can make the chorizo for this recipe at home, using lamb instead of pork. Otherwise, you can buy chorizo at Latin markets or gourmet stores, or substitute hot Italian sausage.

Yield: 4 servings

White Bean Stew

2 tablespoons olive oil
2 tablespoons minced shallots
2 cloves garlic, minced
½ cup sliced wild mushrooms

2 cups cooked white or navy beans (page 192)
4 Roma tomatoes, blackened (page 192) and chopped
2 cups Lamb Stock (page 193)

1 tablespoon minced fresh marjoram
¼ teaspoon salt

4 chorizo links (about 8 ounces each), sliced into quarters
2 cups Lamb Stock (page 193)
8 lamb T-bones (about 5 to 6 ounces each)

¼ teaspoon salt
¼ teaspoon black pepper
8 scallions
1 tablespoon olive oil

2 tablespoons chiffonade of fresh mint

To prepare the stew, heat the olive oil in a large skillet or sauté pan and sauté the shallots, garlic, and mushrooms over medium-high heat for about 5 minutes, or until the shallots and garlic are translucent. Stir in the beans, tomatoes and Lamb Stock, reduce the heat, and simmer for 20 minutes. Stir in the marjoram and salt and remove from the heat.

Cook the chorizo in a dry skillet for 5 minutes over medium-high heat, stirring occasionally until crisp and brown. Keep warm.

Prepare the grill. Meanwhile, in a saucepan reduce the Lamb Stock to 1 cup and keep warm.

Season the lamb T-bones with the salt and pepper and grill to the desired doneness, about 5 minutes per side for medium-rare. Brush the scallions with the olive oil and grill for about 3 minutes.

Warm through the White Bean Stew and ladle onto the center of the serving plates. Place the grilled scallions around the outside of the plate, forming a circle. Stack 2 lamb T-bones per plate on top of the stew and place 4 chorizo slices around the lamb. Pour about ¼ cup of the reduced stock over and around the lamb. Sprinkle the mint over the lamb.

Texas Axis Venison
with Wild Chokecherry-Ancho Chile Sauce

Venison is lean and has low levels of fat and cholesterol compared with other meats—about 50 percent less than chicken and up to 70 percent less than some cuts of beef. Most of the venison commercially available in the United States is deer meat, although the term is also used loosely to refer to elk, antelope, moose, and caribou meat. The native fallow, whitetail, and red deer are the most popular varieties with sportsmen, and each has its own distinct flavor characteristics. These varieties are not necessarily available for commercial use. Because venison has little fat (rather like 1 percent milk), and is leaner than other red meat

such as beef or lamb, it's important to marinate it to enhance the natural moisture, or to baste it while it is cooking.

Axis and sika deer, native to the Indian subcontinent, have been introduced into Texas relatively recently and are being raised by the Texas Wild Game Co-operative in Ingram, which is in the Hill Country outside Austin. Of course, coming from Texas, the animals are a lot bigger than ones I've seen in Asia and Indonesia. Farm- or range-raised venison is now available year-round. Previously, venison was generally considered to be a fall or winter game meat, because of hunting season. This

trend is also good news to professional chefs, who have had few sources for venison because it is illegal to sell privately hunted game to restaurants.

Chokecherries are a type of astringent wild cherry native to North America. They are best when cooked in sauces, jellies, or preserves, and they can also be made into wine. Their dark, fruity tones combine wonderfully well with the ancho chiles to match the complex flavors of the venison. Dried cherries can be substituted just as well.

I recommend you serve this dish with wild rice or wild rice cakes.

Yield: 4 servings

Marinade

6 juniper berries
1 sprig fresh rosemary
15 fresh sage leaves

¼ cup tellicherry (black) peppercorns
6 allspice berries
2 tablespoons kosher salt

2 small leeks, sliced in rings
6 cloves garlic, sliced
¼ cup olive oil

4 Axis venison chops (about 6 to 7 ounces each)

Wild Chokecherry-Ancho Chile Sauce

2 tablespoons olive oil
½ cup venison trimmings
1 cup fresh chokecherries, or ½ cup dried cherries rehydrated in warm water (page 192)

2 cups Venison Stock (page 193)
2 dried ancho chiles, stemmed, seeded, and toasted (page 192)
1 sprig fresh thyme
6 juniper berries, crushed
2 bay leaves

1 tablespoon unsalted butter
½ cup thinly sliced wild mushrooms or domestic mushrooms
1 teaspoon chopped fresh sage

Place all the marinade ingredients in a food processor or blender. (Use a little more olive oil if necessary to allow puréeing.) Purée until smooth. Place the venison chops in a dish, and cover on all sides with the marinade. Cover the dish with plastic wrap and refrigerate overnight.

Bring the venison chops and marinade to room temperature, about 4 hours.

To prepare the sauce, heat the olive oil in a saucepan and caramelize the venison trimmings over medium heat, about 5 to 7 minutes. Add the chokecherries and cook over medium heat for 3 to 5 minutes. Add the stock, toasted ancho chiles, thyme, juniper, and bay leaves. Reduce the liquid by one-third while simmering over low heat, about 12 to 15 minutes.

Remove the pan from the heat and strain the sauce through a sieve into a bowl, pressing down with a spoon or ladle on the solids to force the juices through. Set aside.

In a separate saucepan, heat the butter and sauté the mushrooms over medium-high heat until cooked through, about 2 to 3 minutes. Add the sage and strain off any excess liquid. Add the reserved strained sauce to the mushrooms and keep warm.

Remove the room-temperature venison chops from the marinade. Heat a heavy sauté pan or skillet and sauté the chops for 3 to 4 minutes per side over medium heat for mediumrare.

Allow the chops to rest for a few minutes before serving. Transfer to serving plates and pour the sauce around the chops.

Blackfoot Buffalo Ribeye

with Wild Mushrooms, Green Onions, Applewood-Smoked Bacon, and Cheyenne Batter Bread

The Plains Indians, including the Blackfoot and Sioux (among many other tribes), depended heavily on the buffalo, and eagerly awaited the annual migrations of the herds that provided them with meat, clothing, shelter, fire and heat, paints and dyes, candles, drums, and implements. After the buffalo's tragic brush with extinction toward the end of the nineteenth century, they are now making something of a comeback in North America. They are being ranched in herds across the United States, and even on the island of Kauai in Hawaii. Ted Turner, the owner of CNN, is also raising large buffalo herds on his ranches in Montana and Wyoming.

Buffalo is appearing more frequently on restaurant menus and in supermarket or specialty-food markets' meat cases (see "Sources," page 199). Buffalo meat has a richer flavor than beef, and is healthier because it has an average of 20 percent less fat. Buffalo is expensive, but will probably become less so in the future. It is the perfect meat for stewing in chili, and the less expensive cuts can be braised. Beef or veal ribeye can be substituted for the buffalo.

Yield: 4 servings

Marinade

3 cups red wine
6 tablespoons (2 jiggers) gin
½ onion, diced
1 carrot, diced
1 stalk celery, diced

1 tablespoon chopped fresh thyme
1 tablespoon chopped fresh rosemary
3 cloves garlic, crushed
4 black peppercorns, crushed

12 juniper berries, crushed
2 bay leaves
Zest and juice of 1 lime

4 buffalo ribeye steaks (about 10 ounces each)

Cheyenne Batter Bread

2 cups milk
¾ cup cornmeal
1 tablespoon peanut oil
½ white onion, sliced

1 tablespoon seeded and minced red bell pepper
1 tablespoon seeded and minced yellow bell pepper
1 tablespoon seeded and minced poblano chile

3 cloves garlic, roasted (page 192)
3 tablespoons grated Parmesan cheese
3 eggs

2 cups Veal Stock or Beef Stock (pages 194 and 193)
3 sprigs marjoram
½ cup diced bacon (preferably applewood smoked)

2 tablespoons unsalted butter
1 cup sliced chanterelle mushrooms
½ cup sliced scallions

Salt and freshly ground black pepper to taste
2 tablespoons olive oil

Mix all the marinade ingredients together in a large bowl. Place the ribeye steaks in the marinade, making sure they are completely covered. Cover the bowl with plastic wrap and marinate for at least 2 hours at room temperature, and preferably overnight in the refrigerator.

Preheat the oven to 350 degrees. Butter an 8-inch baking pan.

To prepare the bread, mix the milk and cornmeal together at medium speed in a bowl of an electric mixer fitted with a paddle attachment. Heat the oil in a small skillet and caramelize the onion over medium-high heat, about 5 minutes. Add to the bowl, along with the bell peppers, poblano, garlic, and cheese. Then add the eggs, one at a time, and thoroughly incorporate. Mix for 45 seconds longer until the batter is smooth.

Transfer the batter to the prepared pan. Bake in the oven for 25 minutes, until firm and golden brown.

Meanwhile, heat the stock and marjoram in a saucepan and reduce by half over high heat. Strain, and keep warm.

Heat the bacon in a sauté pan and sauté over medium heat for 5 minutes. Add the butter, chanterelles, and scallions and sauté for 5 minutes longer. Season with salt and pepper.

Remove the buffalo steaks from the marinade and pat dry with paper towels. Heat the olive oil in a large skillet or sauté pan and pan-fry the buffalo steaks over medium-high heat for 4 to 5 minutes per side for medium rare.

Transfer the steaks to serving plates, and garnish with the mushroom-scallion mixture, spooning some on top and some at the side. Cut the batter bread into squares and place beside the buffalo. Pour the sauce around them. ➛🐃

DESSERTS

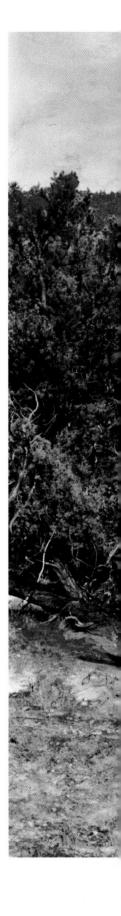

Piñon Tacos

Mango Rice Pudding Brûlée

Mexican Chocolate Silk Pie

Cold Lemon Soufflé
with Garden Berries

Chocolate Pound Cake
with Cajeta Ice Cream

Warm Spiced-Pecan Waffles
with Bourbon Peach-Pecan Sauce and Sweetened Crema

Navajo Peach Crisp

Wild Honey and Blackberry Sorbet

Roasted Dixon Peach Soup
with Sweet Strawberry Sauce

Sweet Coconut Tamales
with Caramelized Pineapple and Brazilian Rum Sauce

Taos Root Beer Float
with Sassafras Granita, Mexican Vanilla Bean Ice Cream, and Molasses Snaps

Piñon Coffee Helado Profiteroles
with Cajeta Sauce

Ibarra Chocolate Flan
with Crispy Phyllo Crust

Desserts are a relatively recent addition to Southwestern cuisine and were originally based on the Hispanic culinary tradition. The Spanish brought the concept of dessert to the New World, although desserts were primarily consumed on special holidays, at religious celebrations, or on feast days. They were a sign of affluence because they were made with processed, expensive flours, rare sugar, and dairy products. In New Mexico today, desserts such as natillas (custards) and biscochitos (cookies) are still most closely associated with the Christmas season. Flans, custards, and cooling fruit-based desserts that have their origins in this tradition have long been favored in the Southwest, and many of the desserts in this chapter follow in this style.

Common characteristics of Southwestern desserts are strong, natural flavors, usually provided by fruits and nuts, with dairy products, flour, sugar, and processed ingredients playing a minimized role. It was the Spanish who brought with them many kinds of soft fruit and dairy products. Until then, the only types of naturally occurring forms of sweetness available were native wild fruits, which were relatively scarce, and honey, which bees collected from desert and mountain wild flowers.

With modern transportation techniques, the use of tropical fruit grown in southern Mexico, Central and South America, and the Caribbean has also become a welcome feature of Southwestern desserts.

One of the great gifts that the New World gave to all cuisines is chocolate (xocolatl, or "bitter water" in the Aztec language). The Aztecs drank an unsweetened mixture of chocolate, chiles (such as the high-fructose, naturally sweet dried ancho), and spices that was believed to be an aphrodisiac. The cacao beans that are native to Central America and from which chocolate is derived were highly prized and used as currency. (A hundred beans would buy a slave.) They were also used in feasts and rituals in pre-Columbian Mesoamerica. It was Cortés, not Columbus, who carried cacao beans back to Europe, and it was the Spanish that used sugar to sweeten chocolate. Thereafter, it became immensely popular in the Old World, especially as a Lenten drink. (No solids are allowed during this fasting period, and chocolate is high in calories and acts as a mild stimulant.) One of the most evocative sights and smells in all of Mexico today is the stores that grind chocolate powder to the customer's taste, made with roasted cacao beans, cane sugar, cinnamon or can-ela, and almonds that are all heaped in tubs or barrels. In Oaxaca, in southern Mexico, you can mix your own blend.

To the surprise of many who think of New Mexico as semiarid high desert or forested mesas and mountainsides, fruits and nuts abound, especially along the Rio Grande Valley. Apple, peach, plum, and apricot orchards were planted by the missions and the early Spanish settlers, and soft-fruit orchards have remained prominent in northern New Mexico, especially in communities such as Velarde, Dixon, and Chimayo. Some of the best raspberries you'll ever taste come from Mora, nestled high in the eastern Sangre de Cristo mountains. Melons, cherries, and pecans are major crops in southern New Mexico, and pine (piñon) nuts grow on the bushy trees that dot the landscape everywhere in the northern part of the state. In the fall, you'll see trucks parked by the roadside and families shaking the trees and knocking branches with sticks to release the pine cones that contain the nuts. Pine nuts were an important source of protein and calories for the Native Americans of the Southwest, especially in winter when other food sources were scarce.

Piñon Tacos

This recipe is Suzy Dayton's version of the one Kim Peoples, the opening pastry chef at Coyote Cafe, created as a tongue-in-cheek dessert, poking gentle fun at the ubiquitous corn tacos made with the hard U-shaped shells. These shells are familiar across the United States but are unknown south of the border. It also puts a Southwestern spin on the concept of the French tuile. The original dessert was featured in a 1989 Life magazine article, titled "Dinner of the Decade," when we paired it with a dessert enchilada and an ancho ice cream-blue corn "quesadilla" to create a different kind of "combination plate."

This dessert taco can be filled with all kinds of things—fruit or ice cream with cajeta sauce, for example—or it can be served plain, as a cookie, or dipped in chocolate.

Yield: 4 to 6 servings

Tacos

1¼ cups pine nuts
½ cup unsalted butter, softened
6 tablespoons brown sugar

6 tablespoons white sugar
1 egg
½ tablespoon vanilla extract

⅓ cup all-purpose flour
¼ teaspoon baking soda

Filling

1 cup mascarpone cream
1 cup heavy cream
¼ cup white sugar

1 tablespoon finely chopped orange zest

1 tablespoon Grand Marnier or other orange liqueur

Garnish

Fresh berries

Orange segments

Cajeta Caramel (page 178), optional

Preheat the oven to 350 degrees. Place 1 cup of the nuts in a single layer on a cookie sheet and toast until golden brown, about 10 to 15 minutes. Let cool and finely chop, or grind in a food processor.

In a mixing bowl, cream together the butter and both sugars until light and fluffy. Add the egg and vanilla, and beat until smooth. Stir in the flour, baking soda, and ground nuts and mix until the dough is just incorporated.

Cover a cookie sheet with parchment paper. Take a tablespoon of the dough and drop it in a circle on the cookie sheet. Repeat for the remainder of the dough, keeping a few inches between each circle as the dough will expand when baked. Press a few of the remaining untoasted pine nuts on top of each circle of dough.

Transfer the cookie sheet to the oven and bake for 7 to 9 minutes, or until golden brown. Let cool for a minute and then remove from the sheet with a spatula, draping them over a rolling pin or broom handle while still soft, so they form a U-shape. Let cool completely until hardened like a taco shell. Store carefully because the "tacos" are very fragile.

Whisk together all the filling ingredients in a mixing bowl until the mixture is stiff and peaks form. Keep chilled.

Place a piñon taco on each serving plate and carefully spoon in the filling. Garnish with berries and orange segments, and the Cajeta Sauce, if desired. ❧

Mango Rice Pudding Brûlée

A few years back, I was in London and passed the office of Dr. Phang, a Chinese dentist. (I swear, this is true.) If you were a pastry chef, and a good one at that, and you wanted a last name that would be perfectly apropos for your profession, what would it be? I think our former pastry chef, Kimberly Sweet, just about takes the cake; it wasn't even a nom de cuisine—she was born with it. This recipe, which combines rice pudding (a Middle Eastern tradition of sweetened rice introduced to Europe by the Arabs), with creamy French brûlée and the tropical mango (originally Indian but now very much a part of the repertoire of Mexican tropical fruit), was inspired by Kimberly Sweet's creation. It's an excellent example of how a single dish can represent the convergence of many diverse culinary traditions.

People are surprised when they discover the rice pudding in such an elegant dessert; they usually associate it with childhood and Grandma. It may be a comfort food, but infused with cinnamon, dried cherries or blueberries, or puréed fresh fruit, rice pudding becomes a wonderful medium for a variety of interesting flavors.

Yield: 6 servings

½ cup long-grain rice
1 cup water
2 cups milk
1 cup heavy cream

1 vanilla bean
¾ cup sugar
2 eggs plus 3 egg yolks
Pinch of salt

2 very ripe mangoes, peeled, pitted, and puréed

Place the rice in a saucepan, add the water, and bring to a boil. Reduce the heat to a simmer and cover the pan. Cook for about 20 minutes, or until the water is absorbed and the rice is tender. Let cool.

Preheat the oven to 325 degrees.

Place the cream and milk in a separate pan. Split the vanilla bean lengthwise and scrape the seeds into the pan. Add ½ cup of the sugar and bring to a boil. Remove from the heat. Temper the eggs and yolks by steadily adding the hot cream mixture, while whisking constantly. It is important to stir constantly and not to let the mixture boil.

Strain into a clean bowl, and then whisk in the cooked rice, salt, and mangoes. Pour into six 8-ounce (1-cup) ramekins and place, uncovered, in a water bath, by filling a large baking pan with enough water to reach halfway up the sides of the ramekins.

Bake in the oven for 30 to 45 minutes or until set. Cool and chill for at least 3 hours before serving. To serve, top each ramekin with ⅔ tablespoon of the remaining sugar and caramelize under a broiler.

Mexican Chocolate Silk Pie

This dessert, a version of Star's Chocolate Silk recipe, which was created by pastry chef Emily Luchetti, is a new interpretation of a classic Southern dessert—the silk pie. The key to success here is using a good-quality bittersweet chocolate. My favorite is Valhrona, but a good Swiss or Dutch brand will work well, too. The Hawaii Vintage Chocolate Company (see "Sources," page 199), which grows the only cacao beans in the country, also makes an excellent brand. Hawaii has the ideal tropical climate for growing beans, and like coffee, cacao prefers well-drained mountain slopes and rich, volcanic soil.

This dessert can also be made with Mexican Ibarra chocolate, which contains almonds, cinnamon, and sugar as well as cacao. This gives it a rougher texture and a rather less refined flavor.

While this recipe does not call for Mexican chocolate, it contains similar ingredients. If you can find long, fragile canela sticks, use them instead of cinnamon. Canela is a different, softer type of evergreen tree bark and it has a mellower, more aromatic flavor. The fresher it is, the more fragrant it will be; if it smells dusty, it's old and not worth buying.

Yield: 8 to 10 servings
(one 10-inch pie)

Crust

2½ cups pecans, toasted (page 192) and coarsely chopped
¼ cup brown sugar

1½ teaspoons ground cinnamon
¼ cup melted unsalted butter

Filling

18 ounces bittersweet or semisweet chocolate (not unsweetened)
10 tablespoons unsalted butter, at room temperature

½ cup sugar
4 eggs
1 teaspoon ground cinnamon
½ cup heavy cream
½ teaspoon almond extract

¼ cup finely chopped toasted almonds (page 192)

Topping

1 cup chilled heavy cream
3 tablespoons sugar

1 teaspoon vanilla extract
2 tablespoons grated chocolate

¼ cup finely chopped toasted almonds (page 192)

To prepare the crust, pulse the chopped pecans in a food processor. Transfer to a bowl and mix with the sugar, cinnamon, and butter. Press the mixture into a 10-inch springform pan (covering the bottom and 2 inches up the sides) and chill until needed.

To prepare the filling, melt the chocolate in a double boiler and cool to room temperature. In a mixer, cream the butter and sugar together until light and fluffy. At medium speed, whip in the eggs, melted chocolate, and cinnamon, and set aside. In a separate bowl, whip the cream and almond extract to soft peaks and fold immediately into the chocolate mixture. Fold in the almonds. Spoon into the chilled crust, and chill for at least 2 hours.

To prepare the topping, whip the cream, sugar, and vanilla together to form firm peaks. Spread on top of the pie, and sprinkle with the grated chocolate and almonds. ▰

Cold Lemon Soufflé
with Garden Berries

There is nothing quite like a cooling, refreshing dessert after a spicy meal, especially on a hot summer day. We usually add this dish to our dessert menu in August, when the first raspberries of the season reach us from the Salmon Ranch in Mora, high up in the mountains on the other side of Taos. There, the cool, wet climate is ideal for ripening berries. I think the best, most flavorful raspberries in the United States are grown there.

This dessert can be prepared ahead of time (but I recommend no more than one day ahead), and it holds up well. It has a delicious, creamy texture, yet it is not as rich as ice cream. You can add a little ginger for a variation in flavor, and any type of fresh berry can be used. Try to use the Meyer variety of lemons if you can find them—they're more aromatic and less sour than regular lemons. But if you use Meyer lemons, use ¼ cup less sugar.

Yield: 6 to 8 servings

½ cup fresh lemon juice
Zest of 1 lemon, finely chopped
2 eggs
1 cup sugar

Pinch of salt
4 egg yolks
2 cups heavy cream, whipped to
  stiff peaks

3 egg whites
1 cup fresh raspberries or diced
  strawberries

In a large stainless steel bowl, combine the lemon juice, zest, whole eggs, 5 tablespoons of the sugar, and salt. Whisk in a double boiler until the mixture thickens, and let cool. Cover and chill if not using immediately; this lemon-curd mixture can be made up to 3 days ahead.

Whisk together the egg yolks and 2 tablespoons of the sugar until the mixture thickens and turns pale (known as the "ribbon" stage). Fold into the lemon curd. In a clean bowl, whisk the egg whites, slowly adding the remaining sugar to form a stiff meringue. Fold into the lemon curd mixture and gently mix.

Transfer the mixture into 6 or 8 ramekins and smooth off the tops (or fill a 10-inch buttered and sugared soufflé mold with the mixture). Chill for at least 6 hours, and preferably overnight. Serve garnished with the fresh berries.

Chocolate Pound Cake
with Cajeta Ice Cream

Pound cakes were originally named because they were made with a pound each of flour, butter, eggs, and sugar. Pound cakes date back to the American colonial period, when they were typically flavored with a little vanilla or lemon. This recipe departs from the classic formula but the result is a dense, rich, moist cake. Here again, the quality of the chocolate is the key (and the butter like-wise)—so don't skimp because it will be very noticeable. Using the paddle attachment of a mixer to combine the ingredients is important, because it produces a fluffy, rich texture that hand-beating cannot achieve. Take care to bake evenly at the correct temperature; if the oven is too hot, the cake will be too crusty and dry. It keeps well if wrapped tightly and stored in a cool place.

Cajeta is Mexican goat milk caramel, and is used in many traditional Mexican desserts. It is less sweet than regular caramel, which I far prefer, and it has an appealing, rustic quality to it. The best cajeta I have tasted comes from goats raised around Celaya and San Miguel de Allende, in the Mexican state of Guanajuato.

Yield: 6 to 8 servings
(one 8½ x 4½ x 2½-inch loaf pan or a 9-inch bundt pan)

Cajeta Ice Cream

1 cup Cajeta Caramel (recipe follows)	2 cups milk 2 cups heavy cream	½ cup sugar 8 egg yolks

Pound Cake

3 eggs ⅔ cup milk 3 tablespoons water	½ tablespoon vanilla extract ¾ cup good-quality cocoa powder 2 cups sugar ½ teaspoon salt	½ teaspoon baking powder 1⅓ cups all-purpose flour 1 cup butter, softened

Prepare the Cajeta Caramel and set aside.

To prepare the ice cream, bring the milk, cream, and sugar to a boil in a heavy-bottomed saucepan. Remove from the heat. Place the egg yolks in a bowl and temper by slowly adding the hot (but not boiling) cream mixture, while whisking constantly. It is important to stir constantly. Cook for 1½ minutes over medium heat and strain into a clean stainless steel bowl set over ice water. Add the Cajeta Caramel and whisk together until smooth. Chill and pour into an ice cream machine. Freeze according to the manufacturer's directions.

Preheat the oven to 350 degrees.

In a mixing bowl, whisk together the eggs, milk, water, and vanilla. Sift together the cocoa, sugar, salt, baking powder, and flour into the bowl of an electric mixer fitted with a paddle attachment.

Mix in the butter and half of the liquid ingredients and when moistened, increase the mixing speed to medium-high. Beat together for 2 minutes, turn down the speed to low and add the remaining liquid, stirring until incorporated.

Pour into a greased and floured loaf or bundt pan and bake for about 1 hour or until an inserted toothpick comes out clean. Remove from the pan and let cool on a wire rack. Slice and serve with the ice cream.

Cajeta Caramel

Yield: 2 cups

4 cups evaporated goat's milk
2 cups milk

5 teaspoons cornstarch
½ teaspoon baking soda
1½ cups sugar

6 tablespoons water
Juice of ½ lemon

Bring both milks to a boil in a heavy saucepan, while stirring, and reduce the heat to a simmer. Mix together the cornstarch and baking soda in a small bowl and add just enough of the hot milk mixture to dissolve the dry ingredients. Beat well with a whisk and pour back into the remaining hot milk. Stir with a whisk and continue to simmer.

In another heavy saucepan, heat the sugar, water, and lemon juice and caramelize over high heat until light golden brown. Wash down the sides of the pan frequently with a pastry brush dipped in water, to prevent sugar crystals from forming. Remove from the heat and let the sugar cool until the bubbles have subsided.

Slowly add half of the hot milk mixture to the cooled sugar mixture. Stir together and pour into the remaining milk mixture in the saucepan. While stirring continuously, cook at a low boil until the caramel is thick and dark, about 1 hour. Remove from the heat and let cool.

OPPOSITE PAGE *Wild Honey and Blackberry Sorbet*

Wild Honey and Blackberry Sorbet

*F*ruit sorbets are one of my favorite dessert choices with Southwestern meals. Their distinctive, ripe flavors, unadulterated by creams or butters, are light, refreshing, and wonderfully cleansing to the palate. Honey makes a more flavorful alternative to sugar, and some wild honeys really taste of the flowers and blossoms from which the bees gather their nectar. I like to use the strongly flavored Taos honey from northern New Mexico, made from mountain wildflower and orchard-blossom nectar.

*B*lackberries are widely cultivated, but nothing beats using hand-gathered wild blackberries that require a little work to pick. This sorbet can be served with *Piñon Tacos (page 173)* or some other light, crispy cookie.

Yield: about 1 quart (6 servings) • *Photo page 179*

1¾ **cups water**
½ **cup wild honey or regular honey**

1 **vanilla bean**
1 **pound fresh blackberries**

1 **tablespoon fresh lemon juice, or more to taste**

Place the water and honey into a saucepan. Split the vanilla bean lengthwise, scrape the seeds into the pan, and add the bean pod to the pan. Bring to a boil, remove from the heat, and transfer to a mixing bowl. Let cool.

Add the blackberries to the saucepan, and then transfer the mixture to a food processor or blender and purée. Strain into a mixing bowl. There should be about 2 cups of strained juice. Add the lemon juice, mix together thoroughly, and pour into an ice cream machine. Freeze according to the manufacturer's directions.

OPPOSITE PAGE *Roasted Dixon Peach Soup*

Roasted Dixon Peach Soup

with Sweet Strawberry Sauce

Dixon is a small, predominantly Hispanic settlement in the Rio Grande Valley, about two-thirds of the way to Taos from Santa Fe. Nearby towns, like Embudo and Velarde, were also settled centuries ago and the orchards that were established back then have been replanted and still yield fruit that, in some cases, are no longer commercially available. One of the growers in the sheltered mountain valleys there is Sylvia Vergara, whose seven-acre farm is in Montecito, just outside Dixon. Sylvia is a descendent of early Spanish colonists, and her strong personal sense of connection to the land was fostered at an early age by listening to her grandmother's stories and songs. Sylvia grows organic apples, pears, apricots, peaches, wild cherries, and raspberries, which she processes for her outstanding La Carreta line of food products (see "Sources," page 199). These include apple cider syrup, apricot jam, wild plum preserves, wild cherry syrup, and a range of flavored vinegars.

Cold fruit soups were popularized by French nouvelle cuisine, and they're an excellent way of eating sweet fruit in a healthful way. It's very important that you use fully ripe fruit, for both flavor and texture. Alternative presentations would be to top the soup with a delicate fruit salsa, or to serve it with cookies, such as almond biscotti or New Mexican biscochitos.

Yield: 4 servings • *Photo page 183*

Sauce

1 pint strawberries	**2 tablespoons sugar**	**1 teaspoon fresh lemon juice**

Thyme Simple Syrup

1 cup sugar	**1 cup water**	**3 fresh thyme sprigs**

Soup

4 large ripe peaches	**⅓ cup sugar**
2 tablespoons softened unsalted butter	**½ to ¾ cup Riesling wine, or other white wine**

Assorted fruits, for garnish (such as raspberries, peach slices, blueberries, and currants)

To prepare the sauce, place the strawberries, sugar, and lemon juice in a blender or food processor and purée. Strain into a bowl and chill.

For the simple syrup, dissolve the sugar in the water and bring to a boil in a saucepan. Turn off the heat, add the thyme, and let steep for 30 minutes. Chill until needed. Strain before using.

Preheat the oven to 375 degrees.

To prepare the soup, rub the skin of the peaches with the butter and roll in the sugar. Cut a small "x" in the top of each peach and place in a baking pan. Bake in the oven for 20 to 25 minutes, or until soft. Remove and let cool.

Peel the peaches and remove the pits. Transfer to a blender or food processor and purée with the Riesling and enough of the simple syrup to thin. (You will not use all of it; taste as you go.) Chill in the refrigerator.

To serve, ladle into chilled soup bowls. Drizzle some of the sauce over the top of the soup and garnish with the fruit.❧

OPPOSITE PAGE *Sweet Coconut Tamales*

Sweet Coconut Tamales

with Caramelized Pineapple and Brazilian Rum Sauce

Sweet tamales are a rarity in the United States, but tamales dulces are a centuries-old Mexican tradition. In northern Mexico, sweet tamales are standard fare for feast days and holidays such as the Day of the Dead. Often, sweet tamales are brightly colored with the dye from different fruit juices, which also contribute to their sweetness.

In this recipe, the inspiration for the tamales comes from the more tropical regions of Mexico, where coconuts, pineapples, and rum sugar cane are all grown. The sauce is based on the Brazilian Daiquiri cocktail that's a trademark at Coyote Cafe. To make the drink, we take light, amber, and dark rums and marinate ripe pineapple in them with brown sugar and

vanilla beans for two weeks. The result is a sweet, flavorful, nectarlike drink that even non-rum drinkers take to. For this recipe you can substitute plain rum and seeds scraped from half of a vanilla bean if you don't happen to have a batch of daiquiris fermenting on your kitchen counter.

Yield: 6 servings • *Photo page 185*

Rice Pudding Tamales

4 cups water	¼ cup sugar	Several long strips orange zest
⅔ cup long-grain rice	⅓ cup sweetened flake coconut	Several long strips lemon zest
3 cups milk	½ vanilla bean	

Caramelized Pineapple

½ cup sugar	1 teaspoon fresh lemon juice	1 fresh pineapple, peeled, cored and cut into ½-inch dice

Brazilian Daiquiri Sauce

½ cup sugar	½ cup unsalted butter
1 teaspoon fresh lemon juice	¼ cup Brazilian Daiquiri or dark rum plus seeds from ½ vanilla bean
½ cup heavy cream	

7 dried corn husks

To prepare the tamales, bring the water to a boil in a saucepan. Add the rice and cook at a slow boil for 10 minutes to blanch; drain and discard water.

Transfer the blanched rice to another saucepan and add the milk, sugar, and coconut. Split the vanilla bean lengthwise, scrape the seeds into the pan, and add the bean pod to the pan. Bring this mixture to a boil over medium heat. Reduce the heat to a simmer and cook, stirring occasionally, until mixture starts to thicken, about 30 minutes. Add the zests to the saucepan and cook for 10 to 15 minutes longer, stirring more and more frequently until the mixture is the consistency of cooked oatmeal.

Transfer this mixture to a mixing bowl. Stir the mixture as it cools, and when cool to the touch remove and discard the zests and vanilla bean pod. Place a piece of plastic wrap directly over the pudding and refrigerate until cold.

To form the tamales, divide the rice pudding between six 12 x 12-inch squares of plastic wrap. Roll up the plastic wrap to form a cylinder and twist the ends tightly to make a tamale about 3½ inches long and 1½ inches in diameter. Chill until needed.

To caramelize the pineapple, place the sugar and lemon juice in a large heavy pan or skillet and caramelize over medium-high heat until deep amber in color. Add the pineapple and stir until the caramel liquefies again. Cook over medium-low heat until the pineapple is caramel colored, about 10 minutes. Let cool.

To prepare the sauce, place the sugar and lemon juice in a large heavy pan or skillet and caramelize over medium-high heat until deep amber in color. Meanwhile, bring the cream to a boil in a separate saucepan while stirring. Remove the sugar mixture from the heat and stir in the cream. Whisk in the butter and then the Brazilian Daiquiri or rum and vanilla bean seeds.

Remove the chilled tamales from the refrigerator. Carefully unwrap and discard the wrap. Tear one of the corn husks into 6 narrow strips. Crimp one end of a corn husk and tie with one of the narrow strips; repeat for the remaining husks, and place one husk on each serving plate. Place a rice pudding tamale on top of each husk. Spoon some of the carmelized pineapple on top of the tamale and drizzle the sauce over and around it. ❧

OPPOSITE PAGE ***Piñon Coffee Helado Profiteroles***

Taos Root Beer Float

with Sassafras Granita, Mexican Vanilla Bean Ice Cream, and Molasses Snaps

One mantra of the Old West was "Old Whiskey, Fast Horses, Wild Women and Root Beer." Many saloons used to make their own root beer from sassafras. This was one of the few nonalcoholic beverages to be consumed on a wide scale in saloons back then. It also happened to be a favorite of mine when I was growing up. I well remember consuming many a Hires root beer float, with

plenty of ice cream, down at the local pharmacy soda fountain. (I can still see the Hires barrel sitting on the counter.) I marveled at the skill required to consume it properly and the need to maintain the delicate balance that existed between the fizz of the soda and the rate at which the ice cream dissolved to prevent it from spilling everywhere.

This fun, whimsical recipe is my reinterpretation of that classic, based on my favorite brand of root beer—Sioux City, which features a wonderful cowboy-ornamented dark brown bottle. The sassafras tree, native to North America, yields a bark that is used for flavoring; the leaves are dried and used to make filé powder. Sassafras was originally used for medicinal purposes.

Yield: 4 servings

Mexican Vanilla Bean Ice Cream

1½ cups milk	6 tablespoons sugar	4 egg yolks
½ cup heavy cream	2 Mexican vanilla beans	

4 bottles Sioux City or other premium root beer

Molasses Snaps

½ cup unsalted butter, softened	¼ cup dark molasses	¼ teaspoon baking soda
⅓ cup dark brown sugar	1 tablespoon powdered ginger	¼ teaspoon salt
	1⅓ cups all-purpose flour	

To prepare the ice cream, place the milk, cream, and sugar in a heavy-bottomed saucepan. Split the vanilla bean lengthwise, scrape the seeds into the saucepan, and add the bean pod to the pan. Bring to a boil. Remove from the heat and let steep for 20 minutes. Return the mixture almost to a boil. Place the egg yolks in a bowl and temper by slowly adding the hot (but not boiling) cream mixture, while whisking constantly. It is important to stir constantly. Cook for 1½ minutes over medium-high heat and strain into a stainless steel bowl set over ice water. Let chill (about 15 minutes) and pour into an ice cream machine. Freeze according to the manufacturer's directions (this will yield about 3 cups).

Pour 2 of the bottles of root beer into a shallow pan. Place in the freezer and freeze until solid. Scrape with a fork to separate into crushed ice crystals *(granita)*, and then return to freezer.

For the Molasses Snaps, cream together the butter and sugar in a mixing bowl until light and fluffy. Add the molasses, ginger, flour, baking soda, and salt, and stir to thoroughly incorporate into a dough. Chill for 30 minutes.

Preheat the oven to 350 degrees. Roll out the snap dough to a thickness of ¼ inch and cut with a cookie cutter. Place the dough on a cookie sheet lined with parchment paper and bake in the oven for 10 minutes.

To serve, fill 4 chilled tall glasses with the crushed ice crystals and 2 scoops each of ice cream. Pour ½ bottle of root beer over each and serve with the Molasses Snaps.

Piñon Coffee Helado Profiteroles
with Cajeta Sauce

Profiteroles *are the light, airy pastries filled with ice cream, flavored whipped cream, or pastry cream and drenched in a rich chocolate sauce. They are a fun dessert for all ice cream lovers, and especially for kids. This recipe offers a Southwestern twist on a French classic, and is easy to make—I made my first profiteroles when I was starting out in the* business taking French cooking classes in San Francisco. Profiteroles are best when fresh; refrigerating or freezing them toughens the pastry dough.

We use our own Coyote Cocina piñon coffee (see "Sources," page 199) that's a blend of French, Colombian, and Mexican beans as well as pine (piñon) nuts. This coffee makes a good souvenir item—the scent of piñon will remind you of the Southwest. When making the cajeta, use a heavy-bottomed saucepan and don't reduce it too quickly or the milk will "fry" on the bottom and burn. You can add some rum, brandy, or vanilla for more flavor, and use the cajeta together with chocolate sauce, if you like.

Yield: 4 servings • *Photo page 187*

Piñon Coffee Ice Cream

1 cup milk
1 cup heavy cream

6 tablespoons sugar
¼ cup ground piñon coffee
  (Coyote Cocina blend)
4 egg yolks

Profiteroles

6 tablespoons water
3 tablespoons unsalted butter

2 tablespoons sugar
¼ teaspoon salt

⅔ cup all-purpose flour
2 eggs

Cajeta Caramel (page 178)   **Powdered sugar, for garnish**

To prepare the ice cream, bring the milk, cream, sugar, and coffee to a boil in a heavy-bottomed saucepan. Remove from the heat and let steep for 30 to 45 minutes, tasting for the desired intensity of coffee flavor. Strain out the coffee grounds with a fine mesh strainer and return the mixture almost to a boil. Place the egg yolks in a bowl and temper by slowly adding the hot (but not boiling) cream mixture, while whisking constantly. It is important to stir constantly. Cook for 1½ minutes over medium heat and strain into a stainless steel bowl set over ice water. Chill and pour into an ice cream machine. Freeze according to the manufacturer's directions (this will yield about 3 cups).

To prepare the profiteroles, preheat the oven to 400 degrees. In a small saucepan, bring the water, butter, sugar, and salt to a boil. Remove from the heat and add the flour all at once, stirring to make a paste. Return the pan to medium-low heat, and stir the mixture constantly with a wooden spoon for about 2 to 3 minutes, until it forms a dryish ball in the center of the pan.

Transfer the dough to the bowl of an electric mixer and beat in the eggs one at a time, mixing well after each one is incorporated. Using a spoon or a pastry bag, drop (or pipe) the mixture into 12 small mounds on a cookie sheet lined with parchment paper.

Bake in the oven for 20 to 25 minutes, until golden brown. Remove from the oven and reduce the heat to 300 degrees. Pierce the profiteroles with a knife or skewer to release the steam, and return to the oven for 10 to 15 minutes to dry out the insides. Remove the profiteroles from the oven and let cool.

Meanwhile, prepare the Cajeta Sauce.

To serve, slice the profiteroles in half horizontally and fill with the Piñon Coffee Ice Cream. Dust with powdered sugar and drizzle with the Cajeta Sauce.

Ibarra Chocolate Flan
with Crispy Phyllo Crust

Ibarra is the famous brand of Mexican chocolate (see "Sources," page 199) made with ground almonds, cinnamon, and vanilla. It's molded into flat, round disks and packed in bright yellow and red striped boxes. Ibarra is not actually used in this recipe because it does not produce the fine texture this flan should have. Instead, we duplicate the taste of

Ibarra by adding cinnamon and almonds. Flan is a traditional, even quintessential, Southwestern dessert in the Spanish and Mexican tradition. It is the one dessert item you'll find on most menus between Mexico City and Santa Fe. Flan makes a great medium for assertive flavors—like oranges, lemons, cinnamon, pine nuts, berries, anise, and

licorice. Steeped vanilla beans, mint, and even basil can also be used. Don't plan on making these flans at the last minute, because the caramel takes time to set, and be sure to cook them slowly so the egg doesn't curdle. This recipe gives the flan a completely different dimension with the addition of the light, flaky crust.

Yield: 4 servings

Phyllo Crust

¼ cup ground almonds
1 teaspoon ground cinnamon
¼ cup sugar

4 sheets phyllo dough, covered with a damp towel

6 tablespoons unsalted butter, melted

Caramel

1 cup sugar

½ cup water

1 teaspoon fresh lemon juice

Flan

1 cup heavy cream
1 cup milk
6 tablespoons sugar

2 sticks canela, each about 4 inches long, or 1 stick cinnamon
½ cup chopped toasted almonds (page 192)

2½ ounces good-quality bittersweet chocolate, finely chopped (about ½ cup)
1 egg plus 3 egg yolks

Preheat the oven to 425 degrees.

To prepare the crust, mix together the almonds, cinnamon, and sugar in a bowl. Cut the phyllo sheets in half vertically and horizontally, creating 4 equal rectangles per sheet. Brush each rectangle with a little melted butter and sprinkle with some of the almond mixture. Take 4 of the rectangles and layer them on top of each other. Repeat for the other 3 phyllo sheets. Work quickly while cutting and coating phyllo, always keeping the resting sheets covered with a damp towel, to prevent them from drying out.

Place four 6-ounce (¾ cup) ramekins upside down on a cookie sheet. Carefully mold the phyllo crusts over and around the ramekins so they form an inverted "nest." Bake in the oven for about 15 minutes, or until crispy and browned. Set "the nests" aside and wash the ramekins.

For the caramel, place the sugar, water, and lemon juice in a saucepan. Bring to a boil, and cook until the mixture reaches a deep amber color. Remove from the heat and immediately ladle 2 tablespoons into each of the 4 clean ramekins. Let the caramel set.

Meanwhile, to prepare the flan, bring the cream, milk, sugar, canela, and almonds to a boil in a heavy saucepan. Turn off the heat and let steep for 30 to 45 minutes. Strain into a clean saucepan and return to a boil. Turn off the heat and stir in the chocolate to melt.

Place the egg and yolks in a bowl and temper by slowly pouring in the hot chocolate mixture, while whisking constantly. Strain again and pour into the ramekins on top of the hardened caramel.

Reheat the oven to 325 degrees. Place the ramekins in a water bath, by putting enough water in a large baking pan to reach half-way up the sides of the ramekins when they are sitting in the pan. Cover the water bath with foil and bake for about 30 minutes or until the flans are set. Let cool and chill for at least 3 hours before serving.

To serve, loosen the flans by running a knife around the inside edges of the ramekins. Invert the ramekins and carefully drop the flans into the phyllo "nests."

OPPOSITE PAGE *Ibarra Chocolate Flan*

Basic Techniques

Blackening Tomatoes and Tomatillos

Blackening tomatoes and tomatillos gives them a more rustic, robust, and complex flavor. To blacken, remove the stems (tomatillos should also be husked and rinsed) and place on a rack under a broiler or over a gas flame until the skins blister, crack, and blacken. This technique replicates the traditional method of blackening them over open fires or grills. Do not allow tomatoes and tomatillos to become overly blackened or they will taste bitter.

Clarifying Butter

Clarified butter is used to cook at high temperatures (non-clarified butter will burn). To clarify butter, melt in a pan over low heat, and let sit for 5 minutes. The milk solids will collect in the bottom of the pan. Skim the surface foam and pour the liquid through a sieve lined with cheese cloth. Discard the solids.

Cooking Beans

In general, it is not necessary to soak beans before cooking them. Soaking helps soften old beans, but these days, beans tend to be fresh, and soaking only loosens the husks, which makes for messy beans. To cook, place beans in pot and add water to cover by at least 1½ inches. Simmer uncovered for 45 minutes to 1 hour, or until tender. Do not add salt until the last 15 minutes or so of cooking: adding salt earlier will make the beans tough. Add more water as necessary to keep the beans covered.

Oven-Roasting Tomatoes

This technique removes the excess moisture from the tomatoes and concentrates the flavor. Preheat the oven to 250 degrees. Cut the tomatoes in half and place them cut side up on a wire rack or on a baking sheet. Sprinkle with a little salt. Roast in the oven for about 3 hours. If desired, you can place a sliver or two of fresh garlic in the middle of each tomato half (discard the garlic after the tomatoes are roasted). If not using immediately, the tomatoes can be stored in a jar in olive oil.

Rehydrating Cherries

To rehydrate cherries, place in a bowl and cover with hot water. Let soak for 20 minutes, or until soft.

Roasting Corn

As with chiles, this technique provides additional flavor dimensions, especially an appealing smokiness that particularly enhances the natural flavor of corn. Cut the corn kernels from the cobs with a sharp knife. Heat a large, heavy-bottomed sauté pan or skillet over high heat until almost smoking. Place no more than two layers of the corn kernels in the pan at a time, and dry-roast for 4 to 5 minutes until smoky and dark, tossing continuously.

Roasting Garlic

Roasted garlic is mellower, sweeter, and more subtle in flavor than raw, fresh garlic. Place unpeeled garlic cloves in a heavy-bottomed cast-iron skillet and dry-roast over low heat for 30 to 40 minutes, until the garlic softens. Shake the skillet occasionally. Alternatively, roast the garlic cloves in the oven for 20 to 30 minutes at 350 degrees. When roasted, you should be able to squeeze the garlic out of the cloves.

Roasting, Peeling, and Blistering Fresh Chiles and (Sweet) Bell Peppers

Roasting chiles or bell peppers (which are botanically chiles) concentrates their natural sugars and develops more complex, robust, and smoky flavors. This technique also facilitates peeling the tough skin, which can be bitter.

To roast, place the chiles or bell peppers on a wire rack over a gas flame, on a grill, or under a broiler. Blister and blacken the skins evenly without burning the flesh. Transfer to a bowl, cover with plastic wrap or a clean kitchen towel, and let steam for 15 to 20 minutes. You can then remove the skin with your fingers or with the tip of a knife. Remove the seeds and internal ribs if the recipe calls for you to do so. (Removing the seeds and membranes diminishes the heat of the chiles.) When it is important to retain the color of the chiles or bell peppers, it is preferable to blister them in hot oil instead of blackening them. To blister chiles, heat ¼ cup canola oil until just smoking, and turn the chile in the oil for 45 seconds. Transfer to a bowl, cover with plastic wrap, and let steam for 10 minutes. The chile can then be handled as above. *Warning: Do not touch your face or eyes after handling chiles until you have thoroughly washed your hands. If you have sensitive skin, wear rubber gloves when handling chiles.*

Toasting Dried Herbs and Spices

Toasting gives herbs and spices a more intense flavor. To toast herbs such as oregano and spices such as coriander and cumin, place in a dry skillet over low heat. Toast for about 1 minute, or until fragrant, stirring frequently. Do not scorch or herbs or spices will become bitter tasting.

Toasting Nuts

Toasting brings out the natural richness and full flavors of nuts. To toast, place in a hot, dry skillet and toast over medium heat for 5 to 7 minutes, until lightly browned, stirring occasionally. Smaller nuts such as pine nuts or sliced almonds, will take 3 to 5 minutes. Alternatively, nuts may be toasted on a cookie sheet in a 250-degree oven for 5 to 10 minutes, depending on the type of nut.

Toasting, Rehydrating, and Puréeing Dried Chiles

In Southwestern cuisine, it is most common to toast and rehydrate dried chiles before puréeing them. To do so, stem and seed the dried chiles, and dry-roast in a single layer in a dry cast-iron skillet, or on a baking sheet in a 250-degree oven, for 2 to 3 minutes. While toasting, shake occasionally and do not allow to burn or blacken, or the chiles will taste bitter. Transfer the chiles to a bowl and add enough hot water to cover. Let stand for about 20 minutes until they are rehydrated and soft. When soft, drain and transfer chiles to a blender or food processor. Taste the soaking water and if it is not bitter, add enough to the blender to make puréeing possible. If the water does taste bitter, use a little plain water. Purée the chiles and strain. Chiles can be puréed ahead of time; if you do not use them in a day or two, freeze them.

Note: To make chipotle chile purée, you can toast and rehydrate dried chipotles and then purée, or purée canned chipotles in adobo sauce.

Basic Recipes

Beef Stock

Yield: 8 cups
Follow the directions for Brown Duck Stock, but use 4 pounds of beef bones and extend cooking time by 1 to 2 hours, or until a full-flavored stock is achieved.

Brown Duck Stock

Yield: 8 cups
4 pounds duck bones (from 2 to 3 large ducks)
12 cups (3 quarts) cold water
1 onion, halved
1 carrot, sliced
½ stalk celery, sliced
2 cloves garlic, crushed
1 bay leaf
1 sprig fresh thyme, or a pinch of dried thyme leaves
3 to 4 sprigs parsley
4 peppercorns, crushed
4 to 6 tablespoons tomato purée

Wash the bones in cold water and cut them into 3- to 4-inch pieces. Place the bones one layer deep in a roasting pan, and roast in a 375-degree oven for 20 to 40 minutes, or until russet colored, stirring occasionally. Transfer the bones to a stockpot and reserve the fat. Place a cup or two of the water in the roasting pan and deglaze

it over medium heat. Add this liquid to the stockpot with the bones. Add the remaining cold water and bring to a simmer. Sauté the vegetables and garlic in a small amount of the reserved fat for 6 to 8 minutes over medium heat, or until evenly browned. Drain well and add them to the simmering stock with the herbs, peppercorns, and tomato purée. Return the stock to a simmer and cook for 5 to 6 hours, skimming any impurities that rise to the surface. Add water as needed to keep all ingredients just covered. Strain the stock, remove any fat or impurities from the surface, and refrigerate or freeze until needed. This stock will keep for 3 to 4 days in the refrigerator.

Brown Poultry Stock

Yield: 8 cups
Follow the directions for Brown Duck Stock, but use 4 pounds chicken bones (from 2 to 3 large chickens).

Chicken Stock

Yield: 8 cups
4 pounds chicken bones (from 3 large chickens)
12 cups (3 quarts) cold water
1 onion, halved
1 carrot, diced
4 stalks celery, diced
1 bay leaf
1 sprig fresh thyme, or a pinch of dried thyme leaves
3 to 4 sprigs parsley
3 peppercorns, crushed

Wash the bones in cold water and cut them into 3- to 4-inch pieces. Place the bones in a stockpot and cover with the cold water. Bring to a boil, then reduce the heat to a simmer. Skim any impurities that rise to the surface. Add the vegetables, herbs, and peppercorns, and continue to simmer for 5 to 6 hours, skimming any fat or impurities that rise to the surface. Add water as needed to keep all ingredients just covered. Strain the stock, remove any fat or impurities from the surface, and refrigerate or freeze until needed. This stock will keep for 3 to 4 days in the refrigerator.

Fish Stock

Yield: 8 cups
5 pounds white fish bones (such as halibut or sole)
10 cups cold water
1 small onion, diced
½ carrot, sliced
1 stalk celery, sliced
4 ounces mushroom stems or trimmings
1 branch fresh fennel (optional)
1 bay leaf
1 sprig fresh thyme, or a pinch of dried thyme leaves
4 sprigs parsley
4 peppercorns, crushed

Wash the bones in cold water and place in a stockpot with all other ingredients. Bring them to a simmer and skim any foam or impurities that rise to the surface. Add water as needed to keep all ingredients just covered. Simmer for 30 to 40 minutes. Strain the stock, remove any impurities from the surface, and refrigerate or freeze until needed. This stock will keep for 3 days in the refrigerator.

Lamb Stock

Yield: 6 cups
1½ pounds lamb trimmings (and additional meat is necessary)
8 cups (2 quarts) cold water
1 small onion, halved
½ carrot, sliced
2 sprigs fresh parsley
3 peppercorns
2 dried or canned chipotle chiles

Place the lamb trimmings in a shallow roasting pan and roast in a 350-degree oven for 30 minutes, or until brown. In a stockpot, bring the water to a boil over high heat, add the trimmings, vegetables, and chipotles, and reduce the heat to medium. Skim any impurities that rise to the surface. Reduce the heat to low and simmer, uncovered for 5 to 6 hours, skimming any impurities that rise to the surface. Add water as needed to keep all ingredients just covered. Strain the stock, remove any impurities from the surface, and refrigerate or freeze until needed. This stock will keep for 3 to 4 days in the refrigerator.

Lobster Stock

Yield: 4 cups

2 to 3 pounds lobster shells, preferably raw
1 tablespoon olive oil
½ onion, diced
½ small carrot, diced
1 cup white wine
5 cups Fish Stock or Chicken Stock
1 bay leaf
1 sprig fresh thyme, or a pinch of dried thyme leaves
3 sprigs parsley
3 peppercorns, crushed
3 juniper berries, crushed (optional)
2 tablespoons tomato purée

Crack the shells with a mallet to release as much flavor as possible. Heat the oil in a stockpot and sauté the shells over moderate heat for 6 to 8 minutes, or until bright red and fragrant. Add the onion and carrot and sauté for 4 to 5 more minutes, stirring often. Add the remaining ingredients and bring to a boil. Reduce the heat to a simmer and skim any impurities that rise to the surface. Simmer for 30 to 45 minutes or until full flavored. Let sit, undisturbed, for 30 minutes. Strain the stock, remove any impurities from the surface, and refrigerate or freeze until needed. This stock will keep for 3 days in the refrigerator.

Pork Stock

Yield: 8 cups

Follow the directions for Brown Duck Stock, but use 4 pounds pork bones and extend cooking time by 1 to 2 hours, or until a full-flavored stock is achieved. If desired, add a few dried red chile flakes (chile caribe) and 1 to 2 oregano sprigs, or a pinch or dried Mexican oregano.

Veal Stock

Yield: 8 cups

Follow the directions for Brown Duck Stock, but use 4 pounds of veal bones and extend cooking time by 1 to 2 hours, or until a full-flavored stock is achieved. If desired, add a few dried red chile flakes (chile caribe) and 1 to 2 oregano sprigs, or a pinch or dried Mexican oregano.

Vegetable Stock

Yield: 4 cups

1 tablespoon vegetable oil
1 small onion, diced
1 carrot, diced
½ stalk celery, diced
1 small leek diced
¼ small bulb fennel, diced (optional)
½ small turnip, peeled and diced (optional)
1 Roma tomato, diced
1 clove garlic, chopped
¼ cup white wine
1 small bay leaf
1 sprig fresh thyme, or a pinch of dried thyme leaves
3 sprigs parsley
3 peppercorns, crushed

Heat the oil in a stockpot. Sauté the vegetables and garlic over medium heat for 8 to 10 minutes, stirring often. Do not allow them to brown. Add the white wine, water, herbs, and peppercorns, and bring to a boil. Reduce the heat to a simmer and cook for 45 minutes. Strain the stock, remove any impurities from the surface, and refrigerate or freeze until needed. This stock is best when used the day it is made.

Venison Stock

Yield: 8 cups

Follow the directions for Brown Duck Stock, but use 4 pounds venison bones and extend cooking time by 1 to 2 hours, or until a full-flavored stock is achieved. Add a few crushed juniper berries, if desired.

GLOSSARY

The following ingredients are frequently used in Southwestern cooking and in the recipes in this book. When helpful, we have also listed the Spanish terms for the ingredients.

Achiote (*annatto*): This spice, which takes the form of small brick red seeds, is a trademark of Yucatecan cuisine and the markets of that region. It is usually available in solid blocks of red paste and has a distinctive, iodine-like flavor that gives an earthiness to chicken, pork, and fish. It is used commercially to dye Cheddar cheese and butter to make them look more appetizing. Before grinding the seeds, soften them by boiling for 1½ hours, and be careful when working with them because their natural dye will stain.

Adobo: A vinegary sauce that may also be used for pickling. Meat, vegetables, or chiles prepared in adobo sauces are described as being *en adobo*. For example, *chiles chipotle en adobo* are canned, dried, smoked jalapeño chiles stewed with onions, tomatoes, vinegar, and spices. Pork *en adobo* refers to pork served with a red chile sauce.

Allspice (*pimienta inglesia; pimentia de Jamaica*): A cousin of clove and black pepper, allspice is a berry native to the Yucatán. Well named, it tastes of a combination of cloves, pepper, cinnamon, and nutmeg. It makes an excellent seasoning for meats and game.

Anaheim chile: Closely related to, and interchangeable with, the New Mexico chiles.

Ancho chile: Dried anchos are the most widely used dried chiles in Mexico. They are brick red to dark mahogany in color, wrinkled, and have broad shoulders (the word *ancho* means "wide"). This chile is at its best when it is very flexible and aromatic. It has sweet fruity flavors, mainly with hints of dried plum and raisin.

Annatto: *See* achiote.

Arugula (*rocket*): A salad green native to the Mediterranean, arugula has a soft texture and a sharp, peppery flavor.

Avocado (*aguacate*): I prefer the purplish black, bumpy-skinned Haas avocados with their rich, buttery flesh, to the smoother green-skinned Fuertes, which are more watery. The Haas variety, which is in peak season in the first half of the year, also keeps better. Buy avocados a few days before you plan to use them, because they are usually sold before they are ripe.

Balsamic vinegar: Made from Italian red wine, balsamic vinegar is full and flavorful, but relatively mild. It is aged in wooden casks for any length of time between two and forty years. We use it mainly for salad dressings and with sautéed tomatoes and vegetables to complement grilled fish and chicken.

Bell Peppers: Also referred to as sweet peppers, bell peppers come in a variety of colors— red, yellow, green, purple, and orange, and are the mildest type of chile. They vary greatly in sweetness and flavor, though most are crisp and refreshing. They should not be substituted for fresh chiles, although they may be combined with them. The green bell pepper, which has an overpowering taste, tends not to marry well with other Southwestern flavors. Roasting and peeling bell peppers gets rid of the tough outer skin and improves their flavor.

Bibb lettuce: A salad green with a tender texture and sharp flavor that goes well with other greens.

Black beans (*frijoles negros*): Actually a very dark purple color, black beans are also called turtle beans. They are native to Central and South America and are used widely in the Caribbean. With their strong, smoky flavor and mushroomlike overtones, they are my favorite beans.

Cajeta: *See* goat's milk caramel.

Canela: There are more than 150 varieties of cinnamon, which is the inner bark of the *Cinnamomum* tree. Canela, originally from Sri Lanka, is a lighter brown and has a softer texture and milder, sweeter flavor than the more common Malabar cinnamon from India. Canela is also thinner and more fragile and usually comes in sticks 3 to 5 inches long and ¼ to ½ inch wide. I prefer to use canela in most recipes because it more closely matches the warm, earthy tones of Southwestern cuisine. Because canela is regarded as a lower grade of cinnamon, it is less expensive; however, it may be more difficult to find. You can substitute regular cinnamon if you can't get canela.

Cayenne: Bright red, thin-fleshed chile. Fiercely hot, sweet, and intense, it is similar in flavor to red Thai chiles and is related to the tabasco chile. It is used fresh in salsas and, when dried, as cayenne powders.

Cebollitos: These small Mexican onions are sweeter than scallions and have a bulb that's larger at the base.

Chiffonade: A French term for a technique that entails slicing greens or herbs into thin strips or ribbons.

Chile caribe: Also known as red pepper flakes. The crushed, flaky (not ground) version of the dried New Mexico red chile, the California chile, or other similar varieties. These are the chile flakes that are used as a pizza topping in Italian restaurants.

Chile molido: A finely ground powder of New Mexico chiles that varies in heat from mild to medium to hot according to the amount of seed ground along with the dried chiles. Like paprika, chile molido is useful as a dry spice for seasoning.

Chile pasado: This is the name given to ripe, fresh red New Mexico or Anaheim chiles that have been fire roasted, peeled, and dried. This process concentrates the natural flavors and heat of the chiles, making them sweeter and hotter than regular dried red New Mexico chiles that are strung in ristras.

Chipotle chile: The brown, wrinkled chipotle is the dried form of the fresh, ripe jalapeño chile smoked slowly over the dried foliage of the chile plant. It is very hot and has a wonderful toasted, smoky flavor that contains tones of leather, coffee, and mushrooms and a marked aftertaste of pure capsicum, the ingredient in chiles that gives them their heat. The chipotle is also available canned in adobo sauce, which is prepared by stewing the chiles with onions, tomatoes, vinegar, and spices. I love the flavor of chipotles, and at Coyote Cafe we most often use them puréed in soups, sauces, and salsas.

Chokecherries: A type of wild cherry native to North America, chokecherries are best when cooked in sauces, jellies, or preserves.

Chorizo: Spicy, coarsely ground pork sausage, usually in crumbled or patty form rather than in a casing.

Cider vinegar: This is the most common type of vinegar used in Southwestern cuisine. Made from apple cider, good-quality cider vinegars are available from health food stores.

Cilantro: Also known as fresh coriander and Chinese parsley, cilantro is common in Asian cuisines and is the most widely used herb in the world. We use it by the case at Coyote Cafe. An aromatic member of the parsley family, its pungent, sweet, and intense flavor "brightens" salsas; it is an important element, both for its flavor and color, in sauces such as pipiáns and moles that use green chiles.

Cinnamon: *See* canela.

Clove (clavo de especia): Clove, which is indigenous to Madagascar and Zanzibar, matches the other spicy flavors of central Mexican cooking. It is a very strong spice and is best when it is not detectable, but used as a background ingredient. If you want an especially mild flavor, discard the bulb at the end of the clove berry and use only the remaining stem.

Comal: A comal is a flat or slightly curved cooking surface, made of earthenware or very thin metal, that is usually placed over a charcoal fire.

Corn husks (hojas de maíz): No part of the maize plant is wasted in Southwestern cuisine. Dried corn husks, after they are soaked in water to make them soft and pliable, are used to wrap tamales. They will keep for up to a year if stored in a dry place.

Cornmeal (harina de maíz): Cornmeal is used as a thickener and as a filling or principal ingredient. Commercial cornmeal is processed with metal rollers that extract the germ and its natural oil, making it less moist and flavorful. Stone-ground cornmeal retains the germ and has a superior flavor, especially when used in corn bread or polenta. However, it also has a shorter shelf life because the germ can become rancid, and it is usually less evenly ground. Cornmeal is ground in two consistencies: fine and coarse.

Crema: A soured cream equivalent to crème fraîche, crema is made from heavy cream, preferably unpasteurized, and a culture such as that in buttermilk. Its flavor is more interesting than sour cream's. Crema adds a richness to beans and has a pleasant, cooling effect on hot spicy dishes.

Cumin (comino): The cumin plant is indigenous to the Southwest and Mexico. The flavor of roasted and ground cumin seeds is better than that of cumin powder. This is a pervasive, earthy spice that combines wonderfully with dried chiles.

Dice: When recipes in this book call for ingredients to be diced, they should be cut into ¼-inch cubes. Fine dice refers to ⅛-inch cubes, and large dice to ⅓- or ½-inch cubes.

Duck (pato): A great favorite of mine and of our customers at Coyote Cafe, duck is too often neglected in home kitchens. It has one of the most versatile and consistently enjoyable flavors and has a richness that goes perfectly with a great Pinot Noir. The legs and breasts should be cooked separately; the legs should be braised slowly until well done; the breasts should be grilled rare to medium rare.

Duck fat (manteca de pato): The rendered by-product of cooking duck or making confit (a method of preserving high-fat meats by cooking them slowly in their own fat so that the fat seals the meat), duck fat has a richer flavor than that of lard or butter. It is available in cans from gourmet specialty stores.

Egg wash: Egg washes are brushed on the top of unbaked breads to give them a crisp, shiny crust. The mixture usually consists of 1 egg, 2 tablespoons water, and a pinch of salt.

Empanada: A turnover that's usually baked or deep-fried, *empanada* means "cooked in pastry" in Spanish.

Epazote: Also known as wormseed, Mexican tea, and stink weed, epazote grows wild and is most easily purchased in potted form from nurseries. But beware: it propagates with abandon and can spread like wildfire if not carefully controlled. It is most frequently used in Southern Mexico. Do not be put off by the aroma of this herb, which is reminiscent of kerosene. It has an untamed flavor that I am partial to, and once you get used to it, you'll love it, too. The young, small leaves are best. It goes very well in stews and with seafood. It is also cooked with beans of all types to reduce their gaseousness.

Fatback: The pure white fat from the back of pork loins, fatback should be ordered fresh from your butcher. Use it to make fresh lard or for adding to sausage—pork does not have enough fat of its own.

Fresno chile: This thick-fleshed, very hot chile is sometimes mistaken for a red jalapeño, although the two are of different varieties and the Fresno is broader at the shoulders.

Frisée: A member of the escarole family, has curly green leaves with white or light green outer edges. It is crunchy and slightly bitter.

Garlic (ajo): One of the foundations of Southwestern cuisine, garlic is used almost exclusively at Coyote Cafe in its roasted form. Dry-roasting brings out its sweetness and eliminates any harshness. Garlic provides the bass notes or earthy tones that mix well with cumin and other roasted spices and herbs, and roasted peppers and tomatoes. Buy the freshest garlic; if you must chop it ahead of time, cover it with olive oil because it will oxidize when exposed to air.

Ginger (jengibre): Ginger is a rhizome or root that is native to Asia and is now grown in the Caribbean, where it is more commonly used than it is in Mexico or the Southwest. It comes in both fresh and powdered forms. I prefer fresh, young ginger, which usually comes from Hawaii and is small, with a reddish brown papery skin. It is very tender, has a delicate floral flavor, is much less tough and fibrous than good-quality dried ginger.

Goat's milk (leche de cabra): Goat's milk is rich and extremely popular in Mexico. It can be bought from goat farms or health food stores or pharmacies that stock it for those who are allergic to cow's milk.

Goat's milk caramel (cajeta): This wonderful, rich dessert sauce has a unique, tangy flavor. As the name indicates, the essential ingredient is goat's milk.

Guajillo chile: Brick red to burgundy in color, smooth with some large folds or wrinkles, the guajillo (literally "little gourd") is the dried form of the mirasol chile. It has medium heat, an earthy flavor, and the dusty, fruity aroma of plums and raisins, with a slight tobacco finish.

Güero chile: Güero is a generic term for yellow chiles and usually applies to pale yellow tapered chiles, such as the Hungarian wax, banana, or Santa Fe grande. Güero chiles have a slightly sweet, sharp, intense waxy taste and vary in potency from medium to hot; they are primarily used to make yellow moles.

Habanero chile: Green, yellow, or orange, lantern-shaped (like a small bell pepper), the habanero is used extensively in the Yucatán and is the hottest of all chiles. I would estimate that the habanero is between fifteen and twenty times stronger than the serrano, and it can have a caustic effect both internally and externally. In spite of the fierce heat, it has a wonderful flavor.

Hoja santa: This herb is also known as the "root beer plant" because of its sassafraslike flavor. Fresh licorice mint leaves, dried anise seeds, or fresh fennel tops can be substituted for hoja santa.

Huitlacoche: Pronounced WHEAT-la-coch-hay, this gray-black fungus grows on corn kernels inside the husk and has a wonderfully rich flavor like that of morel mushrooms. It is a popular Mexican delicacy, although it is known in the United States as "night smut."

Jalapeño chile: The jalapeño is the best known and most widely eaten hot chile in this country. It may be used fresh or roasted and is excellent in quesadillas, salsas, and soups, or with cheese on nacho chips. It is commonly pickled. Fresh ripe jalapeños, when dried and smoked, are known as chipotles.

Jícama: Jícama is a tropical root that looks like a large turnip and has a thin brown skin. The crisp white flesh has the texture of an apple or radish, but the taste is considerably milder—more like that of a water chestnut, for which it may be substituted. In the Southwest, it is usually peeled and eaten, uncooked, in salads.

Julienne: Thin, equally wide strips, usually measuring 2 to 3 inches in length and ¼ inch wide.

Juniper (enebro): Juniper berries are gray-blue and have an aromatic, woodsy fragrance. Native Americans of the Southwest traditionally used them in teas and medicines, and juniper trees are still a common feature of the landscape. Juniper is a natural match for venison, because the deer commonly graze on the bushes. Like rosemary and sage, juniper will nicely flavor meat when added to a grill.

Limes (limas): Whenever possible, use Mexican limes for the recipes in the book. (They are basically the same variety as the more familiar Florida key limes.) Mexican limes do not have the sour juice and diminished perfume that are characteristic of the more popular and widely available Persian limes.

Marjoram (mejorana): Related to mint and thyme, marjoram has a sweetness that goes particularly well with corn, cilantro, and ripe tomatoes. We most often use fresh marjoram when a subtle, fresh, herbal flavor is called for and oregano would be too strong. Wild marjoram is available in New Mexico and in other parts of the Southwest.

Mascarpone: A rich Italian cream cheese that is often sweetened and whipped to accompany fruit and desserts.

Masa: The cornmeal dough used to make tortillas and tamales.

Masa harina: Finely ground cornmeal used to prepare masa.

Mexican oregano (orégano): We use Mexican oregano only in its dried form, never powdered. Drying seems to narrow its strong and sometimes overwhelming range of flavors. Mexican oregano is more pungent and "weedier" than regular dried oregano and should be dry-roasted before it is used. If substituting regular dried oregano, use a little extra.

Mint (menta): Mint is frequently used in the Yucatán, often to balance the aftertaste of cilantro. At Coyote Cafe, we find it gives spicy dishes a deliciously clean finish in the mouth.

Mizuna: New to the Southwest, mizuna is a medium green Japanese lettuce with a pointed leaf and a mild, peppery flavor that gets stronger as the plant matures. It is slightly crunchy and can be substituted for watercress.

Mustard greens: Mustard greens have bright, light green leaves with frilly, scalloped edges and a soft texture. They have a sharp, pungent mustardlike flavor that makes it ideal for mixed salads. They can also be sautéed as a vegetable with Southern-style dishes such as chicken or crab cakes.

New Mexico green chile (fresh): Light to medium green, the New Mexico green chile varies in strength from medium to very hot. This is the basic chile in New Mexican cuisine, with sweet, clean, and salty flavors. The New Mexico green is usually available fresh year-round, but in the fall they are roasted in huge quantities so that they can be frozen and enjoyed throughout the winter. They freeze well, and frozen New Mexico greens are better than canned. If they are unavailable, substitute a mixture of Anaheims and roasted jalapeños.

New Mexico green chile (dried): Very dark olive green, the New Mexico green chile is rarer in its dried form than is the New Mexico red. The wonderful sharp, pungent capsicum flavors of fresh green chiles are captured in the dried product. Unfortunately, because of the labor involved, it is wildly expensive, but, like dried wild mushrooms, a little goes a long way. Try it ground as a seasoning on steaks, chicken, or pork instead of black pepper.

New Mexico red chile (fresh): A ripe version of the New Mexico green, the New Mexico red is a dark, deep intense red. In northern New Mexico in early October, particularly in the Velarde Valley, much of the chile crop is left on the vine to turn bright red and ripen in the crisp fall sun. These chiles are then tied into bunches— the familiar *ristras*—to dry. During a few short weeks, we use as much fresh New Mexico red chile as possible at Coyote Cafe. They are fleshy, hot, and sweet, and, like the green chiles, can also be roasted for sauces, soups, and chutneys.

New Mexico red chile (dried): Dark brick red, smooth, and tapered, this is truly a king of dried chiles. It has a variety of tones, ranging from those of toasty, dried corn and dried berry, to rich tomato; sometimes there are hints of apple and orange. This chile should be used on its own with a minimum of spice or herbal accompaniments.

Oak leaf lettuce: Available in red and green varieties, this lettuce has lobed leaves the same shape as oak leaves. It has a medium, garden-green flavor and a semisoft texture. It is useful as an attractive garnish around the edge of salads.

Pine nuts (piñones): Pine nuts are a native staple crop of Southwestern Pueblo Indians, who use them mostly in ground form in breads and porridges. Native pine nuts, which have a more marked taste of resin, are more scarce now. Increasingly, the nuts are being imported from Europe and China. They are terrific eaten raw and, when ground, make a delicious flour for desserts. Evergreen piñon trees

cover the landscape in many parts of the Southwest, including New Mexico. They tend to be small and grow mostly at elevations above 5,000 feet.

Poblano chile: The poblano is the fresh green form of the ancho chile. It is dark green, tapers down from the shoulders to a point, is medium to hot in strength. It is always used cooked or roasted and never eaten raw. Roasting gives the poblano a smoky flavor. We use them all the time at Coyote Cafe. They are essential for chiles rellenos and any other stuffed chile dish because they have a thick flesh. Very hot poblanos should be seeded and deveined.

Prickly pear (tuna): The greenish yellow or purple, egg-sized fruit of the cactus has a bright red flesh and tastes somewhat like sour cherries. Ripen it at room temperature until it exudes a perfume. It should be handled carefully and the spines removed. Cut the prickly pear in half and scoop out the flesh. It can be used in salsas, sorbets, or sauces, especially for venison.

Quail (corndíz): Quail, a native Southwestern bird, is my favorite fowl. The subtle, desert flavor should not be overwhelmed by sauces that are too strong or spicy. Quail is best roasted or, ideally, browned in clarified butter and then roasted so that its exterior does not cook too fast.

Queso fresco: A fresh, unripened, moist cheese made from partially skimmed milk, queso fresco is mildly salty, somewhat sharp, and has a pleasant creamy color. It may be replaced by a moist farmer's cheese, dry cottage cheese, or a mild feta cheese.

Radicchio (red chicory): A crisp lettuce that originated in Italy, radicchio is primarily used for its maroon or purple color. It has a slightly bitter flavor and a crunchy texture. It should be used sparingly in salads, preferably mixed with other lettuce, and is wonderful grilled as a vegetable with garlic, oil, herbs, and balsamic vinegar.

Ramekins: Straight-sided dishes, usually with walls of 1½ to 2½ inches, and a diameter of 2½ to 4 inches. Ramekins are used for custards, stuffings, and timbales.

Red leaf lettuce: Best before it fully matures, red leaf lettuce has a relatively green flavor, a mild sweetness, and a soft texture.

Rice vinegar: Because this light, mild Japanese vinegar has a lower acidity than cider vinegar, it is best for fish, pickling, and escabeche dishes. Buy only the unseasoned kind. Its natural sweetness complements hot chile flavors. It is available in the Asian foods section of stores and markets.

Romaine lettuce: This lettuce has sweet, green flavor and a crunchy texture. It is the best lettuce for shredding and using in tacos or in Southwestern fillings.

Roma tomatoes: We prefer to use the versatile, plum-shaped Roma tomatoes at Coyote Cafe because they have thicker pulp, less juice, and go best with Southwestern ingredients. Do not refrigerate Roma tomatoes, because their flavor disappears when they are cold.

Sage *(salvia)*: Sage grows wild throughout New Mexico and in parts of Texas, where it is a primary source of food for grazing lamb and deer. Wild sage is much stronger than the garden variety and is a wonderful herb, especially when used sparingly with game, fowl, and meat. Related to mint, wild sage may be added to a wood fire when grilling.

Serrano chile: Bright green or red, cylindrical with a rounded end, the serrano has a clean, biting heat and a pleasantly high acidity. I favor serranos in fresh salsas. This chile is good when roasted and pickled and will liven up a Bloody Mary.

Shallots *(chalotes)*: Originating in the Middle East, shallots are members of the onion family and have small elongated bulbs, usually with a papery reddish brown skin. They have a subtle, complex flavor, which is stronger than that of onions but less pronounced than garlic's.

Spanish sherry wine vinegar: This premium vinegar is aged and has a subtle sweetness and rich flavor that goes well with heavier sauces, especially those with a tomato base.

Squash blossoms *(flores de calabaza)*: Squash blossoms have been a feature of Mexican and Southwestern cuisine for thousands of years. These deep yellow, fragrant flowers, measuring between 4 and 6 inches long, are commonly used deep-fried and stuffed with goat cheese, sautéed as a vegetable, added to quesadillas, soups, and ravioli, or as a garnish. The male flowers are best and should be used immediately after picking; they are in season throughout the summer.

Tamarind *(tamarindo)*: These coffee-colored, sticky pods can be found in Latin or Asian markets. It is also available as a bottled, ready-made paste. It is a flavoring used most often in Mexico in fresh fruit drinks called *liquados*. It is also used as a flavoring in Worcestershire sauce and cola drinks. We use it at Coyote Cafe in sauces, marinades, and as a dessert flavoring.

Thyme *(tomillo)*: The flavor of thyme reflects the aromas of the open range and complements lamb and venison particularly well. Used both dried and fresh, its wild taste makes it a great ingredient in soups, sauces, and stocks.

Tomatillo *(tomates verdes)*: A plum-sized, bright green fruit that was cultivated by the Aztecs, the tomatillo is covered with a light green papery husk. Tomatillos look like small green tomatoes and have a taste that is not dissimilar. Actually, it is a member of the Cape gooseberry family. Its tart flavor, which includes tones of unripe apple, rhubarb, or green plum, marries perfectly with serrano chiles, cilantro, and garlic. Tomatillos develop a toasty sweetness when blackened on a comal or roasted. They complement green chiles. After the tomato, the tomatillo is the most widely used salsa ingredient and forms the base of most Mexican green sauces.

Vanilla *(vainilla)*: Native to the New World and cultivated by the Aztecs, who used it to flavor chocolate and other foods and drinks, the vanilla plant is a member of the orchid family. Probably the best vanilla comes from Tahiti, although it is also grown in Madagascar and Indonesia as well as in Mexico. Buy whole vanilla pods (rarely used now in Mexico) or pure liquid extracts. Vanilla is mostly used to flavor desserts, ice cream, and drinks.

Wild mushrooms *(hongos)*: Wild mushrooms were used in pre-Columbian times. Varieties such as chanterelles, cèpes, portobellos, morels, and porcini grow in the mountains of New Mexico. They have an intense flavor that goes well with hearty Southwestern ingredients, especially game. Cook wild mushrooms as you would the domestic variety. If you cannot find fresh wild mushrooms, use dried cèpes or morels, or as a last resort, buy domestic mushrooms with opened caps. They have a full mature flavor that white button mushrooms lack.

Zest: The outer, colored layer (not the pith) of citrus fruit that contains the concentrated aromatic oils.

*American Spoon Foods
1668 Clarion Avenue
P.O. Box 566
Petoskey, MI 49770
(800) 222-5886
Preserves, condiments, and sauces.

Blue Corn Connection
3825 Academy Parkway South NW
Albuquerque, NM 87109
(505) 344-9768
Blue cornmeal.

Bountiful Cow
1521 Center Drive-B
Santa Fe, NM 87505
(505) 473-7911
Cheeses.

B. Riley
670-A Juan Tabo Boulevard NE
Albuquerque, NM 87123
(505) 275-0902 or
(800) 427-1756 (in New Mexico only)
Herbs (including epazote and hoja santa) and fresh mushrooms.

*Bueno Foods
2001 4th Street SW
Albuquerque, NM 87102
(505) 243-2722
Chiles, hoja santa, epazote.

*Casados Farms
P.O. Box 1269
San Juan Pueblo, NM 87566
(505) 852-2433
Chiles.

Casa Lucas Market
2934 24th Street
San Francisco, CA 94110
(415) 826-4334
Chiles.

*The Chile Shop
109 East Water Street
Santa Fe, NM 87501
(505) 983-6080
Chiles.

Cost Plus
2552 Taylor Street
San Francisco, CA 94133
(415) 928-6200
Cooking equipment and a wide variety of gourmet products.

*Coyote Cafe General Store
132 West Water Street
Santa Fe, NM 87501
(800) 866-HOWL or (505) 982-2454
Beans, chiles (including canned chiles in adobo sauce), Ibarra chocolate, blue cornmeal, canela, spices, herbs, tamarind, La Carreta vinegars, Coyote Cocina Howlin' Hot Sauce, Buckaroo barbecue sauce, and piñon coffee.

*Dean and Deluca
560 Broadway
New York, NY 10012
(212) 431-1691
Chiles, oils, vinegars, beans, and rices.

Elizabeth Berry
Gallina Canyon Ranch
144 Camino Escondido
Santa Fe, NM 87501
(505) 982-4149
Beans and specialty produce.

*Glenn Burns
16158 Hillside Circle
Montverde, FL 34756
(407) 469-4356
Huitlacoche.

Golden Circle Farms
1109 North McKinney
Rice, TX 75155
(903) 326-4263
Hoja santa and epazote.

Hawaii Vintage Chocolate Company
4614 Kilauea Ave., Ste. 435
Honolulu, HI 96816
(808) 735-8494
Premium-quality bittersweet and white chocolate.

*Stuart Hutson
Chile Gourmet Catalog
Rancho Mesilla Inc.
P.O. Box 39
Mesilla, NM 88046
(505) 525-2266
Chile pasado, dried frozen chiles (including New Mexico chiles), smoked chile pasado, and pecans.

*K-Paul's Louisiana Mail Order
824 Distributor's Row
Harahan, LA 70183
(800) 457-2857
Andouille and other sausages.

*La Palma
2884 24th Street
San Francisco, CA 94110
(415) 647-1500
Chiles and corn husks.

Los Chileros
P.O. Box 6215
Santa Fe, NM 87501
(505) 471-6967
Chiles.

*Mercado Latino
245 Baldwin Park Boulevard
City of Industry, CA 91746
(915) 595-3195
Chiles.

*Mi Rancho
464 7th Street
Oakland, CA 94607
(510) 451-2393
Chiles.

*Monterrey Foods
3939 Cesar Chavez
Los Angeles, CA 90063
(213) 263-2143
Southwestern and Mexican food products.

*Pendery's
304 East Belknap
Fort Worth, TX 76102
(800) 533-1870
Chiles, original chile blends, pine nuts, sauces, vinegars, and spices.

*Preferred Meats
2050 Galvez Street
San Francisco, CA 94124
(415) 285-9299
Chorizo, buffalo, venison, naturally raised beef, free-range chickens, squab, quail lamb, veal, apple-smoked meats, and more.

San Francisco Herb Co.
250 14th Street
San Francisco, CA 94103
(800) 227-4530
Herbs and spices.

*Taxco Produce
1801 S. Good Latimer Expressway
Dallas, TX 75226
(214) 421-7191
Chiles and other Southwestern ingredients.

Ten Speed Press/Celestial Arts
P.O. Box 7123
Berkeley, CA 94707
(510) 845-8414
Mark Miller's other publications, including two full-color chile identification posters (fresh and dried) and a full-color Indian corn identification poster, The Great Salsa Book, The Great Chile Book, Coyote's Pantry, and Coyote Cafe: Foods from the Great Southwest. Also offers Alice Waters's full-color tomato-identification poster.

*Texas Wild Game Cooperative
P.O. Box 530
Ingram, TX 78025
(210) 367-5875
Game, meats, and fowl.

Sylvia Vergara
La Carreta
Box 70
Dixon, NM 87527
(505) 579-4358
Vinegars, preserves, syrups, and sauces.

*Williams-Sonoma
100 North Point Street
San Francisco, CA 94133
(800) 541-1262
Cooking equipment and various gourmet products.

*Offers mail-order service.

MENU INDEX

Recipes for dishes with an asterisk appear in this book.

1987

Grilled New York Strip
Dry-Aged Steak with Chimayo Chile-Onion Essence, and Served with Green Chile Ranch Fries

Seafood Grill
Scallops, Salmon, Shark, and Seabass in a Yucatán Achiote Sauce, and Served with Mole Verde and Baby Squashes

Coconut Cocada

Ibarra Torta

Assorted Fruit Sorbetas

Piñon Tacos

Friday-Sunday August 21-23

Coyote Marisco Platter
Mixed Seafood Platter with Mako en Escabeche, Scallop Ceviche and Shrimp Barra Vieja

Sopa de Corn and Jaiba
Sweet Summer Corn with New Mexican Green Chiles, Texas Blue Crab, and Red Chile Crema

Fried Squash Blossoms
Lighlty Floured Golden Squash Blossoms Stuffed with Herbed Cheese and Fried and Served with Salsa Fresca

Duck Tamales
Confit of Duck with a Mole Sauce Made with Dried Chiles and Fruit

*Blue Crab Cakes
Fresh Texas Blue Crab Sautéed in Sweet Butter with Green Chile Chutney

Grilled Tuna
Fresh Hawaiian Tuna Brochette with Texas Wild Boar Bacon and a Tamarind Glaze

*Pailliard of Fresh California Salmon
with Chipotle Crema and Squash Salsa

*Texas Axis Venison
with Wild Chokecherry-Ancho Chile Sauce

Red Chile Quail
Fresh Texas Bobwhite Quail Marinated in Dried Chiles and Wild Mushrooms and Served with Baby Greens

Grilled Fillete
Prime Aged Beef with Tomatillo Chipotle Salsa and Budin of Wild Mushrooms and Potatoes

Coyote Cajeta Caramelizada

Strawberry Bagatelle

Blackberry Shortcake

Assorted Fruit Sorbetas

Pueblo Pork Roast
Sweet Corn and Bean Succotash, Wilted Greens, and Chive Mashed Potatoes

*Acoma Pueblo Quail
with Chicken-Apple Sausage Stuffing and Cider Glaze, Crispy Carrot Hash, and Angel Fire Potatoes

*Blackfoot Buffalo Ribeye
Wild Mushrooms, Green Onions, Applewood-Smoked Bacon, and Cheyenne Batter Bread

*Navajo Peach Crisp

Pueblo Pumpkin Plate
Tesuque Pumpkin Cookies, Pumpkin-Piñon Bread, and Spiced Pumpkin Ice Cream

Warm Sweet Picuris Pudding
Apricot and Vanilla Custard Sauces

Mescalero Melon Platter

Watermelon Ice and Lime-Clove "Snakes"

Navajo Sage Bread

Chile Caribe Bread

*Pollo en Escabeche
Pickled Chicken Salad in Aromatic Spices

*Crepas de Elote con Salmón
Corn Crepes with Cured Salmon

*Sopa de Pato
Roasted Duck Soup with Wild Mushrooms and Vegetables

*Ensalada de Espinaca y Piñon
Salad of Young Spinach and Abiquiu Greens with Pine Nuts

Tamale de Pato Manchamantel
Duck Tamales with a Spicy Chile, Pineapple, Banana Sauce

Marisco Arroz
Mixed Shellfish in a Red Chile Rice

*Pato en Parrilla
Pecan Grilled Maple Duck with Velarde Apricot Chutney

*Atún Verde en Parrilla
Grilled Fresh Tuna with Tomatillo Salsa and Spicy Green Rice

Rosbif Asado con Honga de Caza
Roasted Dry Aged Standing Rib Roast Served with Wild Mushroom Butter and Sweet Corn with Smoked Chile

*Cordero Yucatán
Roasted Lamb Yucatán-Style with Cinnamon Rice

Pecan Torte

Crème Brûlée

Fruit Empanaditas

Chocolate Rum Babas

Friday, August 19

Cinnamon Buckwheat Bread

Orange Cumin Bread

*Sopa de Calabacitas
Yellow Summer Squash Soup with Red Chile Crema

Tostados en Pato Conserva
Southwestern Corn Pizza with Duck Confit

Res Crudo Picante
Raw Beef Fillet with New Mexican Spices and Chiles

Pasta de Flor de Calabaza
Squash Blossom Ravioli with Fresh Ricotta

*Tamales de Camarón
Shrimp Tamales Served with a Green Mole Sauce

*Ensalada Mixta en Naranja
Arugula and Orange Salad with Mixed Greens

Salmón con Gazpacho Salsa
Sautéed Fresh Pacific Salmon with Ripe Tomatoes, Cucumber, and Sweet Red Onion Salsa

Filet de Puerco Chipotle
Grilled Marinated Pork Tenderloin Served with a Peanut-Smoked Chile Sauce and a Green Pipían

*Bistec de New York en Parrilla
Pecan-Grilled Aged New York Steak Served with Tobacco Onion Rings

Cordoníz Asado Relleno con Ostiones
Roasted Fresh Quail Served with Chile Cornbread and Oyster Stuffing

Chocolate Brandy and Vanilla Churros

Buttermilk Tart
with Fresh Berries

Assorted Tropical Fruits
with Caramel Ice Cream

Devil's Food Cake
with White Chocolate Filling

Saturday, August 20

Corn Bread

Chile Bread Sticks

*Sopa de Palomino
Roasted Cherry Tomatoes and Garden Greens Soup

Salchicha Merida
Grilled Spicy Sausage Merida Style with Fresh Corn Relish

*Ostiones Yucateca
Fresh Pacific Oysters Cooked in a Spicy Black Pepper Sauce

Ensalada de Jaiba
Romaine Salad with Fresh Gulf Crab and Lemon Cream Dressing

*Tamales de Venado
Texas Axis Venison Tamales Served with a Mole Sauce

Torta de Congrejo
Crab Cakes with a Tamarind-Smoked Chile Sauce and Fresh Mint

Pollo Barbacoa
Grilled Free-Range Chicken Breast Served with Smoked Sweet Red Pepper Barbecue Sauce with Goat Cheese Dressing

Ensalada de Langosta
Lobster Salad with Roasted Red, Green, and Yellow Sweet Peppers and Baby Corn

Costillas de Cordero Asado
Roasted Rack of Lamb Served with Wild Sage Aioli; a White Bean Gratin with Blue Corn Crust

Filete de Res en Recado
Grilled Marinated Fillet with Dried Green Chile Jerky Sauce and Fire Onions

Cinnamon Berry Torta
with Cajeta

*Mango Rice Pudding Brûlée

Chocolate Truffle Cake

Fruit Sorbetas y Galletas

Sopa de Maíz y Queso
Roasted Summer Corn Soup with Smoked Chile and Cheese

Ensalada de Camarones
Salad of Smoked Shrimp and Abiquiu Greens with Mango

*Tamales de Langosta y Salmón
Salmon and Lobster Tamales with a Smoked Tomato and Jalapñeno Sauce

Carpaccio con Ostiones Ahumados
Raw Sirloin of Beef with Smoked Oyster and Smoked Oyster-Chipotle Mayonnaise

*Salmón a la Parrilla
with Pecan-Grilled Sweet Green Scallions and Corn-Red Pepper Salsa

*Cordoníz Asado con Relleno de Chorizo
Roasted Fresh Quail with Blue Corn-Chorizo Stuffing

Bistec de Nueva York
Pan-Fried Aged New York Steak with Ranchero Sauce and Chile Onion Rings

Cordero Hidalgo
Roasted Young Lamb with Tomatillo Chipotle Sauce and Cactus Salad

Lemon Ice Cream
with Mexican Cinnamon Brandied Cherries

Bittersweet Chocolate Steamed Pudding
with Cajeta Creme Anglaise

Fresh Apple Pie
with Cajeta

Orange Savarin
with Fresh Raspberries

*Sopa de Tarascan
Roasted Tomato, Bean, and Chile Soup from Pátzcuaro

Camarones Asado de Fuego con Melon
Fire-Roasted Spicy Shrimp with Summer Melon Salad

Ensalada de Salmón Curtido
Elizabeth's Abiquiu Greens with Chile-Cured Salmon

Tamale de Carnitas
Seasoned Pork Tamale with Spicy Chile-Pineapple-Banana Sauce

Flores de Calabacitas
Fried Abiquiu Squash Blossoms with Fresh Tomato Salsa

Tartare de Bistec
Southwestern-Style Spicy Steak Tartare with Blue and Yellow Corn Chips

*Lomo de Puerco
Pan-Roasted Pork Loin Stuffed with Wild Cherries and Ancho Chiles

Pato Con Tomatillo
Grilled Breast and Braised Leg of Duck with Tomatillo Sauce and Gratin of Yellow Squash and Cheese

Filete con Ostiones Ahumados
Grilled Prime Angus Fillet with Smoked Oysters and Pico de Gallo

Coulibiac de Salmón
Fresh Pacific Salmon Cooked in a Red Chile Brioche Crust

*Mexican Chocolate Silk Pie

Anise Almond Cake
with Raspberries and Strawberries

Strawberry Cointreau Granita

Ginger Crème Brûlée

*Sopa de Limón
Yucatán-Style Chicken and Chile Soup with Lime

*Tortillas de Maíz
Griddle-Fried Fresh Corn Cakes with Gulf Shrimp and Chipotle Butter

Tartare de Salmón
Fresh Pacific Salmon Tartare with Red Chile Croutons

Ensalada de Avocado y Mango
Fresh Abiquiu Greens with Ripe Avocado and Mango

Pollo Asado con Pipían
Free-Range Chicken Stuffed with Pesto of Red Chile and Pumpkin Seeds

Cordero a la Parrilla con Naranjas y Serranos
Grilled Lamb Loin Chops with Orange-Serrano Sauce

Rosbif Asado
Roasted Dry-Aged Rib Roast with Corn Salsa

Atún a la Parilla
Grilled Fresh Tuna on a Bed of Black Beans, Goat Cheese Crema, and Cilantro Pesto

Bittersweet Brownies
with Strawberry Ice Cream and Fresh Strawberries

Mascarpone Cheesecake
with Biscotti Crust

Bourbon Pecan Tart
with Cajeta

Lemon-Ginger Cake
with Berries and Whipped Vanilla Cream

*Summer Sweet Corn and Yellow Squash Soup
Garnished with Fresh Squash Blossoms and Herbs

Spicy Southwestern Salmon Tartar
with Red Chile Croutons and Cucumber Salad

*Salad of Smoked Duck Breast
with Mango Sauce and Field Greens

*Green Chiles Rellenos
Stuffed with Picadillo of BBQ Brisket

Grilled Fillet of Beef
in a Rich Bay Leaf Sauce

Fresh Gulf Crab Cakes
with Spicy Avocado Salsa and Garden Salad

Roasted Stuffed Cornish Game Hens
in Canela-Orange Sauce

Roasted Pastores Ranch Leg of New Mexico Spicy Lamb
with a Ragout of Summer Vegetables

Hazelnut Ice Cream Sandwich
with Chocolate and Espresso-Caramel Layers

Canela-Crusted Pecan Tart
with Honey Apple Ice Cream

Bourbon Banana and Fudge Mousse Cake

Lemon Scented Vanilla Wafers
Layered with Mixed Fresh Berries

Friday, August 17

Golden and Red Tomato Painted Soup Garnished
with Maine Lobster and Minted Olive Oil

*Albóndigas Oaxacan-Style
in Rich Tomato-Smoked Chile Sauce

*Wild Mushroom Tamales
with Roasted Tomatillo and Wild Mushroom Sauce

Grilled Shrimp in Orange-Chipotle Tamarind Sauce

*Grilled Brochette of Fresh Eastern Sea Scallops
on a Serrano-Cucumber-Avocado Salsa

*Pan-fried Dry-Aged Ribeye Steak
with Bricklayers Salsa and Oven-Roasted New Potatoes

Grilled Smoked Maple Duck Breast
with Peach-Green Chile Chutney

*Roasted Rack of Lamb
with Pecan Crust and Roasted Corn Salsa

Ginger Flan
with Barbados Rum Caramelized Pineapple

Gingerbread Tartlett
with Warm Spiced Apples and Cinnamon Ice Cream

Bittersweet Chocolate Eclairs
with Praline Glazed Bananas

Cold Lemon Soufflé
with Garden Berries

*Fresh Corn Soup
with Chile Pasado, Gulf Shrimp, and Queso Fresco

Corn Cakes Layered
with Carnitas with Peach-Green Chile Chutney

Fresh Gulf Crab Cakes
with Basil Salsa and Field Greens

Beef Carpaccio
with Arugula Red Chile Mayonnaise and Pine Nuts

*Grilled "Rocky" Free-Range Chicken Breast
with a Roasted Chile Poblano-Corn Sauce

Fresh Pacific Salmon
with a Blue Corn-Piñon Crust with Spicy Tomato Vinaigrette

Dry Aged Beef Fillet
with Green Chile Jerky Sauce and BBQ Onions

*Tenderloin of Pork
with Roasted Tomatillo and Wild Mushroom Sauce

Banana Cream Pie
with Macadamia Nut Crust and Toasted Coconut with Fudge Sauce

*Chocolate Pound Cake
with Cajeta Ice Cream

Sweet Almond Cornmeal Cake
with Fresh Peaches and Raspberries

Velarde Apple Sorbet
with Blackberry Sauce

Thursday, August 15

Savory Herbed Flatbread

Buckwheat Walnut Bread

Southwest Painted Soup of Roasted Garden Eggplant and Sweet Red Pepper,
with Green Chile Crema

*Sweet White Corn and Wild Boar Bacon Tamales
with Fresh Apple Chutney

Grilled Sea Scallop Salad
with Sangre de Cristo Wild Mushrooms and Roasted Tomato-Chive Vinaigrette

*Fresh Washington Manila Clams
in a Spicy Broth of Smoked Chile, Tomatoes, Orange Zest, and Roasted Garlic

Grilled Pacific Salmon
with Authentic Yellow and Green Moles Oaxacan-Style, with Roasted Corn Ragout and Red Chile Fried Salmon Skin

Roasted Loin of Pecos Rabbit
Wrapped with Smoked Applewood Bacon, Served with a Basil-Walnut Pesto and Rabbit Raviolis with Thyme Sauce

Roasted Herb-Crusted Leg of Colorado Lamb
with a Stuffing of Sun-Dried Tomatoes, Olives, Garlic Breadcrumbs, and a California Syrah Essence

Grilled Breast of Free-Range Chicken
Stuffed with a New Mexican Herbed Goat Cheese and Mushroom Duxelle, with Fried Polenta and Wilted Summer Greens

Summer Pie of Ripe Peaches and Raspberries,
Served with Vanilla Ice-Cream and Raspberry Sauce

Toasted Almond Tartlets
with Fresh Poached Apricots and Almond Crème

Mascarpone Sorbet
with a Melange of Garden Berries

Cinnamon Crepes Stuffed
with Warm Brandied Cherries, Sweetened Crema, and Bittersweet Chocolate Sauce

Friday, August 16

*Green and Red Chile Brioche

Sun-Dried Tomato Olive Bread
Trio of Field-Ripened Texas Melons Served with Preserved Meats of Bresola, Prosciutto, and House-Cured Duck Ham

Roasted Sweet Corn and Gulf Crab Chowder
with Pasilla de Oaxaca Chiles and Crumbled Queso Anejo

*Spicy Pacific Tartares
Tuna with Serrano-Cilantro Mayonnaise and Salmon with Smoked Chiles

*Garden Field Salad of Maple-Smoked Duck
Served with Andouille Sausage and Apple Cider-Glazed Shallot Vinaigrette

*Grilled Gulf Snapper
with Savory Stew of White Beans, Sun-Dried and Oven-Roasted Tomatoes, with Lemon Zest and Fresh Parsley

Roasted Fresh Guinea-Fowl Stuffed with Herbs,
Served with Hill Country Spoon Bread and Fresh Summer Vegetables

Grilled Marinated Rack of Colorado Lamb
with an Orzo Piñon Ragout, Served with Grilled Eggplant Topped with Picante Olive Tapenade

Grilled Dry-Aged Rib-Eye Steak
with Jalapeño Mustard Glaze, Served with Grilled Leeks and Fried Pepper Rings

Mixed Melon Granita
Served with Almond and Hazelnut Tuilles and Iced Spearmint Syrup

Sweet Ripe Freestone Peaches Poached in Vino Santo
Served with Crumbled Pistachio Biscotti

Cinnamon Filo Basket
with Fresh Summer Fruits and Cajeta Ice Cream

Bittersweet Chocolate-Almond Cake
with Praline

Saturday, August 17

Parmesan Bread Sticks

Sweet Buttermilk-Chive Roll

Five-Grain Bread

Marinelli's Exclusive Iced New Zealand Rock Oysters
with a Trio of Spicy Tropical Salsas

Essence of Maine Lobster and Garden Summer Tomatoes
with Fresh Basil and Peppercress

Guajillo Chile Corn Enchilada Stuffed
with Local Goat Cheese and Grilled Diced Vegetables, Served with a Wild Mushroom and Tomato Butter Sauce

Green Chiles Rellenos
with Gulf Crab, Mango Habanero Sauce, and Cucumber Sauce

Fresh Lobster and Shrimp Torta
with Roasted Corn, Wild Mushrooms and Tomatoes, and Served with Basil Oil and Tomato Coulis

Fresh Roasted Sonoma Quail Stuffed
with Spicy Chorizo, and Served with Cactus and Tomato Salad, Buttermilk Corn Cakes, and Wilted Mustard Greens

Grilled Marinated Pork Tenderloin
with Mango-Habanero Barbecue Sauce, Zucchini Strings, and Pecan Sun-Dried Cherry Wild Rice

*Grilled Beef Tenderloin
with Serrano-Blackened Tomato Butter, Roasted-Garlic Mashed Potatoes, and Carmelized Onion Toasts

Iced Melon Compote
Served with a Trio of Summer Sorbets

Chilled Ginger-Blueberry Soufflé
with Tahitian Vanilla Cookies

Chocolate Mascarpone Ice-Cream
with Espresso Sauce and Amaretto-Hazelnut Biscotti

*Warm Spiced-Pecan Waffles
with Bourbon Peach-Pecan Sauce and Sweetened Crema

Thursday, August 20

Elizabeth's Squash Blossoms

Anasazi Bean Soup
with Sage-Piñon Fry Bread

Hopi Blue Corn Cakes
with Pemmican Sausage and Apple Butter

*Prairie Field Salad
with Native Goat Cheese Fritters and Apple-Cinnamon Oil

Apache Barbecued Salmon
Wrapped in Corn Husks with Sweet Peppers

*Lemon-Sage Bread

Corn-Caribe Bread

*Pan-Seared Nambé Trout
Crusted with Sunflower Seeds and Stuffed with Crab Slaw

Friday, August 21

Elizabeth's Squash Blossoms

Painted Soup
Tomatillo Verde with Avocado and Yellow Tomato-Habanero with Fresh Shrimp Tamales

*Veracruz Tortas
of Fresh Lobster and Corn, Queso Fresco, Sweet Pepper Salsa, and Basil Oil

*Crispy Conejo Empanadas
with Yellow Mole and Tortilla Salad

Wild Mushrooms Squash Blossoms
Tomatillo-Chipotle Sauce

*Ancho-Black Bean Bread

Masa Harina Bread
with Caramelized Onion

Seared "Torres" of Fresh Gulf Tuna
Savory Burrito Verdura and Salsa Trio

*Pollo Huitlacoche
Free-Range Chicken Breast Stuffed with Goat Cheese and Corn, Huitlacoche Sauce, Fresh Corn Tamales, and Field Greens

*Poblano Lobster Rellenos
with Roasted Sweet Corn Salsa and Manchamantel Sauce

Grilled Antelope Chop "Colima Style"
Blackberry-Guajillo Chile Sauce, Grilled Green Onion Polenta, and Runner Bean Ragout

Bittersweet Chocolate and Roasted Banana Pastel
Ibarra Helado and Caramelized Bananas

Coconut Rice Natilla
Tropical Mango Sorbete and Crispy Churros

Pecan Crepas
with Cajeta Caramel and Fresh Berries

Queso Napolitano
Sweetened Cream Cheese with Orange and Chocolate Truffle Center

Saturday, August 22

Elizabeth's Squash Blossoms

*Layered Spicy Eggplant and Sweet Pepper Tostadas
with Aged Rio Grande Goat Cheese, Lemon Oil, and Fresh Herbs

Red Chile Cabrito Enchilada
Avocado Salsa and Black Bean Sauce

Abiquiu Squash Blossom Soup
Crispy Blossom Fritters

Cornmeal Torta
Ragout of Green Chile, Lobster, and Posole

*Roasted Garlic-Chipotle Bread

*Green Chile-Apple Bread

*Adobe-Style Range Chicken
with Red Chile Jus, Roasted Summer Vegetables, Painted Pony Beans, and Mesilla Valley Pecans

*Piñon-Crusted Fresh Halibut
with a Red Chile Shrimp Sauce

Loin of Wild Boar
Stuffed with Piñon-Sage Sausage, Green Chile, and Red Onion Salsa

*Grilled Local Lamb T-Bones
with Chorizo-White Bean Stew and Fresh Mint

Chocolate Bizcochito-Crusted Tart
with Chocolate Almond Ice Cream

Fig Empanaditas with Lemon Sorbet
with Melon, Ginger, and Fig Salsa

Dixon Plum Cobbler
with Praline Ice Cream and Sweet Wine Syrup

Velarde Apricot Soup
with Mora Raspberry Sorbet

Thursday, August 19

*Wild Oregano Breadsticks

Sunflower/Millet Bread

*Plains Venison Jerky Soup
Rich Venison Broth Flavored with Mustard Greens, Corn, and Squash (photo on page 36)

*Gallina Canyon Squash-Blossom Pudding
with Elizabeth's Ranch Arugula Salad (photo on page 100)

Smoked Pecos Rabbit Tamales
Carmelized Onion Masa and Red Chile Honey Jus

*Wild Forest Mushroom and Seared Scallop Salad
with Asparagus, Chipotle Vinaigrette, and Grilled Jalapeño Corn Bread (photo on page 55)

*Blue Corn-Crusted Salmon
with Elizabeth's Haricot Verts, Chanterelles, and Basil Oil (photo on page 137)

"Corned" Rack of Pork
with Three Green Chile and Wild Rice and Sweet Corn Tamales

Roasted Pemmican Stuffed Quail
Venison Stuffing and Roasted Corn Sauce

Pueblo Rack of Lamb
Wrapped in Indian Fry Bread with Black Beans and Pena Blanca Goat Cheese

Summer Squash Spice Cake
with Mexican Marigold Syrup and Molasses Brittle Ice Cream

*Wild Honey and Blackberry Sorbet
(photo on page 179)

Suzy's Sweet Corn Pudding
with Maple Ice Cream and Bourbon Sauce

*Roasted Dixon Peach Soup
with Sweet Strawberry Sauce (photo on page 183)

Friday, August 20

New Mexican Blue Corn Muffins

Wild Rosemary-Pecan Bread

*Mission White Bean Soup
Clear Vegetable Broth with Dried Green Chile, Sun-Dried Tomatoes, and Aged Anejo Cheese (photo on page 40)

Escabeche of Sweet Pepper Rajas
Topped with Artichokes, Fava Beans, and Guajillo Chile Oil

*Sierra Blanca Lamb Tamale Tarts
with Achiote Masa, Pinto Beans, Garlic Custard, and Tomatillo-Chipotle Sauce (photo on page 105)

*Crab Enchiladas con Chile Amarillo
Crab Rolled in Green Chile Corn Crepes with Blackened Yellow Tomato Sauce and Pickled Carrot-Jicama Slaw
(photo on page 72

Chimayo Chile Seared Halibut
with Shrimp Stuffed Squash Blossom and Basil Shrimp Sauce

Canela and Allspice Cured Range Chicken
Dixon Apple and Squash Fritters and Red Chile Roasted Garlic Aioli

Roasted Loin of San Marcos Venison
with Blue Corn Enchiladas with Four Cheeses, Rajas, and Sweet Basil

*Stuffed Loin of Pork
with Fig and Thyme Stuffing and Green Chile-Apple Chutney (photo on page 155)

Dixon Plum Empanaditas
with Canela and Mascarpone Cream

*Sweet Coconut Tamales
with Caramelized Pineapple and Brazilian Rum Sauce (photo on page 185)

Mesilla Valley Pecan Tuile Torta
with Chocolate Mousse and Three Chocolate Sauces

*Taos Root Beer Float
with Sassafras Granita, Vanilla Bean Ice Cream, and Molasses Snaps

Saturday, August 21

*Pumpkin Seed Pipián Bread

*Jalapeño Corn Bread

*Yellow Tomato Gazpacho
with Crab and Sweet Pepper Sauce (photo on page 44)

*Huitlacoche Tamales
with Tomatillo Verde Salsa and Huitlacoche Sauce (photo on page 82)

Rabbit Confit Empanada
Wrapped in Phyllo with Chipotle Jus and Corn Relish

*Sweet Clam Ensalada
with Salsa Fresca, Seaweed and Frisée Salad, and Crispy Tortillas (photo on page 60)

*Sweet Lobster and Mango Marengo
On Yucatán Black Bean Cakes with Cucumber Salad (photo on page 141)

*Roast Chicken Picadillo
with Quinoa Grain Salad, Olives, and Caperberries (photo on page 120)

Fillet of Beef Huitlacoche a la Parrilla
with Elizabeth's Baby Green Beans and Creamer Potatoes

Squab Con Chile Rojo
with Purée of Potato and Wild Mushroom, Red Chile-Squash Blossom Sauce, and Crispy Squab Livers (photo on page 128)

Tropical Sorbet Terrine
with Coconut, Guava, and Mango

Piñon Coffee Helado Profiteroles
with Cajeta Sauce (photo on page 187)

*Ibarra Chocolate Flan
with Crispy Phyllo Crust (photo on page 191)

La Cueva Raspberry Tart
with Mexican Vanilla Ice Cream

INDEX

NOTES

NOTES

NOTES

NOTES

NOTES

NOTES

MORE FROM MARK MILLER

The Great Chile Book
by Mark Miller with John Harrisson

A full-color photographic guide to one hundred varieties of chiles—fifty each of fresh and dried, including a brief description, tips for use, and a heat rating. The book also gives a history of the chile in Mexican and Southwestern tradition, and recipes from the Coyote Cafe.

$14.95 paper, 160 pages.

The Great Salsa Book
by Mark Miller with Mark Kiffin and John Harrisson

This companion to *The Great Chile Book* is filled with sparkling color and features ten kinds of salsa—tomato and tomatillo, chile, tropical, fruit, corn, bean, garden, nut, seed and herb, ocean and exotic. Each section has descriptions, recipes, instructions on dicing, and accompaniments (and, of course, a heat scale).

$14.95 paper, 160 pages.

Coyote Cafe
by Mark Miller

The first cookbook from Mark Miller and his acclaimed Coyote Cafe. Includes more than 175 recipes for everything from cocktails to desserts, and is illustrated with full-color images that capture the flavor of the Southwest.

$25.95 cloth, 216 pages.

Coyote's Pantry
Southwest Seasonings and at Home Flavoring Techniques
by Mark Miller and Mark Kiffin

Mark Miller and Coyote Cafe head chef Mark Kiffin have combined their talents to present the joys of making authentic, natural condiments and accompaniments at home, with 125 recipes for salsas, chutneys, flavored oils and dressings, sauces and pasta toppings, marinades and glazes, and much more.

$25.95 cloth, 144 pages.

Chile Pepper Posters

These sumptuous chile identification posters show thirty-one fresh chiles and thirty-five dried ones, with heat ratings and cooking tips for each. With their unique pre-Columbian borders and vivid photography, these framing-quality prints make a fabulous addition to any wall.

Fresco (fresh) $15.00, Seco (dried) $15.00. Set of both posters $25.00.

Indian Corn of the Americas Poster

This portrait depicts a striking array of colorful corn, along with descriptions of the history and varieties of this quintessential American grain. Available on a maize or black background.

Maize $15.00, Black $15.00. Set of both posters $25.00.

Purchase these titles from your local bookstore or order direct from the publisher. Please include $3.50 shipping and handling for the first item, and 50 cents for each additional item. California residents include sales tax. Write for our free catalog of more than 500 books, posters, and tapes.

Ten Speed Press / Celestial Arts Box 7123, Berkeley, California 94707 (800) 841-BOOK